THE
GARDENER'S
GUIDE

THE
GARDENER'S
GUIDE

Compiled by David Squire

Published by Salamander Books Limited
LONDON • NEW YORK

A SALAMANDER BOOK

Published by Salamander Books, Ltd.,
129-137 York Way,
London N7 9LG,
United Kingdom.

ISBN 0 86101 560 6

Distributed by Hodder and Stoughton Services,
PO Box 6, Mill Road, Dunton Green,
Sevenoaks, Kent TN13 2XX

CREDITS

Compilation and introduction by: David Squire
Contributing authors: Bob Legge, David Papworth,
Noël Prockter and Michael Upward
Editor: Lisa Dyer
Designer: Stonecastle Graphics Ltd.
Line artwork: Maureen Holt and David Papworth
Filmset: SX Composing Ltd.
Colour separation: Scantrans Pte Ltd., Singapore

Printed in Italy

Pictured on the cover, left to right: Styrax japonica, Lavatera trimestris 'Silver Cup', Hemerocallis 'Pink Damask', Rembrandt tulip, Colchicum speciosum, Rosa damascena versicolor, Chaenomeles × superba 'Coral Sea', Polemonium foliosissimum, Freesia 'Red Star', Dahlia 'Wotton Cupid'.

Pictured on page 1: Tulipa 'West Point' and Tulipa 'China Pink', lily-flowered tulips.

Pictured on page 3: A crimson-pink Weigela.

Pictured opposite: The white flowers of Crambe cordifolia in a colourful garden border.

CONTENTS

AN INTRODUCTION TO GARDEN PLANTS

The range of garden plants is amazingly wide, from diminutive alpines and ephemeral annuals to trees, shrubs and conifers. The plants in this all-colour book are arranged alphabetically according to their botanical (scientific) names. Also listed are any other scientific names by which the plants are known. This enables plants which have had their names changed by botanists – but are still sold under an earlier name – to be identified. Many plants have several common names and these too are included. If you know plants only by their common names there is a comprehensive index of these at the back of this book.

With all plants, there is fundamental information gardeners wish to know, such as the best soil, aspect, and sowing seasons. And, at-a-glance, this data is highlighted under each plant name. The nature of each plant – whether annual, biennial, herbaceous perennial, bulbous, shrub, tree or conifer – is indicated, together with a description of the plant.

Nomenclature and Classification of Plants

Every plant's botanical name is usually formed of two parts – the generic and the specific. The generic is the first name and indicates the genus to which the plant belongs. Consider this to be the equivalent of a surname, indicating the family name. The second name is the specific name and defines the actual plant. This is the botanical equivalent of a christian name.

In addition, there is sometimes a varietal name. These further names usually result from humans' endeavours to produce plants with special attributes. Correctly, a variety raised in cultivation is a cultivar, while those that occur naturally are varieties. Both cultivars and varieties are indicated by single quotation marks around their names and these names are positioned after the specific name.

Some plants are hybrids and result from crossing two species. Hybrids are indicated by placing a cross between the generic and specific name. For instance, *Aster × arendsii* and *Hymenocallis × festalis*. A few plants are generic hybrids and have resulted by the crossing of plants from two different genera (the plural of genus). These are indicated by a large cross before each plant's name. For example, the leyland cypress (X *Cupressocyparis leylandii*) is a cross between the monterey cypress (*Cupressus macrocarpa*) and the nootka cypress (*Chamaecyparis nootkatensis*). Rarely, a plus sign is placed before the generic name to indicate a graft hybrid. For example, + *Laburnocytisus adamii* results from a graft between the common laburnum (*Laburnum anagyroides*) and the purple broom (*Cytisus purpureus*).

Types of Plants

A wide range of plants are found in nature, some short-lived, others outliving human beings by centuries. The following are the major categories of plant types.

Annuals, although short-lived, are some of the most popular plants, creating bright splashes of colour. During one season, they grow from seed, develop flowers and produce seed for sowing the following year. Some annuals are half-hardy and need to be raised in warmth in a greenhouse or sunroom in late winter or early spring, ready for planting into a garden when all risk of frost has passed. Others are hardy and can be sown outside in either spring or early summer.

Some plants that are not true annuals are raised as annuals. For example, the well-known wax flower (*Begonia semperflorens*) is a greenhouse perennial grown as a half-hardy annual. Lobelia (*Lobelia erinus*) is a half-hardy perennial usually raised as a half-hardy annual, while the well-known alyssum (*Lobularia maritima* but better known as *Alyssum maritimum*) is a hardy annual invariably sown as a half-hardy annual.

Below: Saxifraga 'Southside Seedling' is an alpine and has white flowers speckled with red.

Below: Although fragile-looking, Galtonia candicans is a hardy bulbous plant.

Below: The narcissus is well-known as a bulbous plant. This is Narcissus tazetta, a particularly beautiful type with clusters of highly fragrant yellow flowers on one stem.

Above: Because of its stature, this shrub looks like a tree. The stems arising from soil-level indicate it is a shrub. Trees are distinguished by having only one central stem, a trunk.

Biennials are sown one year for flowering during the following year. Usually they are sown during early summer or midsummer, and subsequently thinned or transplanted into nursery beds. In autumn they are then planted into their flowering positions. Some plants that are not true biennials are also grown in this way.

Herbaceous perennials are popular border plants, creating vivid colour every year. During autumn, herbaceous perennials die down to soil-level, surviving winter in a dormant state. In spring, the roots send up fresh shoots. Herbaceous perennials create most of their new shoots around the outside of the clump, and after a few years the centre becomes old and woody. At this stage, the whole clump can be lifted and young pieces from around the outside replanted.

Alpines are those plants that, in nature, grow in alpine regions and thrive above the tree-line but below the permanent snow-line. In garden terms, however, it has come to mean any plant grown in a rock garden. True alpines are very hardy and survive low temperatures, but garden alpines are soon damaged by water and cold.

Bulbs are store-houses of energy and colour. Most flower in late winter and spring, but a few bloom in summer. Daffodils and tulips are the best known flowering bulbs – the onion is the popular culinary example. Botanically, a bulb is an underground storage organ with a bud-like structure and fleshy, scale-like leaves tightly wrapped around each other. Frequently, the term 'bulb' is loosely used to define other energy-storing underground organs such as corms, tubers and rhizomes. Corms are formed of greatly enlarged stem bases, examples being gladioli and crocuses. Tubers are swollen stems or roots. Dahlias are root tubers, while potatoes are stem types. Rhizomes are either totally underground and slender or thick and partly-buried.

Shrubs have a woody structure and persist from year to year, creating permanent features in a garden. Shrubs differ dramatically from trees, having many stems arising from below or level with the soil's surface. Occasionally, some shrubs, such as *Buddleia alternifolia*, are trained as trees, but this is an exception.

Trees are also woody structures, some living for hundreds of years. They are distinguished from shrubs by having a single, woody stem (a trunk) that grows from soil-level to where the branches arise.

Conifers have tree-like or shrub-like proportions. Some mature to over 30m (100ft) high, while others reveal a ground-hugging habit. Most conifers are evergreen but a few, such as the maidenhair tree (*Ginkgo biloba*), are deciduous and bear a fresh array of leaves each spring. Conifers usually bear their seeds in cones.

Growing Garden Plants
Gardens are usually a medley of plants, creating colour and interest throughout the year. The main influences on their growth are soil, aspect and location.

SOIL Good soil is vital for healthy growth. If it contains too much clay or sand, or is exceptionally acid or alkaline, plants will not grow satisfactorily. Most soils contain balanced amounts of clay, silt and sand, as well as organic materials such as decomposed vegetation.

Clay soils are notoriously difficult to work, retaining masses of water in winter yet becoming bone-dry and hard during summer droughts. However, clay soils are less likely than sandy ones to be short of nutrients. Clay soils can be improved, but it takes several years. Here are a few ways to improve clay soils:
- Dig in copious amounts of bulky organic material, such as farmyard manure, compost, peat or spent mushroom compost.
- Calcium compounds help to make small clay particles cling together and form small lumps, thereby improving aeration and drainage. Liming is the easiest way to add calcium, but do not do this if the soil is already alkaline (see page 8: Alkaline soils).
- To improve a small area quickly, add sand and gravel to physically open up the soil. However, at least 10% of the area needs to be sand or gravel to noticeably improve the soil.
- Concentrate on growing shrubs, trees and perennials, rather than annuals and bedding plants that need seasonal cultivation.

Below: This is a beautiful display of purple grape hyacinth growing along a garden border. These flowers, along with many other perennials, easily grow on ordinary, well-drained soil.

Sandy soils are much easier to work than clay types, but they have drawbacks and, unless plants are chosen carefully, gardening on a dry, sandy soil can be a real struggle.

A light, gravelly or sandy soil lacks an adequate reservoir of nutrients, unless constantly replenished. As well as being short of nutrients, sandy soils lack water for long periods during summer. The superb drainage created by large soil particles is useful for plants adapted to these conditions, but for the majority the lack of moisture can be a disaster.

These are some ways to improve sandy soils:
- Dig in as much bulky organic material – compost, farmyard manure, peat or spent hops – as you can. This is a regular task, as these materials soon decay in well-aerated soils.
- Install a hose sprinkler system for important areas, such as summer flower beds.
- Mulch plants regularly. This involves forming a 5-7.5cm (2-3in) thick layer of well-decayed compost or peat around plants.
- Apply a general fertilizer to flowers each spring.
- When planting, add compost or peat to the soil, and also a sprinkling of bonemeal.

Alkaline soils contain a high proportion of chalk. Although many plants happily grow in these soils, if you wish to plant azaleas (rhododendron) there will be problems. Acid-loving garden plants in chalky soils develop restricted growth and sickly-looking yellowish foliage.

Alkalinity is at the opposite end of the scale from acidity, and in the garden these can be measured on a pH scale, from 0 to 14. The lower the reading the higher the acidity, and the higher the reading the greater the alkalinity. A reading of 7.0 is chemically neutral, but most plants happily grow in 6.5, which is slightly acid. The scale is logarithmic, and therefore potentially misleading. A difference of 1.0 on the scale represents a soil ten times more acid or alkaline. Simple but effective pH soil-testing kits are available from gardening shops and nurseries.

Follow these tips to improve chalky soil:
- Dig in plenty of organic material, especially compost, farmyard manure and peat. If the soil is very alkaline, avoid adding spent mushroom compost as this usually contains limestone and may make the problem worse.
- Apply a mulch, especially peat and pulverized bark, around plants. Water the soil first.
- Apply a general fertilizer in spring. Use acidic fertilizers such as a sulphate of ammonia if a nitrogenous fertilizer is needed. Avoid the use of ammonium nitrate and chalk mixtures as these make soil more alkaline.
- Two minor elements not always present in general fertilizers and often deficient in alkaline soils are magnesium and iron. If necessary, apply these separately.

Acid soils are at the other end of the pH scale from those which are alkaline. Although many gardeners equate acid soils with peaty types, there are also acid clays and acid sandy types. If your soil has a pH reading of less than 6.5, it is acid. Soils that are lower than pH 6.0 may suffer from a deficiency of phosphate but many evergreens and woodland plants will still do well. As long as the pH reading is not too low, it is easy to correct the acidity.

The chart shows that the amount of lime needed to raise the pH depends on the form in which it is applied, as well as the type of soil. As a guide, the following amounts of lime should decrease acidity by 1.0 pH.

SOIL	GROUND LIMESTONE	HYDRATED LIME
Typical loam	380g per sq m (16oz per sq yd)	285g per sq m (12oz per sq yd)
Sandy soil	190g per sq m (8oz per sq yd)	140g per sq m (6oz per sq yd)
Clay soil	575g per sq m (24oz per sq yd)	425g per sq m (18oz per sq yd)

Above: To correct acid soil, apply the appropriate measure of ground limestone or hydrated limestone to suit your soil.

ASPECT AND LOCATION Many of the plants in this book grow quite happily in any aspect, facing north, east, south or west. Tender ones are best in a sheltered position facing day-time sun, while hardier ones survive colder sites.

The majority of shrubs and trees, as well as most herbaceous perennials, have a hardy constitution. Summer flowering bedding plants, however, are not frost tolerant. Because hardy annuals have a relatively short growing season, most need a comfortable position in full sun.

Below: These lovely 'Dwarf Resisto Rose' petunias in the foreground enjoy a sunny position at the front of the border.

Propagating Plants

Increasing plants is a natural pursuit for gardeners. Apart from the satisfaction of producing fresh plants, it enables the exchange of plants with neighbours. Even if you do not have specialized propagation equipment, there are several easy ways to increase plants.

Division is an easy way to increase most herbaceous perennials. In autumn or spring, lift and divide congested plants, replanting young parts from around the outside of the clump.

Layering is a simple method for increasing shrubs with low-growing stems or shoots. Bend the stem or shoot and peg it into the soil. Bending and twisting the stem at soil-level encourages rooting, which may take up to a year. When roots are apparent, sever them from the parent and plant into the garden. Layering is best carried out in late summer and autumn.

Sowing seeds is the main method for increasing annuals (both hardy and half-hardy types) and biennials. Half-hardy annuals are raised from seeds sown in gentle warmth during late winter and early spring. When large enough to handle, the seedlings are pricked off into boxes, later acclimatized to outdoor conditions and planted into the garden as soon as all risk of frost has passed.

During late spring and early summer, hardy annuals are sown directly into the positions where they are to flower. The entire seedbed is marked out into separate areas for individual species and varieties, and seeds are sown in shallow drills about 6mm (¼ in) deep. After germination, thinning out the seedlings should take place.

Biennials are increased from seeds, usually sown in early summer or midsummer. The seedlings are then thinned out or transplanted into nursery beds and planted into their flowering positions in autumn.

Cuttings are a popular way to increase some plants, ensuring that the new plants resemble the parent in every respect. It is an ideal way to increase many shrubs, as well as a few herbaceous perennials.

Pests and Diseases

Garden pests have only two thoughts, reproducing themselves and eating. Unfortunately, they appear always to chew your most precious plants.

Some insects suck sap from soft leaves and flowers, causing mottling and yellowing. Caterpillars (larvae of moths and butterflies) and beetles chew and tear leaves and flowers. Earwigs are notorious pests of flowers, causing severe chewing and tearing. Other pests live wholly or partly in the soil, chewing roots whenever the opportunity arises. A large number of pest-killing chemicals are available and are either sprayed or dusted on plants. There are also insecticides to dust or lightly fork into soils.

Diseases are sometimes difficult to diagnose until well established. Soft parts of plants – leaves and flowers – are especially vulnerable. There is a wide range of chemicals available to control diseases, but good plant husbandry helps to prevent many of them. To help keep plants healthy, follow these tips:
- Do not leave decaying stems and leaves on a plant or, if fallen, on the soil.
- Do not pack plants too closely together as it reduces air circulation. Wet leaves and little air movement encourage the presence of diseases.

***Above:** An easy way to multiply weeping trees or shrubs is by layering. Bend a stem or shoot into the soil. Once the roots are established, sever the stem from the parent and replant.*

- Control pests at the earliest opportunity. They puncture plant tissue and encourage the entry of diseases. Also, sap-sucking pests spread viruses.
- Burn infected plants. Do not leave them to contaminate other plants.

Safety with Garden Chemicals

Do not use insecticides and fungicides indiscriminately. Most gardening chemical products will have information on the suitability of the chemical for particular plants as well as specific information on the application of the treatment. It is wise to follow their recommendations strictly. In general, take care to:
- Carefully read the manufacturer's directions before use.
- Use only at the strength recommended – making a stronger solution will not kill more pests.
- Not spray or dust plants when the weather is windy as this increases the risk of inhaling chemicals.
- Keep all sprays and dusts away from children and pets. And store them out of reach of children.
- Clean all sprayers and containers after use.
- Not spray in strong sunshine, as this may damage plants.
- Certain chemicals may damage particular plants – read the label carefully.
- Many chemicals are toxic to fish – avoid spraying near ponds, especially on windy days.

Abelia × grandiflora

(Glossy abelia)

- **Open sunny spot**
- **Good loamy soil**
- **Late summer/early autumn flowers**

This evergreen to semi-evergreen shrub will reach a height of 1-2m (3.3-6.5ft). Its slender arching branches are slightly downy. The striking, dark green foliage has smooth, pointed leaves, 2.5-6.5cm (1-2.5in) long, pale green beneath and more or less lightly toothed. The white pink-tinged funnel-shaped flowers have a faint fragrance, and are carried on the previous year's shoots in the leaf axils.

This hybrid has a good constitution and makes a vigorous graceful shrub, flowering late in the season. It does quite well on chalk and lime soils. Although there are several other abelias, A. × *grandiflora* is the most reliable. Endeavour to buy pot-grown plants. Take care to remove worn-out stems and very thin twigs in autumn.

Propagate by taking half-ripe cuttings in midsummer and insert them into a propagator with a little bottom heat.

Above: Abelia × *grandiflora* is covered in late summer with slightly fragrant, funnel-shaped, white, pink-tinged flowers.

Right: Abies balsamea 'Hudsonia' forms a neat, slow-growing conifer, ideal for year-round colour in rock gardens.

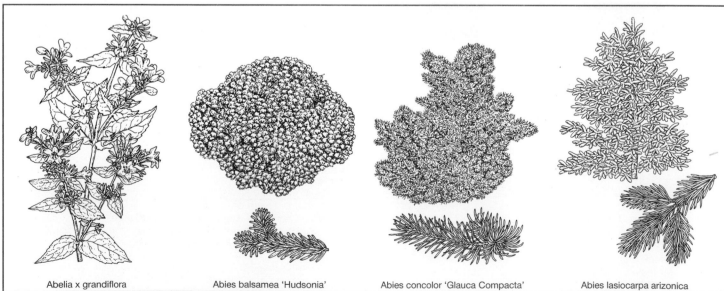

Abelia x grandiflora   Abies balsamea 'Hudsonia'   Abies concolor 'Glauca Compacta'   Abies lasiocarpa arizonica

Abies balsamea 'Hudsonia'

(Balsam fir)
- **Provide shelter when young**
- **Deep moist soil**
- **Slow-growing small bush**

This variety of the balsam fir forms a dwarf, evergreen conifer up to 30cm (12in) tall in ten years, but can reach 75cm (30in) in 30 years. Branches and foliage form a dense, compact bush with a flattish top, spreading to almost 1m (3.3ft) wide.

This is an ideal rockery plant as it remains in scale with other rockery species. The cylindrical cones grow on the upper sides of the branches, and they open and break up when the seed is ripe.

Plant the seeds in late winter for extra stock. Avoid extremes of soil such as boggy situations, pure sand or chalk; but grow in a deep moist well-drained soil. Place in an area protected against hard frost, which can damage the young shoots. This variety is normally pest- and disease-free.

Abies concolor 'Glauca Compacta'

(White fir)
- **Stands heat and dry conditions**
- **Avoid chalky soils**
- **Slow-growing small bush**

This dwarf variety of the North American white fir is one of the best conifers for the rock garden, or even as a specimen for a lawn or a container. It has silver-blue, evergreen foliage that grows in a slightly irregular form, giving it an attractive character. It can take up to 25 years to reach 75cm (30in) tall, with a spread of just over 1m (3.3ft). It prefers a deep moist soil but will tolerate hot and dry conditions; avoid a chalky soil. The winter buds are large and resinous, and open in spring to pale hairless clusters of leaves. The cones, almost 25cm (10in) long, are pale green when young but turn purple as they mature.

This shrub can be grown from seed, but the plants may vary in colour. It is normally propagated by grafting the right shade of leaf on to a dwarf rootstock. The plants are generally free from pests and diseases.

Abies lasiocarpa arizonica

(Cork fir)
- **Prefers humid conditions**
- **Deep moist soil**
- **Slow-growing medium tree**

This medium-sized, evergreen conifer has thick corky bark, and its distinctive winter buds are white and resinous. It will reach 18m (59ft) tall where conditions are good, but the average plant reaches half this size. The leaves are silvery grey in colour. The cones are purple when young.

When the cones start to break up, collect the seed and sow in a seed compost in early spring. Allow the seedlings to grow on in a seed bed for over two years before planting out in their permanent positions. Plant this tree in a deep moist soil that is free or almost free from lime. A slow-growing dwarf cultivar, 'Compacta', has blue-grey foliage, and may take ten years to reach 70cm (28in).

Watch for white waxy wool on the leaves and branches, caused by adelgids. Spray with malathion in late spring to control an attack. If the stems start to die back, spray the tree with a fungicide to deter fungus.

Acaena buchananii

(New Zealand burr)
- **Full sun**
- **Any soil**
- **Ground cover**

This is one of a large family of hardy herbaceous plants, mainly native to New Zealand, which are useful subjects for ground cover and under-planting with dwarf bulbs. They are admittedly invasive, but excellent for a poor soil and a hot dry sunny position. This is not a plant for a damp situation, but it does very well in the cracks of paving stones.

They are grown mainly for foliage, but the spiny seed heads are attractive in their own right. *A. buchananii* has grey-green foliage with yellowish brown burrs. The flowers are insignificant and the leaves small, neat and briar-like in appearance, making a mat no higher than 5cm (2in) tall.

Propagation is simple, by dividing the runners in autumn or spring, making sure there is a good root system to each runner.

Acanthus mollis

(Artist acanthus, Bear's breeches)
- **Sunny position**
- **Well-drained soil**
- **Late summer flowering**

This attractive hardy herbaceous plant has green glossy foliage. The mauve-pink, foxglove-like flowers are rather sparingly produced on stems 1.2m (4ft) or higher. As plants can spread as much as 90cm (3ft), it is advisable not to

Above: *Abies concolor 'Glauca Compacta' is a slow-growing conifer, eye-catching with its silver-blue foliage that forms an irregular outline.*

grow more than one plant in small gardens. Any good fertile soil suits acanthus, provided it is well-drained. Plant in spring. During the first winter, especially in cold districts, give a mulch of leaf-mould or well-rotted garden compost.

Acanthus spinosus is similar to *Acanthus mollis* in many respects, except that it has nasty spines at the end of each dark green, deeply divided leaf. Each leaf is about 60-90cm (2-3ft) long. The flowers of *A. spinosus* are borne more freely than those of *A. mollis*. When the flowers are dried they have a pleasant scent and can be used for winter decorations.

Propagate by seed sown in spring in a cold frame, by root cuttings in late autumn or winter, or by division in spring.

Acaena buchananii

Acanthus mollis

Acer griseum

(Paperbark maple)
- **Sun or light shade**
- **Most soils including chalk**
- **Superb autumn colour**

This lovely small deciduous tree of Chinese origin is ideal for the small or medium garden, as it is slow-growing and takes many years to reach 7.6-9m (25-30ft). It is renowned for its charming peeling bark, which reveals a cinnamon-coloured layer beneath. Each heavily toothed leaf is composed of three leaflets. The green leaves are a pretty dove colour beneath. In autumn the foliage is tinted superb shades of red and orange. If you have space for only one tree, this is a good choice.

This tree grows well on chalky soils and looks best when grown in a lawn, rather than in a border along with shrubs. When growing it in grass, allow ample cultivated ground around the base.

Although the paperbark maple seeds fairly freely, the seeds have a very low germination rate.

Acer japonicum 'Aureum'

(Maple)
- **Sunny position**
- **Most soils, including lime**
- **Foliage throughout summer**

A tree worthy of note is the deciduous Japanese maple, especially the cultivar 'Aureum'. The species *A. japonicum* has typical maple leaves, each with seven to 11 lobes. In spring, before the foliage appears, purplish red flowers are produced. In autumn the foliage turns to tones of rich reddish crimson, providing a stunning display in the garden. It will make a tree 6-9m (20-30ft) high.

The cultivar 'Aureum' rarely grows higher than 6m (20ft), and even then it grows slowly. Its lobed foliage is a pale golden to bright yellow throughout the season. It is a superb small tree or large shrub for the small or medium-sized garden, and has the advantage of growing well on chalk soils.

Shelter *A. japonicum* and the cultivar 'Aureum' from cold winds and late frost, which can damage foliage. Propagate *A. japonicum* by seed in early spring, and 'Aureum' by budding or grafting.

Achillea filipendulina

(Fern-leaf yarrow)
- **Sunny position**
- **Tolerates dry soils**
- **Summer flowering**

The large yellow plate-like flowers of the herbaceous perennial *A. filipendulina* are best seen in the variety 'Gold Plate'. This most

Below: *Achillea filipendulina 'Gold Plate' has bright yellow, flat heads above stout stems.*

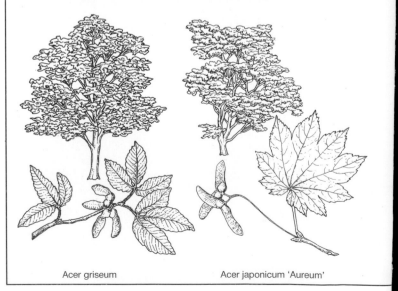

Acer griseum   Acer japonicum 'Aureum'

spectacular plant has flat bright yellow heads at the top of stout erect stems, 1.5m (5ft) tall. Each flower head can be as much as 13cm (5in) across, and the plant can spread as much as 45cm (18in).

Another variety is 'Coronation Gold'. This has pale yellow flat heads, and the 90cm (3ft) stems rise out of grey-green feathery foliage.

Propagate by seeds or division in spring, or by cuttings in early summer. Plant in spring, in good retentive soil. A few peasticks will be needed to protect the heavy heads in wet weather, particularly in windswept gardens.

The tall varieties should be cut down to ground level during the autumn. The flower heads can be dried for winter decoration indoors.

Achillea tomentosa

(Woolly yarrow)
- **Full sun**
- **Poor soil**
- **Summer flowering**

This carpeting, hardy herbaceous plant grows throughout SW Europe and across to central Italy, thriving in full sun on a starvation diet. It is particularly suitable for growing in crevices and dry walls. There are several species in the

Left: *This lovely maple is Acer japonicum 'Aureum'. The foliage turns to rich crimson in autumn.*

wild, but most have flowers that are too weedy and unattractive. *A. tomentosa* is the most popular alpine yarrow in gardens, with softly hairy and ferny grey leaves forming prostrate mats from which rise the flat yellow 4cm (1.6in) wide flower heads on 15cm (6in) stems.

Slugs seem to be partial to the foliage in spring, but metaldehyde pellets will deter them.

Propagation is by soft cuttings in a sand frame between midsummer and early autumn, or by division in spring. Autumn divisions should be kept in a frame over winter.

Aconitum napellus

(Helmet flower, Monkshood, Soldier's cap, Wolf's bane)
- **Full sun; tolerates partial shade**
- **Fertile, retentive soil**
- **Summer and late summer flowering**

This hardy herbaceous perennial is well-known for its spires of delphinium-like flowers. The blue helmet-shaped flowers are held at the top of stout 90-120cm (3-4ft) stems, and clothed with dark green finger-like foliage. Today there are many varieties to choose from. Among the finest are 'Blue Sceptre', with blue and white bicolour flowers, 60cm (24in) stems, and a pretty, dwarf plant 'Bressingham Spire', with 90cm (3ft) stems. *A wilsonii* has flowering stems up to 1.8m (6ft).

Above: *Aconitum napellus, an herbaceous perennial, creates dominant spires of purple flowers in midsummer and late summer.*

To improve flowering, thin out surplus stems and give a mulch of compost in the spring.

Propagate by seeds in spring or by division in spring or autumn. Plant out in late autumn.

Adonis aestivalis

(Pheasant's eye)
- **Sow in spring**
- **Ordinary soil, with added peat**
- **Partly shaded or sunny position**

This hardy annual is of outstanding beauty. The deep crimson petals of the flower contrast vividly with with nearly black stamens in the centre of the cup-shaped flowers. Growing on stems 30cm (12in) high, the leaves are fine, deeply cut, and almost fern-like. It is a beautiful plant for all.

Sow seed in any good growing medium in spring, then prick off and grow on in the usual way. Plant out into final positions in late spring at 30cm (12in) apart. Alternatively, sow seeds where they are to flower in the autumn. Once germinated, make the first thinning at 15cm (6in) spacings. The following early spring complete spacing to 30cm (12in). Germination may be slow.

Ideally suited to the front of a border, they combine very well with other annuals and biennials. When designing an area for these plants, make sure you plan for bold drifts to get maximum effect.

Achillea filipendulina

Achillea tomentosa

Aconitum napellus

Adonis aestivalis

Aethionema 'Warley Ruber'

(Stone cress)
- **Full sun**
- **Any well-drained soil**
- **Evergreen sub-shrub**

The shrubby, hardy, evergreen aethionemas give of their best in a hot dry situation on the rock garden. They thrive on sunny limestone in the Mediterranean region, but in cultivation will tolerate a neutral soil. Do not plant on an acid soil. They form neat plants of bushy habit with blue-grey leaves, and the small pink flowers are borne in clusters. 'Warley Ruber' makes a plant about 15cm (6in) tall.

Removal of the flowering stems is not only a neat practice but assists with the propagation of the plant, as the non-flowering soft growth thus created is ideal for taking cuttings from midsummer onwards. Insert in a sand frame and pot up as soon as roots form. When established they should be pinched out and will then be ready for planting out in the spring.

Agapanthus

(African lily)
- **Sunny position**
- **Moist, fertile soil**
- **Summer flowering**

The blue African lily, *Agapanthus umbellatus*, belongs to the family Liliaceae, but is not, in fact, a lily. It is hardy out of doors only in gardens that are usually frost-free. Today, however, there are some very fine garden forms that are hardy. During the 1950s and 1960s the 'Headbourne Hybrids' were developed from *Agapanthus campanulatus;* they are in varying shades of blue.

All agapanthus plants have lily-like flowers that are arranged in an umbel, like an upturned umbrella. The flowers are borne on stoutish stems, 60-90cm (2-3ft) high. They are deciduous, and the dark green strap-like foliage dies down in the winter, so it is wise to mark the spot where they grow so that when the border is dug over, the plants are not damaged. Choose moist rather than dry soil, but avoid very wet ground.

Propagate by division in spring, as the new growth appears.

Ageratum houstonianum

(Flossflower, Pussyfoot)
- **Sow in spring**
- **Most ordinary types of soil**
- **Tolerates all positions except heavy shade**

Flowering from early summer onwards, these beautiful half-

Below: Aethionema 'Warley Ruber', ideal for hot and dry rock gardens, has clusters of small pink flowers in early summer.

hardy annuals have flowers that resemble small powder puffs. Shown to their best when edging a formal bedding scheme, they are also good subjects for window boxes and containers.

Try to use the F1 hybrids available; these give larger and longer trusses of blooms. The cultivar 'Adriatic' is in this class. Its height is 20cm (8in), and the mid-blue flower is produced above light green hairy leaves. Although most

Above: Agapanthus 'Headbourne Hybrid' creates spectacular blue flower heads at the tops of stiff, upright stems.

cultivars are in the blue range, there are a few whites available.

Sow seed in boxes of growing medium in spring, under glass. When large enough to handle, prick out in the usual way. Plant out in final positions at the end of spring or when the risk of frost has disappeared. Until planting out try to maintain a temperature of 10-16°C (50-60°F); lower than this will tend to check the growth of young plants.

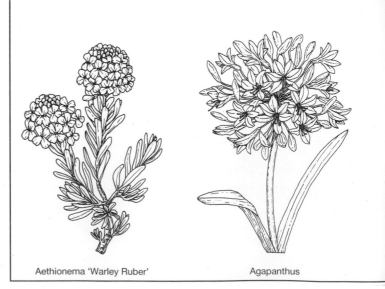

Aethionema 'Warley Ruber'

Agapanthus

Alchemilla mollis

(Lady's mantle)
- **Sunny or shady sites**
- **Avoid very wet ground**
- **Early summer flowering**

The hardy herbaceous perennial *A. mollis* has become very popular for flower arranging. The rounded, silky-haired, pale grey-green leaves and tiny sulphur-yellow frothy sprays of flowers last a long while, beautifying either the flower border or the flower arranger's vase. It is also a superb ground cover plant. Its seeds can be invasive, however. To prevent it spreading, remove the flower heads before the seeds ripen, and this will save many self-sown seedlings appearing where they are not wanted. It grows to about 45cm (18in) in height. *A. mollis* has the useful ability of being able to grow happily in full shade.

Allium giganteum
- **Sunny site**
- **Well-drained soil**
- **Plant with 15cm (6in) of soil above bulb**

This hardy bulbous plant is grown mainly for its decorative flower head, which stands well above other herbaceous plants. The leaves are grey-blue and strap-like, making a clump up to 45cm (18in) in height, with flower heads 10cm (4in) across. The flowers in midsummer are deep lilac. As soon as the flowers die, cut the heads off but leave the stalks to feed the bulb for the following year. Dead leaves and stems should be removed in autumn.

Grow these plants in a sunny place in well-drained soil, and leave untouched for a few years. Then lift, split and replant in spring or autumn with more space around the bulbs. Seeds can be sown in autumn, winter or spring. Leave them for 12 months, then replant in nursery rows out of doors, keeping the soil moist.

Propagate by division in spring or autumn. Plant this species in any good fertile soil, in sun or shade. Insert twiggy sticks for support in windswept locations.

Left: Allium moly, ideal for borders as well as large rock gardens, has clusters of yellow flowers in midsummer.

Watch for slugs and white rot. Infected bulbs should be destroyed.

Allium moly
(Golden garlic, Lily leek, Yellow onion)
- **Sunny site**
- **Well-drained soil**
- **Plant with 7.5cm (3in) of soil over the bulb**

This hardy, bulbous plant is suitable for growing in a rock garden, as it grows only 30cm (12in) tall. It has strap-like grey leaves and bright yellow star-like flowers that form clusters 5cm (2in) wide on the end of the flower stems in midsummer. The plants spread 15cm (6in) and should be planted this distance apart.

Plant the bulbs in autumn in well-drained soil with some moisture; they prefer a sunny site. Leave them for a few years, until the flowers become crowded. Then lift the clump in spring or autumn, split and replant with more space. Alliums can be grown as pot plants provided they are kept cool until the flower buds start to open and then brought indoors. Sow seeds in winter or spring. After 12 months, replant in a nursery bed for two years.

Protect from slugs, and watch for white rot. If white fungus appears at the base of the bulbs, destroy the plants and do not grow alliums in this soil for ten years.

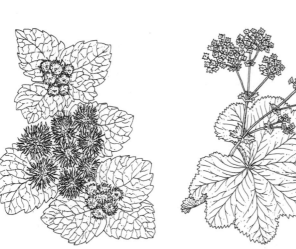

Ageratum houstonianum

Alchemilla mollis

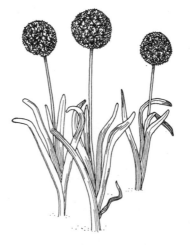

Allium giganteum

Allium moly

Allium narcissiflorum
- **Sunny position**
- **Well-drained soil**
- **Bulbous**

The onion family is widespread throughout the Northern Hemisphere and contains some species that are blatantly rampant but *A. narcissiflorum* – one of the many dwarf and hardy species – is well behaved. Found wild in Northern Italy and Southern France it grows happily in screes, which suggests that it requires free drainage in the garden. It has a wide tolerance of varying soil conditions, and it flowers in midsummer, producing on its 15-35cm (6-14in) flower stem an umbel of bell-shaped flowers of purple-pink hues. It is one of the most attractive of the small onions and does well in a sunny position.

Propagation is simple: collect the seed in autumn and sow it in late winter, and young seedlings will be ready in late spring for autumn planting.

Alstroemeria aurantiaca
(Lily-of-the-Incas, Peruvian lily)
- **Sunny, sheltered site**
- **Well-drained fertile soil**
- **Plant tubers 10-15cm (4-6in) deep**

This tuberous-rooted plant has twisted blue-grey leaves, and grows to a height of 90cm (3ft). Borne on leafy stems, the flowers are trumpet-shaped in orange-reds, the upper two petals having red veins.

Plant the tubers in spring. Cover with a mulch of compost or well-rotted manure in spring. As they grow, support to prevent them being blown over. Dead-head plants to encourage more blooms. In autumn cut stems down to the ground. In spring the plants can be divided, but take care not to disturb the roots unduly. Sometimes the plant will not produce any stems, leaves or flowers during the first season, but once established it can be left for years. Sow seed in spring in a cold frame, and plant out a year later.

Watch for slugs and caterpillars, and use a suitable insecticide if necessary. When the plant shows yellow mottling and distorted growth, destroy it – this is a virus disease.

Althaea rosea
(Alcea rosea)
(Hollyhock)
- **Sow in spring**
- **Heavy and rich soil**
- **Sheltered position but not shade**

Hollyhocks are probably the tallest plants you are likely to grow in an ordinary garden. There are many varieties to choose from but *A. rosea* (now properly known as

Above: Althaea rosea develops tall, rigid stems packed with large, pink, double or single flowers from midsummer.

Right: Alyssum saxatile 'Dudley Neville', with biscuit-yellow flowers, is superb when planted to trail over dry stone walls.

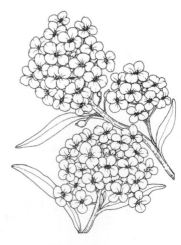

Allium narcissiflorum

Alstroemeria aurantiaca

Althaea rosea

Alyssum maritimum

Alcea rosea) and its cultivars are by far the easiest. Flowers are produced on short stalks directly from the main stem. They range in colour from pink and red to white and light yellow. Up to 10cm (4in) in diameter, they can be single or double.

Treat as a biennial to obtain the tallest plants, by sowing where they are to flower in early summer. Take out shallow drills 23cm (9in) apart. Thin out seedlings in summer to 60cm (24in) apart. The resulting plants will attain a height of about 2.7m (9ft) the following summer.

For annual treatment, sow on site in spring in the same way, and thin out to 38cm (15in) apart. Plants treated in this way will flower in the same year, reaching a height of about 1.8m (6ft).

For best results, give a mulch in spring, and water freely in dry weather.

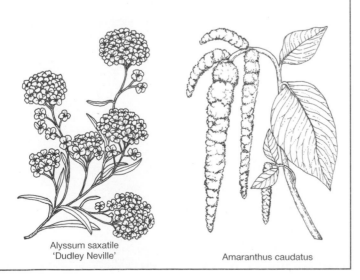

Alyssum saxatile
'Dudley Neville'

Amaranthus caudatus

Alyssum maritimum

(Lobularia maritima)
(Sweet alyssum)
- **Sow in early spring**
- **Ordinary soil**
- **Full sun**

This well-known annual, now properly known as *Lobularia maritima*, has extraordinary resilience, mainly because of its ability to self-seed in great quantities. Some gardeners have difficulty in eradicating it from the garden. Mats of tiny flowers are produced on short stems 7.5-10cm (3-4in) from early summer onwards if plants are sown directly where they are to flower in spring.

Plants can be raised by sowing seeds in boxes of seed-growing medium a month earlier. Prick out the seedlings into a free-draining potting medium when large enough to handle. Plant out in final positions in mid-spring. To prolong the flowering period make a further sowing in late spring.

Commonly used for edging formal beds and borders, this species can also be used effectively with other annuals. Other colours include rose pink, mauve, purple and lilac.

Alyssum saxatile 'Dudley Neville'

(Basket of gold, Golden-tuft alyssum, Rock madwort)
- **Sunny position**
- **Any well-drained soil**
- **Evergreen sub-shrub**

The parent plant, *Alyssum saxatile*, is an evergreen shrubby perennial that can be 20-30cm (8-12in) tall. However, the named cultivars tend to be slightly less vigorous. These include 'Compactum', which lives up to its name at 15cm (6in); 'Plenum', with double flowers; 'Citrinum', with lemon-yellow flowers; and 'Dudley Neville', with unusual biscuit-coloured flowers that are restrained compared to their brilliant relatives.

Propagation of the parent species is easy from seed. Sow in late summer and pot on in autumn, and young plants will be available for the following spring. The named cultivars cannot be guaranteed to come true from seed. They should be increased from cuttings, taken in mid- to late summer and inserted in a sand frame. Pot up in autumn, pinching out the centres to encourage a bushy plant.

Amaranthus caudatus

(Love-lies-bleeding, Tassel flower)
- **Sow in spring**
- **Well-cultivated soil**
- **Sunny location**

This half-hardy annual has long tail-like racemes of crimson flowers which can reach 45cm (18in) in length. The flowers are produced on stems up to 1.05m (3.5ft) tall. Leaves are ovate in shape and green in colour, the latter changing to bronze as the season progresses. *A. caudatus* is used mainly in formal beds as a 'spot' plant to give height. Try them as individual specimens or in groups on a mixed border. The flowers appear in summer.

For borders, sow the seed directly into the open ground in spring in a sunny position. When thinning out seedlings give plenty of room for development, about 60cm (24in) apart.

Raise plants for containers and formal borders by sowing in boxes of good seed-growing medium in early spring. Prick off into pots under glass, and plant out into final positions in late spring.

Below: Amaranthus caudatus is a half-hardy annual with tassel-like, dark maroon-purple flowers.

Right: Amelanchier lamarckii creates a massed display of starry white flowers in spring.

Amaryllis belladonna

(Belladonna lily, Cape belladonna, Naked lady)
- **Sunny sheltered position**
- **Well-drained soil**
- **Plant 15-20cm (6-8in) deep**

This slightly tender bulbous plant has strap-like leaves, lasting from late winter through to midsummer. After the leaves die down, flower stems appear and grow to a height of 75cm (30in). The trumpet-shaped pink or white flowers vary from three to 12 on a stem.

Plant the bulbs in summer in a warm sheltered situation in well-drained soil. Bulbs can be divided in summer and should be replanted immediately. Dead-head flowers as they fade, and remove leaves and stems as they die.

Hippeastrum bulbs, often sold as amaryllis, are tender indoor subjects. Plant one bulb in a 15-20cm (6-8in) pot of well-draining mixture, leaving a third of the bulb exposed. Water a little until the flower stem appears and then water and feed liberally. Bulbs bloom about three months after planting. Prepared bulbs planted in late autumn flower during midwinter.

Below: Amaryllis belladonna, a large bulbous plant, has clusters of fragrant, pink flowers.

Amelanchier lamarckii

(June berry, Service berry, Shad, Snowy mespilus, Sugarplum)
- **Full sun**
- **Any good soil including lime**
- **Spring flowers; autumn foliage**

This small deciduous tree or large shrub has for a long time been erroneously identified as *A.*

canadensis or *A. laevis*. When grown as a small tree it needs to have a main stem about 1.2-1.5m (4-5ft) before the branches start. Young shoots may appear up the main stem; rub these off to retain a clean stem. If grown as a large shrub it can have several stems from the base.

In spring the unfurling silky oval leaves have a coppery to pinkish hue. Before the foliage changes to

a yellowish dark green, clouds of starry white flowers are scattered among the branches. Finally, in the autumn, there is a breathtaking display of orange and red foliage.

Propagate by seed, sown as soon as it has been gathered, or by grafting in spring.

Anacyclus depressus

(Mount Atlas daisy)
- **Sunny scree**
- **Well-drained site**
- **Evergreen**

This attractive hardy, evergreen perennial comes from the Atlas Mountains in Morocco, which might suggest that it is not over-hardy. However, it survives all but the most severe winters and forms a neat mat of grey-green ferny foliage that lies prostrate on the soil. One plant can make a 30cm (12in) spread. The flowers are no more than 5cm (2in) tall and can be 5cm (2in) across. Their attraction lies in the pinky-maroon backing to the petals in bud.

Ideally *A. depressus* should be planted in a well-drained situation in full sun. Never grow in wet conditions. Cover with glass in winter.

Propagation is by seed, gathered carefully by placing a sheet of paper under the seed head when it is quite dry, and shaking them on to the paper. Sow fresh seed in the autumn in a gritty mixture at 7-10°C (45-50°F).

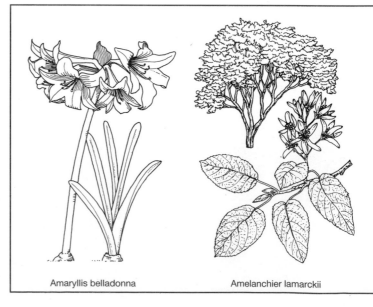

Amaryllis belladonna

Amelanchier lamarckii

Anaphalis yedoensis

(Everlasting, Life-everlasting, Pearly everlasting)
- **Sun or partial shade**
- **Well-drained soil**
- **Late summer or autumn flowering**

This hardy herbaceous perennial has broad green leaves that are white felted beneath, and flat

Above: *Anacyclus depressus, diminutive and ideal for rock gardens, has white flowers with yellow centres during summer.*

papery white flower heads with enchanting yellow centres. These flower heads develop from late summer through to early autumn, reaching up to 10cm (4in) across. Although its foliage dies back in the winter, silvery-white shoots

appear as spring approaches. It will reach a height of 60cm (24in).

When pearly everlasting flowers are gathered for drying, give the stems a good drink before hanging them up to dry off.

A. yedoensis is best when grown in full sun, although it can tolerate the shade of a wall (but not of trees). This plant will soon droop if it becomes too dry at the root.

Propagate by division in autumn, or by seeds sown out of doors in spring. Plant them in any good retentive soil.

Anchusa azurea

(Anchusa italica)
(Alkanet, Bugloss, Italian bugloss)
- **Sunny position**
- **Well-drained soil**
- **Early summer flowering**

Anchusas are tall coarse-growing branching herbaceous perennials that have rough hairy stems and foliage with large, charming forget-me-not blue flowers. There are many excellent varieties: 'Morning Glory' is bright blue and reaches 1.5-1.8m (5-6ft); 'Opal' is an old favourite, soft blue, 1.5m (5ft); 'Royal Blue' is rich royal blue, 90cm (3ft); the late spring to early summer flowering 'Loddon Royalist' is gentian blue, 90cm (3ft). Another variety, 'Little John', has brilliant blue flowers.

Propagation is easy. Cut roots into lengths of about 4cm (1.6in), making a clean cut at the top of

each and a slanting one at the base – this will prevent them being inserted upside down. Place pots of these roots in an unheated frame. Plant out in early to mid-spring. To prevent damage, stake plants early on.

Androsace primuloides 'Chumbyi'

(Androsace sarmentosa)
(Rock jasmine)
- **Open situation**
- **Any soil**
- **Evergreen**

This family of hardy and slightly tender perennials creates neat domes covered in intense white flowers. Not all of them are suitable for growing outdoors, but *A. primuloides* from the Himalaya has a number of varieties that are suitable for the rock garden. The plants form rosettes 3-5cm (1.25-2in) across and these form mats some 60cm (24in) across. The pink flower heads reach no taller than 10cm (4in). 'Chumbyi' is more compact and of more robust constitution.

The well-drained soil should contain some humus. Winter wetness affects the rosettes, so some protection is advisable.

Propagation is by potting up rooted rosettes in early autumn, which will be ready for planting out the following spring after over-wintering under protection.

Anacyclus depressus

Anaphalis yedoensis

Anchusa azurea

Androsace primuloides 'Chumbyi'

Above: Anemone blanda, a spring-flowering plant, is ideal for rock gardens and naturalizing.

Anemone blanda

(Blue windflower, Lily-of-the-field, Windflower)
● **Sun or light shade**
● **Well-drained soil**
● **Plant 5cm (2in) deep**

This spring-flowering cormous plant grows to 15cm (6in) tall. The daisy-like flowers, in white, pink, red-tipped, lavender or pale blue, are 3.5cm (1.4in) across. They make an ideal rockery plant and can be grown under trees.

They tolerate either alkaline or acid soils provided they are well-drained. Soak corms for 48 hours before planting. Plant corms 10cm (4in) apart in autumn. Lift the corms after leaves die down in early autumn. Then divide and remove offsets for replanting. Sow seeds in late summer, and germinate in a cold frame. Transplant seedlings and grow on for two years before moving to final positions.

If plant and soil are treated with a general insecticide you should have little trouble. Stunted yellow leaves and meagre flowers indicate a virus attack; destroy plants before the virus can spread.

Anemone coronaria

(Poppy anemone, Poppy windflower, Windflower)
● **Sunny or lightly shaded position**
● **Well-drained soil**
● **Plant corms 5cm (2in) deep**

This cormous-rooted plant flowers in spring, and the blooms vary from white to blue or red. The 'De Caen' and the new robust 'St. Piran', both with single flowers, and the 'St. Brigid' anemone with double or semi-double blooms have all been developed from this plant. These grow to a height of 30cm (12in) and flowers are up to 7.5cm (3in) across.

Corms should be planted in early autumn, 15cm (6in) apart. By planting in other months, a succession of blooms can be had throughout the year. Corms deteriorate, and should be replaced every couple of years. Anemones can be grown from seed, sown in late summer and kept in a cold frame. Transplant the seedlings, leave for a year, and then move to their flowering position. Treat these plants with a general pesticide to stop insect attack. If the plant looks sick and the leaves turn yellow, destroy it before the virus spreads.

Anemone × hybrida

(Anemone japonica)
(Japanese anemone, Japanese windflower, Windflower)
● **Sun or partial shade**
● **Well-drained ordinary soil**
● **Early autumn flowering**

Of all the many windflowers, the best-known are the many hybrids of the hardy, herbaceous perennial *Anemone × hybrida*. These vary in height from 45cm-1.2m (18in-4ft), and their individual flowers vary in size from 4 to 6cm (1.6-2.4in) across, each with five or more petals. Each flower has a central boss of yellow stamens. Choose from 'Bressingham Glow', a semi-double rosy red, 45cm (18in) tall; 'Luise Uhink', white, 90cm (3ft); 'September Charm', single soft pink, 45cm (18in); 'White Queen', 90-120cm (3-4ft); and 'Honorine Jobert', white, 120cm (4ft).

Propagate by cutting the roots into 4-5cm (1.6-2in) lengths and inserting them in a deep box filled with peat and sand mixture.

Anemone nemorosa

(European wood anemone, Windflower, Wood anemone)
● **Light shade**
● **Well-drained soil with leaf-mould**
● **Plant 5cm (2in) deep**

This hardy anemone has white flowers with a touch of pink or blue

Anemone blanda

Anemone coronaria

Anemone x hybrida

Anemone nemorosa

Above: Antennaria dioica 'Rosea' is a carpeting evergreen with pink flowers in early summer.

Left: Anemone coronaria 'De Caen' has single flowers during spring, in a wide colour range.

on the outside of the petals. The low-growing plant reaches 10cm (4in) high, although some varieties grow to twice this size. The flowers are single, about 2.5cm (1in) across; there are some doubles.

These plants are easily grown from corms, provided they are planted in autumn in a shady place with moist soil. Do not plant in a hot dry position. They will bloom in spring. They may be attacked by a number of insects, such as flea beetles, caterpillars, cut worms, aphids or slugs. These should be treated with a suitable insecticide when damage is seen. Virus and rust disease can affect the plants, leaving yellow spores on the leaves and stems and yellowing of leaves with twisted flowers; if either of these symptoms is seen, destroy the plant.

Antennaria dioica 'Rosea'

(Catsfoot, Ladies' tobacco, Pussy-toes)
● **Any situation**
● **Any well-drained soil**
● **Evergreen**

A useful hardy, evergreen carpeting plant that forms a prostrate mat up to 45cm (18in) across of pointed silvery leaves with short flower stems, 5-10cm (2-4in), producing rich pink flowers. Antennarias are found in Europe, Asia and North America.

'Rosea' is useful on any well-drained soil, the height of the flower varying according to the richness of the situation. Bulbs can be planted under it and it is a useful subject for an alpine lawn.

Propagation is by division in spring or late summer, planted out direct or potted up. It does not succumb to pests or diseases.

Anthemis tinctoria

(Golden marguerite, Ox-eye chamomile, Yellow-flowered chamomile)
● **Full sun**
● **Well-drained soil**
● **Summer flowering**

This species is a free-flowering, hardy herbaceous perennial. The daisy flowers are held on single-flowered stems above a base of parsley-like foliage.

There are several named varieties, varying in height from 60 to 90cm (2-3ft). The pale primrose-yellow 'E.C. Buxton' is 60-75cm (24-30in) tall. 'Loddon' has deep buttercup-yellow flowers, 75-90cm (30-36in) high and of similar height is the bright golden-yellow 'Grallagh Gold', which has flowers almost 6.5cm (2.6in) across. The 60-90cm (2-3ft) 'Wargrave' has lemon-yellow flowers.

Propagate this species by division in spring. To encourage good strong basal growth before winter, cut the plants down as soon as they have finished flowering.

Antennaria dioica 'Rosea'   Anthemis tinctoria

Anthyllis montana
(Mountain kidney vetch)
- **Hot situation in full sunshine**
- **Well-drained dry soil**
- **Evergreen**

The pea family forms a huge collection – some utterly weedy, others quite attractive. Most are happy in any garden soil. Of those suitable for gardens, *A. montana* is the best, forming a small woody bush up to 30cm (12in) tall. The hairy foliage gives a silvery appearance and the flowers are red or red-purple.

This species is best planted in a sunny spot in well-drained gritty soil.

Propagation is by cuttings taken with a heel in summer and inserted in a sand frame. Seed is rarely set, but can be sown in early spring. The plant produces a tap root that resents disturbance, so once planted it should not be moved. It is free of pests and diseases.

Above: Antirrhinum majus 'Royal Carpet' creates colourful masses of yellow, pink and red flowers in summer.

Antirrhinum majus
(Common snapdragon, Garden snapdragon, Snapdragon)
- **Sow late winter/early spring**
- **Light to medium soil**
- **Sunny position**

Snapdragons are some of the best-known summer-bedding

Below: Anthyllis montana has silvery foliage and purplish flowers.

plants. There are many varieties, which range from heights of 23cm (9in) to 1.2m (4ft).

As this is a half-hardy annual, sow seeds in late winter or early spring in a temperature of 16-18°C (60-65°F). Use a peat-based growing medium or make up your own (without nutrients) of equal parts peat and sand. Sow seed thinly and cover only lightly. Seedlings are prone to damping off disease, often caused by a too rich growing medium.

Prick off into boxes when large enough to handle. Harden off and plant out in early summer at 23cm (9in) apart. To make bushier plants, pinch out the central growing point when the young plants are 10cm (4in) high.

Aquilegia Hybrids
(Columbine)
- **Sun or partial shade**
- **Any well-drained fertile soil**
- **Early summer flowering**

The many hybrid strains of this hardy herbaceous perennial are elegant plants. The 'long-spurred hybrids' have rather glaucous foliage. The flowers range in colour from pure white, through yellow to pink, soft rose, red, crimson, purple, and blue. Grow these 90cm (3ft) tall plants in partial shade in the dappled light given by deciduous trees for a longer season of bloom. They do best in well-drained fertile soil that does not dry out.

The Common Columbine (*Aquilegia vulgaris*) and its double form are short-spurred and these, too, come in a variety of colours. They reach 60cm (24in) in height.

Propagate by seeds sown in a cool greenhouse or frame in spring, or out of doors in early summer. Division of named varieties can take place in early spring.

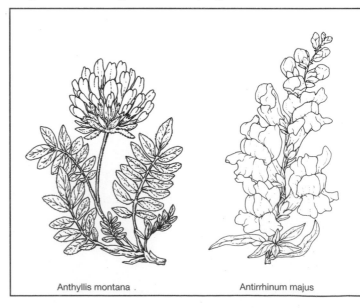

Anthyllis montana .   Antirrhinum majus

Arabis ferdinandi-coburgii 'Variegata'

(Rock cress)
- **Full or partial sunshine**
- **Any soil**
- **Evergreen**

This evergreen perennial, *Arabis ferdinandi-coburgii* 'Variegata' has conspicuous variegated foliage. It forms a tight mat up to 30cm (12in) across that is so attractive as to warrant the removal of the short white flowers borne on 8cm (3.2in) stems. Unlike some plants, it retains its bright variegation throughout the year.

The better known *A. caucasica*, also known as *A. albida*, is really too invasive to be used in a rock garden. Its white flowers appear fleetingly in spring and leave an untidy plant for the rest of the year, though it is admirable for a dry stony bank.

Propagation is by division at almost any time, but it is best in late autumn or early spring. Cuttings can be taken in late summer with a heel or with some old wood at the base.

Arbutus unedo

(Cane apples, Strawberry tree)
- **Full sun**
- **Good fertile soil, including lime**
- **Autumn flowers and fruit**

This tree or large shrub is surely one of the most beautiful flowering evergreens. It grows 4.5-9m (15-30ft) high. Often trees have a gnarled appearance, and the old dark brown bark shreds as trees become established. The glabrous leaves are a dark shining green, leathery and toothed, 5-10cm (2-4in) long, narrowly oval and tapering towards each bud. *A. unedo* will grow where lime is present, which is unusual for ericaceous plants. It also grows well near the sea, where it often bears fruit more freely.

The white pitcher-shaped flowers are freely borne in early and mid-autumn, and often well into winter. At the same time, round orange-red strawberry-like fruit appears. The fruit is very gritty and unpalatable.

Propagate by seed sown in spring, or by cuttings of the current year's wood taken during winter and placed in a propagating frame.

Below: *Arabis ferdinandi-coburgii 'Variegata' forms a tight mat of foliage, variegated green and white.*

Arenaria balearica

(Corsican sandwort, Sandwort)
- **Moist shady situation**
- **Peaty soil**
- **Evergreen**

Arenaria balearica is an attractive, slightly tender, shrubby perennial. It forms a prostrate mat of tiny green leaves, with masses of single white flowers on 2-3cm (0.8-1.25in) stems.

It requires a damp situation and will grow attractively over the face of a damp porous rock or peat block. This plant does not take kindly to direct exposure to sunshine. It may be difficult to establish, but once it settles, it will stay. It is an unobtrusive plant and easy to eradicate if it becomes invasive. Although it spreads, it does so gently. It comes from the Balearics and other Mediterranean islands and can be seen in complete shade between rocks at sea level in Sardinia.

Propagation is by division in early autumn, planting direct. It dislikes being potted up, but this can be overcome by plunging a plant in peat and taking the pieces as they root.

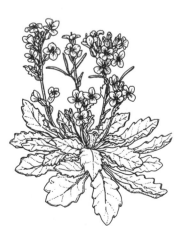

Aquilegia hybrid

Arabis ferdinandi-coburgii 'Variegata'

Arbutus unedo

Arenaria balearica

Aster amellus

(Italian aster, Italian starwort)
- Sunny position
- Retentive well-drained soil
- Late summer and early autumn flowering

This hardy herbaceous perennial has large solitary flowers with golden-yellow centres. There are several clusters of flowers to each strong branching stem, and the grey-green foliage is rough. These plants form a woody rootstock.

Varieties to choose from include: 'King George' which has soft blue-violet 8cm (3.2in) flowers with golden-yellow centres; the large-flowered pink 'Sonia', 60cm (24in) tall; and the compact dwarf 'Violet Queen' 45cm (18in) tall; 'Nocturne' which grows up to 75cm (30in) tall with lavender-lilac flowers; and 'Pink Zenith' which is 60cm (24in) tall with clear pink flower heads.

They object to winter wetness and are happiest in good well-drained retentive soil. They are best planted in spring. Propagate by basal cuttings in spring, or by division where possible.

Below: Aster amellus 'King George' brings late summer colour to hardy herbaceous borders. Plant in soil that does not remain wet during winter, and select a sunny position.

Aster × frikartii 'Mönch'

- Sunny position
- Good well-drained soil
- Summer to autumn flowering

Aster × frikartii 'Mönch' is a hybrid between *A. amellus × A. thomsonii*. Its flowering period is considerably longer than the *A. amellus* varieties. This hardy herbaceous perennial has stout branching stems up to 90cm (3ft)

bearing an abundance of clear lavender-blue flowers with yellow rayed centres, lasting until the frosts begin in autumn. Every collection of hardy herbaceous perennials should possess a plant or two.

Grow this hybrid aster in good well-drained soil in an open sunny position. Make sure that there is sufficient moisture in the soil to sustain the autumn flowers but avoid excessive wetness during the winter months.

Propagate this variety by basal cuttings in spring, or by division where possible. It is best planted in spring.

Left: Aster × frikartii 'Mönch' is bright-faced, with yellow-centred lavender-blue flowers during summer and until the frosts of autumn. Well-drained soil is essential.

Aster novae-angliae

(Michaelmas daisy, New England aster)
- Sunny position
- Good fertile soil
- Late summer, early autumn flowering

This hardy herbaceous perennial forms a tough, vigorous compact rootstock. Beautiful clusters of flowers, each measuring up to 5cm (2in) across, are produced during the late summer and early autumn. The dull green leaves are lanceolate. Several lovely varieties are available, all excellent as cut flowers.

The warm pink flowers of 'Harrington's Pink' were introduced 40 years ago. This variety grows to 1.2m (4ft) in height.

The semi-double phlox-purple 'Lye End Beauty' is 1.35m (4.5ft) tall. Two lovely varieties are both about 1m (3.5ft) tall, 'Alma Potschke' with branching heads of salmon-tinged bright rose flowers, and the startling ruby-red 'September Ruby'.

Propagate these plants by dividing their tough rootstocks in autumn, by placing two strong forks back to back.

Aster amellus

Aster x frikartii 'Mönch'

Right: Astilbe chinensis 'Pumila' is ideal for growing in rock gardens, creating a sea of fluffy, deep pink flowers through summer and into autumn. Moist soil and light shade suit it.

Aster novi-belgii

(Michaelmas daisy)
- **Sunny location**
- **Ordinary fertile soil**
- **Early autumn flowering**

This hardy herbaceous perennial from North America is a well-known border plant, flowering during late summer and into early autumn.

There are many colourful varieties, in heights ranging from 25cm (10in) to 1.2m (4ft). Dwarf varieties include 'Audrey', with mauvish-blue, single flowers; 'Lady in Blue' with semi-double blue flowers; and 'Snowsprite' with white flowers.

Taller varieties include 'Carnival', with cherry-red, semi-double flowers; 'Chequers' with rich violet-purple flower heads; 'Freda Ballard' with semi-double, rich ruby flowers; 'Royal Velvet' with almost double, rich violet-blue flowers and 'White Ladies' with beautiful white blooms.

These plants need a sunny situation in any fertile soil. If mildew attacks the plants, use a fungicide.

To propagate, divide and replant the roots, preferably during early spring.

Astilbe × arendsii

(False goat's beard, Perennial spiraea)
- **Sunshine or partial shade**
- **Moist fertile soil**
- **Summer flowering**

Astilbes are one of the most decorative hardy herbaceous perennials. The arendsii hybrids vary from white, through pale pink, deep pink, coral and red, to magenta. *Astilbe × arendsii* are not only good garden plants, but they also force well under glass in an unheated greenhouse. The foliage varies from light to dark green, with some of the purplish and reddish purple shades. The fluffy panicles of flowers are held on erect stems 60-90cm (2-3ft) tall, but the dwarf varieties are only 45cm (18in).

They will grow in full sun or partial shade and thrive in most soils. There are too many varieties to mention, but all are worth a place in any garden.

Propagate by division in spring. Alternatively, roots may be divided in autumn and potted for forcing or spring planting. Do not cut old flower stems back before spring.

Astilbe chinensis 'Pumila'

(False goat's beard, Perennial spiraea)
- **Moist shady situation**
- **Leafy soil**
- **Herbaceous**

This hardy herbaceous perennial is ideal for growing in a rock garden or small border. It is superb for filling in the gap between spring and autumn, for it flowers in summer through to early autumn.

A. chinensis 'Pumila' produces a 23cm (9in) tall narrow spike of deep pink flowers, slightly flushed with purple, from a base of fern-like leaves. It requires a cool spot, perhaps at the base of a rock where its roots can shelter. Full sun can be tolerated provided there is ample water in summer. Never let this plant dry out.

Propagation is by division in spring, taking care not to split the plants into too small units. The new young plants will certainly need moisture and a shady position while establishing, and should do well in a leafy or peaty soil.

Aster novae-angliae

Aster novi-belgii

Astilbe x arendsii

Astilbe chinensis 'Pumila'

Astrantia major

(Masterwort)
- **Sunshine or partial shade**
- **Retentive fertile soil**
- **Summer flowering**

Astrantia major, the masterwort, is a fascinating hardy herbaceous perennial. Each flower head has outer bracts that are stiff, papery and pointed, and in the centre of each individual flower are many tiny florets. The whole umbel presents a number of star-like flowers. The foliage is palmate. The colour of the flowers is a pure rose-pink, with a pinkish collar of the petal-like bracts. The flowers are held on wiry stems 60cm (24in) high. Other varieties have greenish

Below: Astrantia major, an herbaceous perennial, develops star-like flower heads during summer. Moisture-retentive soil is essential.

white or pale green collars of bracts. One variety, 'Sunningdale Variegated', has leaves prettily splashed with yellow and cream, but as the season advances they lose their variegation unless old flower stems are cut back.

To be successful, astrantias must be in a soil that does not dry out in summer.

Propagate by seed sown as soon as it has been gathered, or by division in spring.

Aubrieta 'Ballawley Amethyst'

- **Open situation**
- **Any well-drained soil**
- **Evergreen**

Aubrietas are low-growing, hardy, evergreen perennials that are almost too well-known to need description. There are a number of species but the best garden plants

come from selected seedlings of *Aubrieta deltoidea*. Cultivation is easy provided you can give it the dry conditions on a sunny bank or dry wall that it requires. It thrives on chalk or in alkaline conditions, where it gives of its best with a colourful spring display. Add lime to the soil if it is acid. There are many named forms, in colours ranging from pale pink through to blue and violet-blue.

To encourage neat plants, cut the dead flower heads off with shears, and by late summer the

Above: Aubrieta deltoidea is startlingly attractive when draped over an old brick wall, perhaps softening the sometimes stark lines created by windows.

new growth should have covered up any untidiness. The plants form mats up to 60cm (24in) wide and the flower heads are 8-10cm (3.2-4in) tall.

Propagation is by division in early autumn. The parent plant, or part of it, is taken to pieces and potted up.

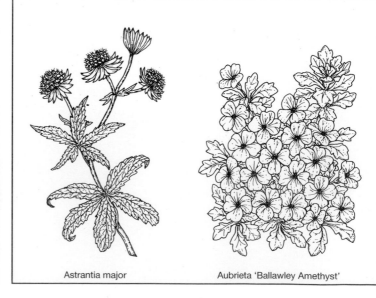

Astrantia major   Aubrieta 'Ballawley Amethyst'

Aucuba japonica 'Variegata'

(Variegated Japanese laurel, Variegated laurel)

- **Shade or sun**
- **Any good soil, including lime**
- **Spring flowers; summer and autumn fruits**

A hardy, evergreen shrub, *Aucuba japonica* grows 2-3m (6.5-10ft) tall and has glossy yellowish spotted green foliage. The cultivar 'Variegata', introduced from Japan in 1783, is sometimes known as *A.j.*'Maculata', but 'Maculata' is a male form whereas 'Variegata' is female. Its purplish flowers produce oval-shaped scarlet berries, provided there is a male form to effect pollination.

In order to have plenty of good young growth, give an annual mulch of leaf mould, but do not fork over the ground.

Propagate by hardwood cuttings 15-23cm (6-9in) long, in autumn, inserted out of doors.

Azorella trifurcata

(Bolax glebaria)

(Fairy moss)

- **Open situation but not direct sunshine**
- **Good drainage but with moisture**
- **Evergreen**

This hardy, evergreen, prostrate plant is sometimes found as *Bolax glebaria* in catalogues. Its natural habitat is South America, where it is native to the Falkland Islands and Chile.

This rock garden plant forms a spreading symmetrical mat on a stony sunny scree, which should have a degree of moisture about. It can also be usefully employed in the alpine house. The hummocks are composed of rosettes of leathery green leaves, and might make a spread of up to 90cm (3ft), but reach only 7-8cm (2.75-3.2in) tall. The flowers are minute and yellow, appearing in midsummer on short stems.

It spreads slowly, and this provides the method of propagation, as the spreading stems root as they move. Remove some rosettes in spring for propagation, and for neatness.

Ballota pseudodictamnus

- **Sunny location**
- **Well-drained ordinary soil**
- **Attractive foliage**

This white woolly hardy perennial has a bush-like habit. It is a good ground cover and looks well throughout the year. The small mauve flowers are almost invisible, so it is the white woolly foliage that is the attraction. Established plants have a woody base. New shoots are smothered with pale, apple-green, egg-shaped, deeply indented leaves. The many-flowered whorls of pale green bracts are widely displayed at each pair of leaves. The lower leaves remain apple-green but those nearer the top of each 45-60cm (18-24in) stem become more and more woolly. Dried ballota is much used by flower arrangers.

In late spring plants need pruning; leaves that have suffered winter damage can be cut back. Propagate by taking heel cuttings in early summer.

Begonia semperflorens

(Wax begonia, Wax plant)

- **Sow in late winter**
- **Light, slightly moist soil**
- **Semi-shade, or some sun**

Of all the half-hardy annuals, the begonia must rank high on the list of most gardeners. A very wide range of this group of plants is available: short, tall or medium in height, green or copper foliage, red, pink or white flowers. However, they are tender and therefore some heat will be necessary at propagation time for good results. Plants are usually 15-20cm (6-8in) high, with a similar spread.

Sow seeds on a peat-based growing medium in late winter. Mix the seed with a little fine sand before sowing to enable it to be sown more evenly. Do not cover the seed. Place in a temperature of 21°C (70°F). When they are large enough to handle, prick off the seedlings in the usual way. Plant out into final positions in early summer, after the danger of frost.

Below: Begonia semperflorens 'Venus' is a superb half-hardy annual for smothering the ground in summer with attractive flowers and waxy foliage.

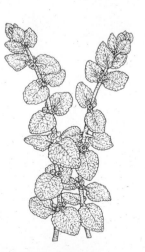

Aucuba japonica 'Variegata'   Azorella trifurcata   Ballota pseudodictamnus   Begonia semperflorens

Begonia × tuberhybrida

(Tuberous begonia)
- **Slight shade**
- **Humid atmosphere, moist soil**
- **Plant flush with the soil**

This tender tuberous-rooted plant creates a mass of large, rose-like flowers from midsummer to late summer. These colourful plants are mainly grown for planting in summer-bedding displays, as well as in containers on a patio.

The range of plants is wide, ranging in height from 30-60cm (12-24in) and up to 38cm (15in) wide. The variety 'Pendula' is superb when grown in a hanging-basket on a patio.

Tubers are started into growth in early spring in 16-18°C (60-65°F). Place the tubers hollow-side uppermost in moist peat, and just level with the surface. As soon as leafy shoots are produced, pot up the tubers individually into 13cm (5in) wide pots, and later into larger ones. Harden off plants in a cold frame and plant out only when all risk of frost has passed.

In late summer, before the first frosts, lift, box-up and place the plants in a frost-free place.

Berberis darwinii

(Darwin's barberry, Darwin's berberis)
- **Sunny position**
- **Good fertile soil**
- **Spring flowers; autumn fruits**

Berberis darwinii is a lovely flowering evergreen shrub that reaches a height of 2-3m (6.5-10ft). Its shield-shaped leaves are dark green, glossy and stalkless. It was discovered in Chile by Charles Darwin in 1835. In spring, bushes are covered with deep orange-yellow flowers tinged with red, on drooping racemes 4-5cm (1.6-2in) long. In late summer to early autumn, oval plum to bluish coloured berries are produced.

It is perfectly hardy, but should be given a position sheltered against drying winds. It does best in moist fertile soils. Prune in spring or after flowering.

Propagate by seed sown in late winter in a prepared seed bed out of doors, or take half-ripe cuttings in late summer.

Below: Berberis darwinii is a widely-grown evergreen shrub with deep orange-yellow flowers tinged red in spring.

Bergenia cordifolia

(Pig squeak)
- **Sunshine or shade**
- **Not fussy about soil**
- **Spring flowering**

Bergenia has gone through a series of generic names: at one time it was *Megasea* and then *Saxifraga*.

In recent years these hardy evergreen perennials have come into their own, partly due to the interest in flower arranging. The large leathery green or dark green foliage often takes on attractive hues of red, crimson and brown-red. Their flowers, displayed on stout stems 30cm (12in) high, rise above the mass of green leathery foliage. The variety *B. cordifolia* 'Purpurea' has large rounded leaves that turn purplish in winter; its flowers are magenta.

Another variety is the pretty white-flowered *B. stracheyi* 'Silver Light' or 'Silberlicht'. The pure white flowers take on a pinkish tint as they age, but are still lovely.

Propagate bergenias by division, immediately after flowering or in autumn. Do not let them dry out.

Below: Bergenia cordifolia is an evergreen border perennial with large, domed heads of magenta flowers during spring.

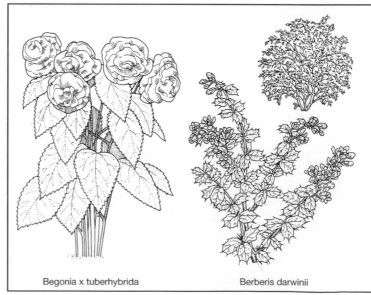

Begonia x tuberhybrida

Berberis darwinii

Betula pendula 'Youngii'

(Young's weeping birch)
- **Open sunny situation**
- **Light sandy fertile soil**
- **Winter/spring catkins; autumn foliage**

Here is a perfect weeping, deciduous tree for a small or medium-sized garden. In spring its weeping branches display the yellow pendent male catkins, which in winter are greenish. The erect female catkins are pale green, enhanced by small dull crimson stigmas. Specimens trained with a leading stem or grafted on to a standard stock produce a dome-shaped tree.

Young trees need secure staking until they are strong enough to stand on their own. Avoid thin chalky soils. Although trees will thrive on fairly fertile soil where lime is present, this weeping birch grows better on lime-free soils. Also, avoid very wet ground.

Propagate by budding In midsummer out of doors on to stocks of *Betula pendula*.

Borago officinalis

(Borage, Cool tankard, Talewort)
- **Sow in mid-spring**
- **Ordinary soil**
- **Sunny location**

This hardy annual is grown for its foliage and flowers and as a valuable addition to summer salads. Usually attaining a height of 1m (3.3ft), the plants are better suited to the middle or back of a large border. Group them together in fours or fives for a bold effect. Larger plants will need staking.

The large leaves are obovate, tending to narrow at the base, covered with hairs (as are the long stems), and a good green in colour. Flowers are generally blue, but purple and white forms occur. The flowers are about 2cm (0.8in) across and resemble five-pointed stars.

This species is very easy to grow. In mid-spring sow the seeds where the plants are to flower. Take out small drills and cover the seed. Later thin them out to 30cm (12in) apart. Flowering begins in early summer.

Dried flowers of borage can be used to enhance the ever-popular pot-pourri; collect blooms before they are fully open.

Brachycome iberidifolia

(Swan River daisy)
- **Sow in mid-spring**
- **Rich soil**
- **Sunny but sheltered site**

The daisy flowers of this half-hardy annual may be lilac, blue-purple, pink or white. Very free-flowering and fragrant, the blooms are produced on compact plants from early summer onwards. It is very

striking when sited towards the front of a border. It can also be planted in containers on a sunny sheltered patio or yard. Wiry stems reach a height of 45cm (18in) and carry light green leaves that are deeply cut. The scented flowers, when fully open, are about 4cm (1.6in) across.

Sow the seed under glass in spring. Use a good ordinary seed-growing medium, and keep in a temperature of 16°C (60°F). When

Above: Brachycome iberidifolia has delicate, scented, daisy-like flowers in a range of colours from early to late summer.

seedlings are ready, prick off in the usual way. Set plants out at 35cm (14in) intervals in late spring. Alternatively, sow seed directly into the border during mid-spring and thin out later. Some support may be necessary. Take care to avoid windy sites.

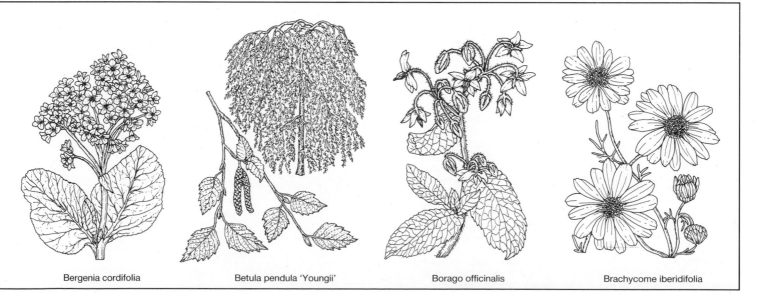

Bergenia cordifolia   Betula pendula 'Youngii'   Borago officinalis   Brachycome iberidifolia

Above: Buddleia alternifolia reveals weeping stems smothered in slightly fragrant, bright lilac-purple flowers in summer.

Buddleia alternifolia
- **Open sunny situation**
- **Good loamy soil**
- **Summer flowers**

This small deciduous weeping tree has lance-shaped, dark green leaves which are narrow and 4-10cm (1.6-4in) long. The bright lilac-purple flowers are slightly fragrant. A well-grown tree makes a delightful sight in full bloom.

To maintain a healthy specimen, cut out the old flowered shoots as soon as the flowers have faded. At the same time, remove any dead or unwanted shoots. Standard trees usually have a main stem 1-1.2m (3.3-4ft) high. Remove all surplus shoots that appear on the main stem.

Propagate by half-ripe cuttings taken during the summer.

Buddleia davidii
(Butterfly bush, Orange-eye buddleia, Summer lilac)
- **Sunny location**
- **Any good soil**
- **Summer flowering**

One common name of this deciduous shrub is derived from its attraction to butterflies. It grows to a height of 3-4m (10-13ft) and the four-angled stems make wide-spreading bushes with an open habit. The lance-like leaves are dark green above and white-felted beneath. The fragrant flower trusses are on tapering panicles.

There are many varieties to choose from: 'Black Knight' is dark purple; 'Harlequin', reddish purple with creamy white variegated foliage; 'Peace', pure white; and 'Royal Red', purple-red.

Annual pruning needs to be done during late winter. Cut back the previous year's growth to within a few buds. Newly planted bushes should have their growths pruned to half their length for the first two or three years.

Propagate by half-ripe cuttings in summer, or by hardwood cuttings in autumn.

Buddleia globosa
(Orange ball buddleia, Orange ball tree)
- **Sunny location**
- **Any fertile soil, including lime**
- **Early summer flowering**

The almost evergreen *Buddleia globosa* is a striking shrub, with orange-yellow ball-like flowers and dark green wrinkled foliage. The downy covering above and tawny felt covering beneath the leaves are outstanding. The lance-shaped leaves are 13-20cm (5-8in) long and 4-5cm (1.6-2in) wide. The honey-scented globose flowers, each about 2cm (0.8in) in diameter, are carried in terminal panicles of eight to ten. Each panicle can measure 15-20cm (6-8in) long. Well-grown shrubs can reach 4.5cm (15ft) in height and spread.

Only in very hard winters will this buddleia become a semi-deciduous shrub; certainly in milder localities it will remain evergreen.

Below: Bupleurum fruticosum has attractive blue-green leaves and clusters of small yellow flowers from midsummer onwards.

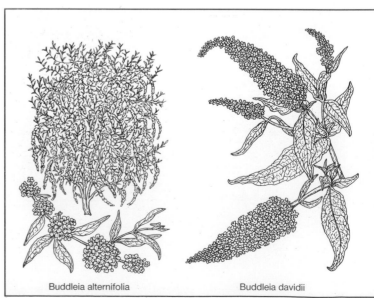

Buddleia alternifolia

Buddleia davidii

Pruning usually entails cutting out all weaker shoots in spring. When they become too large, bushes can be cut back hard in early spring, but flowers will be lost for one season.

Propagate by half-ripe cuttings taken in early summer to midsummer.

Bupleurum fruticosum

(Thoroughwax)
- **Sunny position**
- **Any good soil, including lime**
- **Flowers midsummer/early autumn**

This hardy evergreen or semi-evergreen flowering shrub has a rather floppy habit, and grows 1.5-2.5m (5-8ft) high. It is a must for seaside areas and for chalky soils. Its small yellow flowers are borne on terminal umbels 7.5-13cm (3-5in) across, and carried on purplish young shoots. The alternate narrow blue-green leaves are 5-9cm (2-3.5in) long and 2-4cm (0.8-1.6in) wide.

When the bush becomes untidy and thick, cut it hard back to within about 15cm (6in) of the ground in late spring; by autumn it should become a shapely bush again. With such treatment, a season's flower display will be lost, but the result will be rewarding.

Propagate by taking firm side shoots and inserting them in a cold frame in late summer.

Calceolaria integrifolia

(Slipper flower, Slipperwort)
- **Sunny situation**
- **Well-drained, loamy soil**
- **Summer flowering**

The mention of calceolarias makes many gardeners think of tender plants with pouched flowers. *Calceolaria integrifolia* is a bushy shrub about 1.2m (4ft) tall. Its sage-like opposite dull green leaves are 5-9cm (2-3.5in) long and 2-4cm (0.8-1.6in) wide, have a soft greyish felt beneath and are stalkless. The pouch-like, bright yellow flowers grow in terminal flat-topped clusters.

Although tolerably hardy in many areas, this evergreen shrub appreciates protection from a wall, fence or hedge, and an aspect warmed by the sun. In cold districts, cover plants with dry bracken against frost damage.

Prune in spring if plants have been damaged during winter. If it is severely cut back, this charming shrub will soon break freely from any live wood. Propagate it by softwood cuttings in summer.

Calendula officinalis 'Lemon Gem'

(Pot marigold)
- **Sow in early spring or autumn**
- **Ordinary free-draining soil**
- **Sunny spot**

The very reliable calendulas have beautiful yellow, orange or gold flowers. 'Lemon Gem' has striking double yellow flowers that are formed on compact plants 30cm (12in) high. Free-flowering and pungent, they can be used almost anywhere in the garden.

As this is a hardy annual, seeds can be sown where they are to flower during the autumn or early spring. Take out shallow drills and then lightly cover the seed. Thin out to 15cm (6in) apart. Alternatively, they can be raised under glass to give uniformity for the formal planting areas. Raise during early spring in a frost-free temperature. Autumn-sown plants will be stronger, and flower earlier. Dead-head to prolong flowering.

Below: Calendula officinalis 'Lemon Gem', a pot marigold, creates large, double bright yellow flowers during summer.

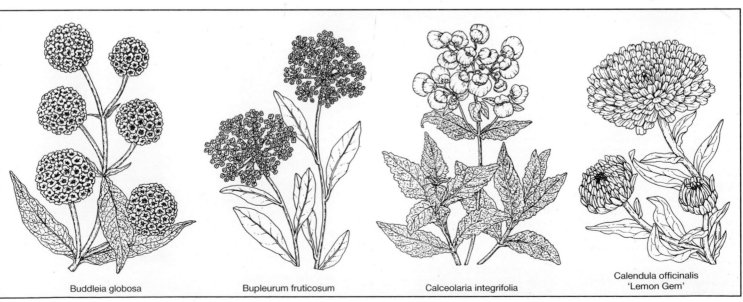

Buddleia globosa

Bupleurum fruticosum

Calceolaria integrifolia

Calendula officinalis 'Lemon Gem'

Callistephus chinensis 'Milady Mixed'

(Annual aster, China aster)
- **Sow in early spring**
- **Any soil, but well drained**
- **Sunny and open position**

A half-hardy annual, the aster is useful for almost any purpose. Many forms have been developed, from 15cm (6in) high to 75cm (30in). A wide range of colours is available and the shape of the flowers can be just as varied, from button types to large chrysanthemum forms. As a moderate choice try the 'Milady Mixture'. The blooms are slightly inward curving and weather resistant. The stems are 25cm (10in) high, and the double flowers are in shades of blue, rose, rose-red and white. They are ideal as bedding plants or as drifts in the annual border.

Early flowering plants should be raised under glass in a temperature of 16°C (60°F) during early spring. Sow the seeds in pots or boxes of any good soil-based growing medium. Prick out into boxes, harden off in the usual way and plant out into final positions, 15cm (6in) apart, in late spring or early summer.

Calluna vulgaris

(Heather, Ling, Scotch heather)
- **Open sunny situation**
- **Any fertile lime-free soil**
- **Flowers from summer to late autumn**

This hardy evergreen shrubby plant can be found growing on moorland and mountains over a wide area in Europe. Today there are many varieties, in a wide range of colours, with single or double flowers. Of the doubles, the 23cm (9in) 'J. H. Hamilton' has bright pink flowers from late summer to early autumn. An old favourite is 'H. E. Beale', 60cm (24in) tall, with sprays of soft pink flowers in autumn; it does well on clay soil. 'Gold Haze' is 60cm (24in) tall, with golden foliage and sprays of white flowers. 'Cuprea', only 30cm (12in) tall, has coppery foliage and light mauve flowers in late summer.

Prune these heathers when flowering has finished by cutting off old flower heads; but if they are

grown for foliage, cut off the dead flower spikes in spring.

Propagate by taking heel or nodal cuttings in summer, or by layering during the spring.

Calochortus venustus

(Butterfly tulip, Globe tulip, Mariposa lily, White mariposa)
- **Full sun**
- **Dry, well-drained sandy soil**
- **Plant 7.5cm (3in) deep**

These bulbous plants thrive in light woodland and open grassland; in light sandy soil they grow to over 45cm (18in) tall. The calochortus forms a spindly plant with insignificant foliage of long slender leaves that appear in early spring. The summer flowers vary from white to yellow, orange, rose, dark red or purple, with very decorative markings, and reach 5cm (2in) across.

Plant in autumn in a sunny situation, with a dry sandy soil that has some leaf-mould in it. The bulbs should be planted 7.5cm (3in) deep and kept away from excessive moisture, so ensure that the soil is well drained. When foliage dies down, keep the plant dry until growth starts again. Then keep it just moist until it flowers. It will grow well in a greenhouse.

Camassia leichtlinii

(Bear grass, Camass)
- **Sun or light shade**
- **Moist soil**
- **Plant 15cm (6in) deep**

This bulbous plant grows to a height of 90cm (3ft) and has pointed sword-like leaves. The

Above: Callistephus chinensis 'Milady Dark Rose' is a dwarf, with long-lasting flowers. Ideal when planted in window boxes.

flowers, on stems that grow above the leaves, are star-shaped in blue or white, about 4cm (1.6in) across, and appear in summer.

This species should be planted in a heavy moist soil with plenty of leaf-mould or peat to prevent drying out by spring winds and summer droughts. The bulbs should be planted in autumn, 15cm (6in) apart. They can be left for a few years; then in autumn lift the bulbs, split up and replant to give them more space. To prevent strength being taken from the bulbs, dead flower heads should be removed. To increase your stock, bulblets can be removed from around the older bulbs in early autumn and replanted

immediately. They should reach flowering size in three years. Seeds can be sown, but may take up to five years to flower.

Camellia × williamsii 'Donation'

- **Sun or partial shade**
- **Good acid or neutral peaty soil**
- **Spring flowers**

These handsome evergreen shrubs are quite hardy, except that their flower buds and flowers can be damaged by frost. Although camellias do well in partial shade, they do equally well in full sunshine. They dislike lime soils. They need an ample supply of sifted leaf-mould or peat. Moisten the peat properly before use.

Today there are many varieties of *Camellia japonica*, but for the small or medium-sized garden there is nothing more beautiful than *C. × williamsii* 'Donation'. Its soft pink semi-double flowers, about 13cm (5in) across, are borne above dark green glossy foliage. The growth is vigorous and erect, reaching a height of 2-3m (6.5-10ft).

Prune camellias when bushes become overgrown. They can be cut back hard after flowering has finished. Otherwise the only pruning needed is to keep bushes shapely.

Propagate by half-ripe cuttings of the current year's wood during the summer under glass.

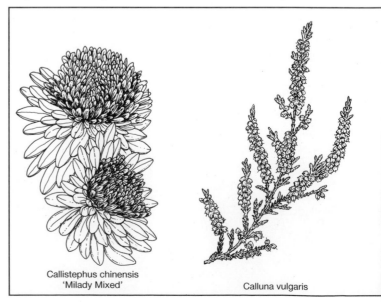

Callistephus chinensis 'Milady Mixed'

Calluna vulgaris

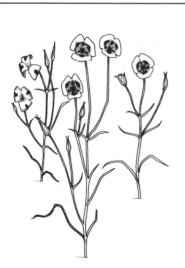

Above: *Camellia × williamsii 'Donation' is an evergreen shrub* with soft-pink, semi-double flowers blooming in spring.

Above: *Campanula cochleariifolia is ideal in rock gardens, creating* thimble-like blue lavender flowers during summer.

Campanula cochleariifolia

(Fairies' thimbles)
- **Any situation**
- **Any soil**
- **Evergreen**

Campanula cochleariifolia (sometimes still listed as *C. pusilla*) is so good-tempered as to be suitable for most soils and situations. This dwarf perennial is native to the European Alps, where it thrives on and around limestone rocks and is happiest in stony ground where it can run freely. Thus in cultivation it enjoys scree conditions where its blue bells can push their way up on 5-8cm (2-3.2in) stems from the heart-shaped basal leaves. Although it spreads, it can be controlled very easily, but it is attractive enough to deter such a move. There are forms ranging from white to deep blue.

Propagation is by division between early autumn and spring, or by soft cuttings in late spring or early autumn.

Calochortus venustus

Camassia leichtlinii

Camellia x williamsii 'Donation'

Campanula cochleariifolia

Catananche caerulae
(Cupid's dart)
- **Full sun**
- **Well-drained light soil**
- **Summer flowering**

This attractive hardy herbaceous perennial forms clumps of hairy grass-like leaves, from which emerge 60cm (24in) spikes each carrying silvery papery bracts and lavender-blue everlasting flowers. The best form, *Catananche caerulea* 'Major', has larger and richer blue flowers. There is also a white variety, 'Perry's White'.

To extend the season of flowering, grow two or more clumps, and cut one down when it comes into flower; this will then bloom later. The flowers can be cut and dried, like everlastings, and used for indoor decoration. All are best in full sun and in well-drained soil. If plants are cut back in early autumn, this enables them to pull through the winter.

Propagate by root cuttings in autumn, or by division in spring, or by seeds sown out of doors in spring.

Ceanothus × delinianus
(Californian lilac, Redroot)
- **Sunny sheltered situation**
- **Any good fertile soil including lime or chalk**
- **Summer to autumn flowering**

Ceanothus × delinianus and its varieties form a group of deciduous shrubs which reach 1.5-2m (5-6.5ft) tall. Most have blue flowers but a few are shades of pink. 'Gloire de Versailles' has enormous panicles of powder-blue flowers; 'Topaz' has bright indigo-blue flowers; and 'Henri Desfosse' is a darker blue than 'Gloire de Versailles'. 'Marie Simon' is rose-pink, and 'Perle Rose' is carmine-rose.

The panicles of flowers are produced on the new wood and for this reason bushes must be hard pruned each year in spring. Cut plants back almost to the base of the previous year's growth. To encourage good growth, feed with a general fertilizer and mulch with well-rotted leaf-mould, good garden compost or farmyard manure (but it must not be fresh).

Propagate in summer by half-ripe cuttings of the current year's growth.

Ceanothus impressus
(Californian lilac, Redroot, Santa Barbara ceanothus)
- **Sunny position**
- **Any good fertile soil, including chalk**
- **Spring flowering**

This evergreen shrub has clusters of deep blue flowers in spring, but even before the flowers open, the dark red flower buds are attractive and make a beautiful display. The almost rounded leaves, 6-10mm (0.25-0.4in) long, are dark green and deeply furrowed, and pale green beneath. This species makes a low-growing shrub about 1.5m (5ft) high and equally wide.

This is one of the hardiest of the evergreen ceanothus species. Even if a treasured specimen is killed by hard frost, these plants are easily propagated. Provided a few cuttings are taken from time to time, young plants can soon replace the loss. After the ceanothus has flowered, shorten the longest shoots; do this every year.

Propagate by half-ripe cuttings of the current year's growth in late summer.

Below: *Ceanothus impressus is a superb evergreen shrub for planting against a wall.*

Cedrus deodara 'Aurea'
(Golden Himalayan cedar)
- **Light shade when young**
- **Good well-drained soil**
- **Slow-growing medium tree**

This beautiful yellow-foliaged evergreen conifer from the Himalayas has a drooping

Below: *Celosia argentea plumosa is a half-hardy annual that creates tall, feathery flower plumes during summer.*

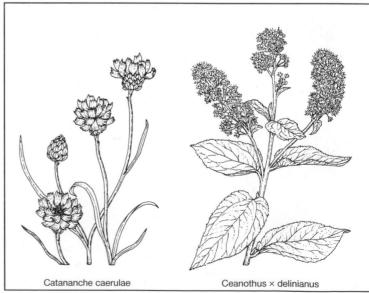

Catananche caerulae   Ceanothus × delinianus

character. It has longer needles than other cedars, about 5cm (2in). The golden colour is noticeable on exposed foliage but becomes more green where strong light does not penetrate. The yellow is less pronounced in winter. The tree grows to 3m (10ft) tall in ten years, but can eventually reach 12m (39ft). The cultivar 'Golden Horizon' is a semi-prostrate variety, reaching 75cm (30in) tall and twice as wide.

Seeds can be sown in seed compost in spring. When the seedlings are 7.5cm (3in) tall, plant them out in a nursery bed. Keep them in a lightly shaded area, as this variety is prone to frost damage when young. Plant out in the final positions after three or four years; stake plants over 45cm (18in) tall. The soil should be well drained with leaf-mould, peat and bonemeal.

Celosia argentea plumosa
(Celosia argentea pyramidalis)
(Feathered amaranth, Prince of Wales' feather)
- **Sow in early spring**
- **Well-drained fertile soil**
- **Sunny sheltered location**

These plants are raised as half-hardy annuals. The variety 'Apricot Brandy' was introduced for its dwarf effect, at most the height will be 40cm (16in). A handsome shade of apricot, the plumes are an

aggregate of both central and basal side shoots. The plants may have plumes up to 50cm (20in) across, and the light green foliage can be overwhelmed by the bloom.

This cultivar makes an excellent bedding subject for formal plantings, but is also invaluable for displays in window boxes, troughs or containers for the patio or yard. Group them together in large pots and place near the front door, to make a pleasant feature for visitors to admire.

Centaurea cyanus 'Blue Ball'
(Bachelor's buttons, Bluebottle, Cornflower)
- **Sow in autumn or spring**
- **Ordinary well-drained soil**
- **Sunny position**

The common native cornflower is a great favourite, but selection and breeding over many years has led to improved strains for the garden. If you decide to grow this plant, try 'Blue Ball', which is very true to type and free from the purple tinge often found in the blues. Strong 90cm (3ft) stems carry the ball-like flowers well above the leaves, which are narrow and lanceolate in shape. Grow this hardy annual in bold groups near godetias and you will have a beautiful contrast of colour during the summer. They are often grown as cut flowers either in the border or in rows in another part of the garden.

Sow seeds in either autumn or spring. Those sown in autumn will make larger plants. Take out drills where the plants are to flower, sow the seed and cover.

Below: Centaurea cyanus 'Blue Ball' is a hardy annual that

Thin out subsequent seedlings to about 45cm (18in). In very cold areas protect autumn-sown seedlings from frost. Give support to very tall types.

becomes smothered with button-like flowers during summer.

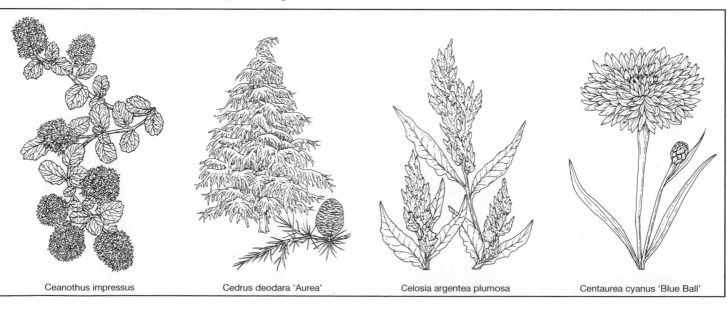

Ceanothus impressus   Cedrus deodara 'Aurea'   Celosia argentea plumosa   Centaurea cyanus 'Blue Ball'

Centaurea macrocephala

(Great knapweed, Knapweed, Yellow hardhead, Yellow hardweed)
● **Full sun**
● **Light, sandy soil**
● **Summer flowering**

This herbaceous perennial is a member of the knapweed family and is a very handsome plant. The strong erect stems are 90-120cm (3-4ft) tall. At the top of each stem appears a round golden flower head, as large as a tennis ball. Each flower is surrounded by rough brown papery bracts forming a collar that protects the inner florets. If situated in the middle of a border, this plant makes an outstanding individual display. The flower heads dry well, and are useful for winter decorations.

Below: Centaurea macrocephala develops large, thistle-like flower heads during summer.

It would be unfortunate not to mention *C. dealbata* 'John Coutts'. This perennial cornflower is free-flowering and, from my experience, can be left in one position for many years. The cornflower blooms are clear pink, on 90cm (3ft) stems.

These plants need full sun, and will do well in a limy soil. Propagate when necessary by division in spring or autumn.

Below: Centaurea moschata 'Dobies Giant' creates a wealth of colour throughout summer.

Centaurea moschata

(Sweet sultan)
● **Sow in mid-spring**
● **Fertile, well-drained soil**
● **Sunny position**

From the Orient, this hardy annual has sweetly scented yellow, purple, pink or white flowers up to 7.5cm (3in) across. Carried on thin stems 45cm (18in) high, the leaves are narrow. This species is ideal for the middle of the border, planted in groups.

Centaurea macrocephala

Centaurea moschata

Centranthus ruber

Ceratostigma plumbaginoides

Plants come into flower in early summer and, from this period, keep dead blooms picked off. This will encourage lower lateral shoots to develop and produce further flowers.

Wherever possible, make sowings directly where plants are to flower, as disturbance can result in considerable losses. To avoid such disappointments, sow in drills in mid-spring in a well-drained border, and thin out the germinated seedlings to 23cm (9in) apart. If possible, make a further sowing a month later to ensure a longer period of bloom. The giant strain is well recommended, and has finely fringed petals.

Centranthus ruber
(Kentranthus ruber)
(Fox's brush, Jupiter's beard, Red valerian)
- **Full sun**
- **Ordinary garden soil**
- **Summer flowering**

Although this hardy herbaceous perennial may be classed as a wilding, it is worth garden space, especially if you have a lime or chalk soil. Plants can often be seen growing on old walls or mortar rubble dumps.

The closely packed heads of red or deep pink flowers are carried on 60-90cm (2-3ft) glaucous stems and foliage. The red flowers are certainly more colourful than the pink ones, and it is as well to

remember this when buying. There is also a white form available, *Centranthus ruber* 'Albus'.

Propagate by seeds sown out of doors during the spring or the seeds can be sown as soon as they are ripe where the plants will eventually flower. Alternatively, plants can be divided in late autumn or spring.

Ceratostigma plumbaginoides
(Leadwort)
- **Any open situation**
- **Any soil**
- **Herbaceous**

This shrubby perennial species is one of the beauties of the garden in autumn, when other plants are dying down. Its red-tinged foliage deepens as autumn proceeds and its 2cm (0.8in) wide terminal cluster of blue flowers arrives from late summer onwards. The plant is completely hardy and unharmed by early frosts, although some say otherwise. It can spread to about 40cm (16in), but cannot be considered invasive, although its roots install themselves fairly firmly.

This is an accommodating plant, but will thrive better in a well-

Right: Cercis siliquastrum is a hardy deciduous tree with clusters of purplish-rose flowers in spring. Its roundish leaves create a foil for the flowers.

drained warmish spot where it will reach its full height of 30cm (12in). Do not plant the ceratostigma in a damp situation.

Propagation is simply by division in spring, just before growth begins. Division in autumn would spoil the plant at its peak.

Ceratostigma willmottianum
(Chinese plumbago, Hardy plumbago, Plumbago)
- **Full sun**
- **Fertile well-drained soil**
- **Late summer and autumn flowering**

This half-hardy deciduous shrub needs to be treated like a fuchsia. It has to be cut back in late winter or early spring to encourage strong growth for the coming season. It makes a wiry bushy plant up to 90cm (3ft) tall. Its small, rough leaves are green, set on brown twiggy stems that are topped by branching shoots bearing clear cobalt-blue flowers. Because it is usually cut back in winter or spring, it is frequently grown in herbaceous borders.

Propagate *C. willmottianum* by softwood cuttings in early summer, inserted in a heated propagator.

Cercis siliquastrum
(Judas tree, Love tree)
- **Full sun**
- **Any well-drained soil**
- **Mid- to late spring flowering**

Legend says that it was on this tree that Judas hanged himself after the betrayal, hence the common name. The sight of its clusters of purplish-rose flowers is certainly unforgettable. They are produced in spring from the joints of the old wood and on the trunks of old trees.

This deciduous tree or outsized bushy shrub reaches up to 7.6m (25ft) in height, and trees nearly 100 years old will be about 9m (30ft) tall.

The roundish leaves are as attractive as the flowers, each having a heart-shaped base, green above and a greyish green below. In midsummer the flowers are followed by pea-shaped pods, 7.5-13cm (3-5in) long.

This species will thrive in well-drained soils, and prefers a milder climate rather than a cold hard one. Transplant at an early stage, as older plants resent disturbance. Propagate by sowing seed under glass in late or early spring. It is beneficial to remove dead wood in late winter.

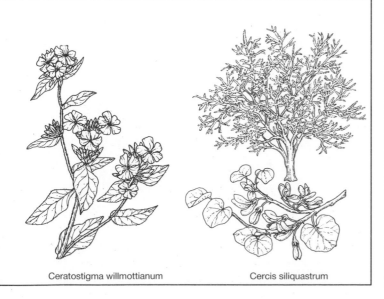

Ceratostigma willmottianum   Cercis siliquastrum

Chaenomeles × superba 'Knap Hill Scarlet'

(Flowering quince, Japonica)
- **Sunny situation**
- **Any good well-drained soil**
- **Spring flowers; autumn fruits**

For a stunning display of bright red flowers throughout the spring months it is hard to beat this superb deciduous shrub. The cup-shaped flowers, each 2.5-4cm (1-1.6in) across, are borne in clusters on spiny twigs clothed in the new spring foliage. During the autumn these give way to golden yellow edible fruits, the quinces. Bushes grow to a height of about 1.2-1.5m (4-5ft) and just as wide.

Other quinces to look out for are *Chaenomeles × superba* 'Crimson and Gold', which forms a dense spreading shrub about 1m (3.3ft) tall, and the many varieties of *Chaenomeles speciosa*, particularly 'Simonii', which bears semi-double bright crimson-scarlet flowers on a slow-growing shrub up to 75cm (30in).

Propagate all these shrubs by seeds sown in spring, by half-ripe cuttings in summer, or by hardwood cuttings in late autumn or winter. Little pruning is necessary except thinning.

Chamaecyparis lawsoniana 'Aurea Densa'

- **Open situation**
- **Ordinary garden soil**
- **Very slow-growing dwarf bush**

This beautiful evergreen conifer was raised in England in 1939. It is a golden-leaved dwarf and grows to 2m (6.5ft), but will take about 30 years to reach half this height. It has densely packed fans of flattened leaves and a regular conical shape. Tiny green cones about 6mm (0.25in) in diameter turn brown as they ripen.

The seeds can be sown, but seedlings can vary greatly. It is better to take cuttings, in an equal mix of peat and sand in a cold frame in spring. Transplant them into nursery beds in autumn and grow on for three years before moving to their final situation.

Normally these plants are free from pests and diseases except for honey fungus.

Right: Chamaecyparis lawsoniana 'Aurea Densa' is a slow-growing, golden-green conifer.

Below: Chaenomeles × superba 'Coral Sea' bears cup-shaped pink flowers during spring.

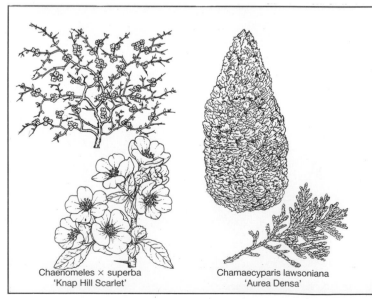

Chaenomeles × superba
'Knap Hill Scarlet'

Chamaecyparis lawsoniana
'Aurea Densa'

Right: Chamaecyparis obtusa 'Nana' is a small and slow-growing evergreen, with dark green foliage. It has saucer-shaped fans of leaves.

Chamaecyparis lawsoniana 'Elwoodii'
- **Open or lightly shaded site**
- **Well-drained garden soil**
- **Slow-growing bush**

Probably one of the best-known cultivars of this evergreen conifer, the 'Elwoodii' is ideal for the small garden and rockery. It is of garden origin from cross-pollination of other cultivars developed from western United States parents. It has a fine blue-green colour, and a column-like shape with tight neat foliage on an upright branch system.

In ten years it can reach 2m (6.5ft) tall and 75cm (30in) wide. In 20 years it reaches 3m (10ft). It can be made to grow more slowly by lifting it each year and replanting in autumn. The cones are green, changing to brown as they ripen. Prune to keep a single leader for a well-shaped bush.

The seeds can be sown, but are unlikely to be true to type. Some growers sow plenty of seed and retain only seedlings that show the colour and characteristics of the parent.

To obtain a plant true to its parent, cuttings should be taken. After they root, keep them in a nursery bed for three years.

Chamaecyparis lawsoniana 'Green Globe'
- **Open or lightly shaded site**
- **Ordinary well-drained soil**
- **Slow-growing dwarf bush**

This dwarf evergreen conifer was raised in New Zealand from United States parents. It is the most compact of the dwarf varieties available. Its fine green colour, combined with its globular form, makes it ideal for a rockery, sink garden, container or border where it can be viewed clearly. It will reach 30cm (12in) in ten years, and should eventually reach twice this size. The sprays of green leaves give a softer outline than that of some other miniature forms. The green cones are 6mm (0.25in) wide, and turn brown as they ripen.

The seed can be sown, but is unlikely to come true. It is better to take cuttings or to graft on to a dwarf stock. Cuttings should be placed in an equal mixture of peat and sand, and when rooted, transplanted into a nursery bed to grow on for three years. Keep the bed well weeded, and then plant them out in their final situations. Place either in the open or in light shade.

Chamaecyparis lawsoniana 'Minima Aurea'
- **Open situation**
- **Ordinary garden soil**
- **Slow-growing dwarf bush**

This dwarf, rounded, evergreen conifer was raised some 60 years ago. The main difference between this variety and 'Aurea Densa' is that the forms of foliage are mainly ranged vertically giving it a distinctive texture. Its rounded form is slightly taller than wide, reaching 50cm (20in) tall by 40cm (16in) wide in ten years, and just over 1m (3.3ft) tall by 80cm (32in) wide in 30 years. The scale-like leaves are golden-yellow and soft to the touch. They need to be placed in open sunlight to retain their brightness. The small cones are green, turning to brown when they ripen.

It is best to propagate by taking cuttings, which should be struck in spring and set in an equal mixture of peat and sand in a cold frame. Plant out the rooted cuttings into a weed-free nursery bed in autumn, grow on for three years, and then plant out.

Chamaecyparis obtusa 'Nana'
- **Open site or light shade**
- **Well-drained garden soil**
- **Very slow-growing dwarf bush**

Developed by the Japanese from the Hinoki cypress that grows in Japan, this evergreen conifer is much sought after for miniature gardens and rockeries. It will reach only 25cm (10in) high and as wide in ten years; after 100 years it may reach 1.5m (5ft). It makes a flat-topped dome, with saucer-shaped fans of tight, dark green leaves. The cones mature within a year.

The ripe seeds can be sown, but are unlikely to grow true. It is better to grow from cuttings. Use a half and half mixture of peat and sand. Grow until they have rooted, and then plant out in a nursery bed. Great care is needed to prevent the plants from being choked by weeds and other plants. After three years, move them to their final positions and keep a space clear around them for a few years. Use a well-drained soil that has been enriched with peat, leaf-mould and bonemeal.

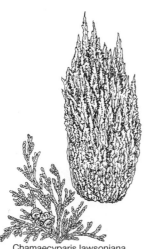

Chamaecyparis lawsoniana 'Elwoodii'

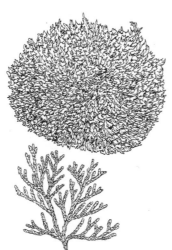

Chamaecyparis lawsoniana 'Green Globe'

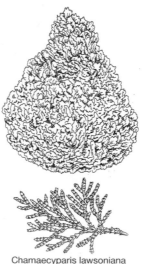

Chamaecyparis lawsoniana 'Minima Aurea'

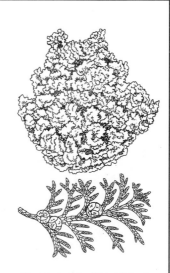

Chamaecyparis obtusa 'Nana'

Chionodoxa luciliae gigantea

(Glory of the snow)
- **Open sunny site**
- **Ordinary soil**
- **Plant 5-7.5cm (2-3in) deep**

This early-flowering bulb grows to 20cm (8in) tall. The strap-like leaves have blunt tips, and the six-petalled violet-blue flowers with white centres are 4cm (1.6in) across. They are ideal for growing in rock gardens, at the front of beds and in grass. They come into flower in late winter and last until spring.

Plant bulbs 5-7.5cm (2-3in) deep and 7.5-10cm (3-4in) apart in the autumn. For a good effect, plant in groups. Lift the plants after several years, divide the bulbs and replant to give more space; the best time is when foliage is dying back. Seeds can be sown in late spring, left for a year and then transplanted into flowering position. Slugs are the worst pest; put down slug bait in the area. Black sooty areas around the flowers are caused by smut. Lift and destroy the infected plants, and spray other chionodoxas with a fungicide.

Choisya ternata

(Mexican orange, Mexican orange blossom)
- **Sheltered, sunny situation**
- **Almost any soil**
- **Spring flowering**

This handsome evergreen shrub is suitable for all except the very coldest areas. Bushes reach a height of 2-3m (6.5-10ft). The dark green glossy leaves 8-15cm (3.2-6in) long, consist of three stalkless leaflets 4-8cm (1.6-3.2in) long, tapering at either end and attached to a 3-5cm (1.25-2in) main stalk. When crushed, the foliage has a pungent smell, and the clusters of white spring flowers have a sweet fragrance. In winter the foliage is useful for floral arrangements.

Although it is hardy, its foliage will often look scorched after frosts, but as the weather improves so will the foliage. After frost damage, cut back shoots as necessary. If bushes have grown out of hand, cut hard back to old wood. For a second crop of the scented flowers, prune back flowered shoots by about 25-30cm (10-12in) as soon as blooming has finished.

Propagate by softwood cuttings taken in summer.

Chrysanthemum carinatum 'Court Jesters'

(Tricolour chrysanthemum)
- **Sow in early spring**
- **Ordinary soil**
- **Sunny position**

This member of the daisy family is one of a number of hardy annual species originating from the Mediterranean area. The plants will grow about 60cm (24in) tall and branch freely under good

Below: Chionodoxa luciliae is a superb late winter and early spring flowering bulb, ideal for planting in rock gardens.

conditions. The daisy-shaped multicoloured flowers, 5-6cm (2-2.4in) across, open from midsummer onwards and last well when cut. Their varied markings are attractive in an annual border. They will continue to flower until autumn frosts.

Sowings may be direct into flowering position when soil conditions are suitable, in early spring. Thin out seedlings to about 20cm (8in) apart to allow for development. This annual will succeed on most soils given good drainage.

The young growths are sometimes attacked by aphids; spray as soon as seen.

Below: Chrysanthemum carinatum 'Double Mixed' is a hardy annual that creates a mixture of bright-faced flowers in summer.

Chionodoxa luciliae gigantea   Choisya ternata

Chrysanthemum maximum

(Daisy chrysanthemum, Max chrysanthemum, Shasta daisy)
- **Sunny location**
- **Any good fertile soil**
- **Summer flowering**

The Shasta daisy, a native of the Pyrenees, is a must for any hardy herbaceous perennial border. The height varies from 60 to 90cm (2-3ft). The flowers are single or double, with plain or fringed petals. On account of the large flat heads, rain and wind can soon knock plants over. Short peasticks should be inserted in the ground before the plants are too advanced to give some support.

One of the best-known varieties is 'Esther Read', 45cm (18in) tall, with pure white, fully double flowers. 'Wirral Pride' is a 90cm (3ft) beauty with large anemone-centred blooms. Another variety is the fully double white-flowered 'Wirral Supreme', 80cm (32in) high. If you prefer a large, fully double frilly-flowered variety, plant 'Droitwich Beauty', 80-90cm (32-36in) tall. A creamy-yellow variety of *Chrysanthemum maximum* is 'Mary Stoker', 80cm (32in) high.

Propagate by softwood cuttings in summer, or by division in autumn or spring.

Right: Chrysanthemum parthenium 'Golden Ball' is an herbaceous perennial with masses of yellow, button-like flowers.

Chrysanthemum parthenium

(Matricaria eximia)
(Feverfew)
- **Sow in autumn or spring**
- **Ordinary soil**
- **Sunny position**

This is a hardy herbaceous perennial which is usually grown as an annual. Several varieties are

available, including 'Golden Ball' which is 25cm (10in) high with ball-shaped, golden-yellow flowers from early to late summer.

Sow seed under glass in spring in a temperature of 13°C (55°F). A good soil-based growing medium will give satisfactory results. Prick out in the usual way, harden off in a sheltered frost-free area, and plant out in late spring. This method will ensure an evenly grown batch of plants, essential for formal plantings. Those grown as pot plants should be pricked out singly into individual pots, gradually moving them into larger pots. Spacing in the garden should be 25-30cm (10-12in).

Cimicifuga racemosa

(Black cohosh, Black snakeroot, Bugbane)
- **Sun or partial shade**
- **Rich fertile moist soil**
- **Summer flowering**

This hardy herbaceous perennial is commonly known as bugbane because of the rather unpleasant smell that is given off by the leaves of some species. Such a name is misleading, however, as no perennial can be more beautiful when its tall branching stems are displaying the feathery sprays of creamy-white flowers during late summer. The stems are 1.5-1.8m (5-6ft) tall. The fluffy flowers droop gracefully above shining green divided foliage. Another fine cimicifuga is *C. japonica*, with snow-white blooms on stems up to 90cm (3ft) tall.

Cimicifugas will grow in dry soils but are far finer where their roots are growing in rich deep well-cultivated soil, preferably moist. These plants need full sun, and must not become dry or starved. Propagate them by seed as soon as it has been gathered, or by division in spring or autumn.

Chrysanthemum carinatum 'Court Jesters'

Chrysanthemum maximum

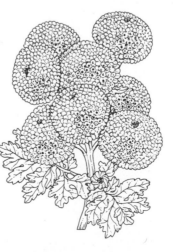

Chrysanthemum parthenium

Cimicifuga racemosa

Cineraria maritima 'Silver Dust'

(Senecio bicolor)

● Sow in early spring
● Ordinary soil
● Sunny location

This half-hardy perennial is grown almost exclusively for its foliage effect in bedding and border arrangements during summer. It is a very fine plant, with intense silver-white foliage deeply dissected, looking like a piece of lace. About 15cm (6in) tall, it makes a pleasing edge to a formal bed.

Only in the mildest areas will this cultivar survive the winter, and therefore propagation is carried out annually. Sow seed during early spring under glass, in a temperature of 16-18°C (60-65°F). Use a good proprietary growing medium for sowing and pricking out. Grow on in slight heat. Harden off in the usual way before planting out in late spring. Early removal of any flower stems and buds that appear will encourage a finer foliage effect.

Below: Cineraria maritima 'Silver Dust' creates a sea of deeply dissected silvery-white leaves.

Cistus 'Silver Pink'

(Rock rose)

● Full sun
● Light, well-drained soil
● Summer flowering

This lovely evergreen shrub hybrid bears clear silvery pink flowers up to 7cm (2.75in) across above lance-shaped evergreen foliage. Each flower has a prominent boss of golden-yellow stamens. 'Silver Pink' is ideal for small gardens as it grows only about 75cm (30in) high. It is poor on acid soils, but perfectly hardy when grown on well-drained moderately rich soils.

For a more vigorous cistus up to 2.5m (8ft) tall choose *Cistus × cyprius*. Its white flowers are enhanced by a blood-red blotch.

The rose-like flowers of cistus last, as a rule, for only a few hours in the morning, and never more than one day. But a regular succession of buds keeps the floral display going for two or three months during fine weather. The plants are hardy except in very severe winters. Propagate by half-ripe cuttings in summer.

Below: Cistus 'Silver Pink' bears clear silvery pink flowers in the summer months.

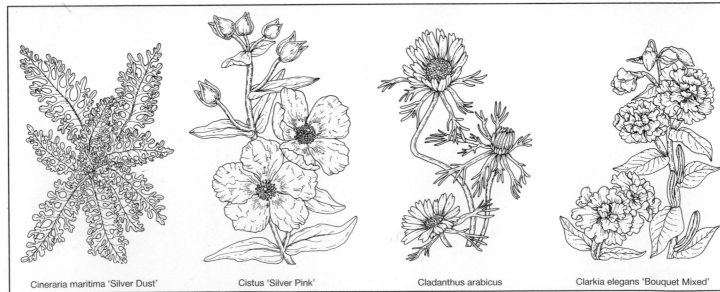

Cineraria maritima 'Silver Dust'   Cistus 'Silver Pink'   Cladanthus arabicus   Clarkia elegans 'Bouquet Mixed'

Cladanthus arabicus
- Sow in spring
- Light and open soil
- Sunny site

A native of Spain, this lovely hardy annual is similar to *Anthemis* but it has the habit of branching just below the flower heads. It starts to bloom in early summer and will continue well into the autumn. Individual flowers are 5cm (2in) across and a deep golden yellow colour. Plants develop into mounds as the season progresses, reaching a height of 75cm (30in). Light green leaves, linear and almost feather-like in shape, make a good setting for the flowers. They are an ideal subject for adding height to a border.

Sow seeds during spring where they are to flower. Make sure that ground conditions are fit for this by lightly raking down the soil. Thin out the seedlings when they are large enough to handle, to 30cm (12in) apart. Dead-head to prolong flowering

Clarkia elegans 'Bouquet Mixed'
(Clarkia unguiculata)
- Sow in spring
- Light to medium soil, slightly acid
- Sunny location

These hardy annuals will give a galaxy of double pink, red, white, lavender, purple and light orange flowers. Ovate leaves are carried on branching erect stems of 60cm (24in). These plants produce flowers about 5cm (2in) across, produced along almost the whole length of the stems and appearing from early summer onwards. For a wonderful display of colour, use towards the centre of a border in bold drifts.

Given good weather conditions, sow seed in flowering positions in spring. Take out shallow drills, sow thinly and cover. Thin out germinated seedlings to 30cm (12in).

Alternatively sow during autumn in mild districts; these will flower the following year from the end of spring onwards. Correct spacing is essential for good growth. Avoid over-rich soils, or fewer flowers will be produced.

Clematis recta
(Herbaceous virgin's bower)
- Full sun
- Ordinary fertile soil
- Summer flowering

This outstanding hardy herbaceous perennial has pinnate glistening dark green leaves. During summer an abundance of billowing sweetly scented white flowers is carried on branching sprays at the top of straggling stems. Each flower forms a star and can be as much as 2.5cm (1in) across. Plants reach a height of 1.2-1.5m (4-5ft), and sometimes higher. Place a few peasticks around the plant, allowing the stems to clamber through them. This will help support the stems and show the flowers to good advantage.

In autumn, when flowering has finished, the mound will be covered with clouds of silvery seed heads.

This fine clematis will thrive in full sun in ordinary garden soil, and also do well in an alkaline soil. A spring mulch of peat or rotted manure will be beneficial. Prune the plant down to ground level during the winter.

Propagate this species by division during the dormant season.

Cleome spinosa 'Colour Fountain'
(Spider plant)
- Sow in spring
- Light, ordinary soil
- In full sun

This is a very exotic, unusual-looking half-hardy annual; the flowers are spider-shaped and scented. 'Colour Fountain' mixture will include shades of rose, carmine, purple, lilac and pink. Stems reach 60-90cm (2-3ft) and carry digitate leaves of five to seven lobes. Some spines may be evident on the undersides of these leaves.

This is extremely useful as a 'spot' plant to give height to formal bedding schemes. As a border plant its height will add character, but care should be taken to position it towards the rear in a sunny place.

To flower in summer, seed will need to be sown under glass in spring. Use a well-recommended growing medium, and keep at a temperature of 18°C (65°F). Prick out the seedlings into individual pots, 9cm (3.5in) in diameter. Harden off gradually and plant out in late spring. The delicately scented flowers will give great pleasure.

Below: Cleome spinosa 'Colour Fountain' has distinctive, slightly scented, spider-like flowers from midsummer to the frosts of autumn.

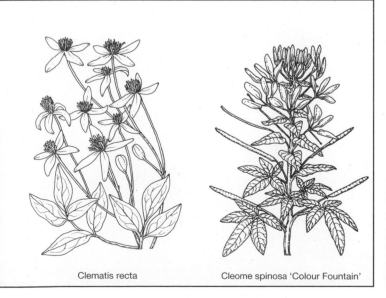

Clematis recta

Cleome spinosa 'Colour Fountain'

Cobaea scandens

(Cathedral bells, Cup-and-saucer vine, Mexican ivy, Monastery bells)
- **Sow in very early spring**
- **Ordinary well-drained soil**
- **Sunny, sheltered location**

Climbers are few among the annuals and biennials, but this glorious flowering climber is a half-hardy perennial usually grown as a half-hardy annual. Individual blooms are up to 7.5cm (3in) long, and bell-shaped. Young flowers are a light green, soon changing to violet-purple. The calyx at the base of the bell usually remains green. This vigorous climber can reach a height of 7m (23ft) and is suitable on a wall that has a trellis.

Grow in a sunny sheltered position for the finest results. Sow seed under glass in early spring, using fresh seed if possible for better germination. Temperature should be maintained at 18°C (65°F). Water freely in dry weather. Sow individually in small pots of a good loam-based growing medium. Harden off gradually, and plant out in early summer.

Coix lacryma-jobi

(Job's tears)
- **Sow in early spring**
- **Any well-drained soil**
- **Sunny, south-facing site**

This is one of a number of annual grasses suitable for beds or

borders. The tear-like seeds are grey-green in colour, tiny and pearl-shaped, growing on stems 60-90cm (2-3ft) tall. Similar in habit to sweet corn, they are very vigorous. Once plants are established they will tend to become pendulous before flowering in summer, after which the pearl-like seeds will be formed. If grouped together, these plants lend an air of strength to an annual border. When ready for harvesting, the hard seeds can be safely used by children for threading on to strings.

Sow seed in early spring under glass, in a temperature of 13-16°C (55-60°F). Use a loam-based compost and sow directly into individual small pots to save later potting on. Plant out into final positions in early summer. Avoid overfeeding, or flowering and seed development will be delayed.

Colchicum autumnale

(Autumn crocus, Fall crocus, Mysteria, Naked boys, Wonder bulb)
- **Sun or partial shade**
- **Well-drained soil**
- **Plant 10cm (4in) deep**

This cormous plant produces large mid- to dark green leaves in spring and early summer. These then die

Below: *Coix lacryma-jobi, an ornamental grass, has drooping, tear-shaped seed heads.*

back, and from the bare earth spring the stemless flowers in autumn. The leaves grow up to 25cm (10in) long. The flowers are 15cm (6in) long, and from each corm come several blooms of lilac, rose or white; one variety has double pink flowers.

The corms should be planted in late summer if purchased corms, or from lifted plants when the leaves die down in midsummer.

Position them 20cm (8in) apart in clumps, where they can get some sun. Grown from seed, they may take seven years to reach flowering; offsets take only a couple of years to mature. The area round the corms should be treated to prevent slug attack.

Below: *Colchicum speciosum has purple flowers with white throats during late summer and autumn.*

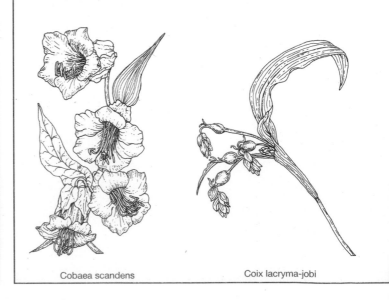

Cobaea scandens

Coix lacryma-jobi

Colchicum speciosum

- **Sun or partial shade**
- **Well-drained soil**
- **Plant 10-15cm (4-6in) deep**

This cormous plant flowers in autumn. The flowers are white, rose, purple, violet or crimson, some with coloured veining. Leaves show in spring and last till early summer, 30cm (12in) long and 10cm (4in) wide, four to each bulb.

It is easily cultivated in ordinary well-drained soil, and increases well in grass. Plant a little deeper than *Colchicum autumnale*, in early autumn. Make sure that the leaves do not choke smaller neighbours in spring. Colchicums can be grown from seed, but take up to seven years to reach flowering. Offsets from existing corms will take only two or three years to flower. Lift corms when the leaves have died down in summer, remove the offsets and replant. Keep slugs off with slug bait; the plants are usually disease-free.

Collinsia bicolor

- **Sow in autumn or spring**
- **Ordinary, moist but well-drained soil**
- **Partial shade**

This very appealing hardy annual can be used in most situations as long as they are not too arid. It is a useful plant because it will tolerate partial shade. It is ideal for the border in a damp shady yard.

Flowers, as its name implies, are two-coloured, having an upper and lower lip formation. The upper petals are usually white and the lower ones lilac to purple. One or two named cultivars are available, mainly pink, and they are worth considering for a change. Their blooms are borne on thin squarish stems carrying lanceolate deep green leaves in pairs. Up to 60cm (24in) in height, they should be grown towards the back of an annual border, preferably near a light yellow subject of a similar height. Use bushy peasticks for support.

Sow seeds where they are to flower, in autumn or spring. Shallow drills will suffice; cover the seeds and thin out when large enough, to 15cm (6in) apart.

Convallaria majalis
(Lily of the valley)

- **Light shade or dappled sun**
- **Retentive fertile soil**
- **Late spring flowering**

Lily of the valley is one of the best-loved sweetly scented hardy herbaceous perennials. This shade-loving plant enjoys liberal supplies of humus in the soil. Sometimes it may be suitable to grow under trees, but this is not recommended, as tree roots take moisture and nourishment from the soil. Some sunshine is preferable, provided moisture and humus are available.

Plant in early autumn. The stoloniferous roots should be placed 7.5-10cm (3-4in) beneath the surface, with the fleshy crowns pointing upwards about 2.5cm (1in) under the surface. Keep the ground moist from spring to autumn. A top dressing of rotted farmyard manure, garden compost or leaf-mould should be given annually. When picking, pull the flower stems carefully, leaving a pair of leaves. If you must have leaves, pull only one from each crown. Propagate by division in early autumn.

Below: Collinsia bicolor creates masses of bicoloured flowers in purple and white from early to late summer.

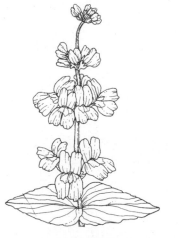

| Colchicum autumnale | Colchicum speciosum | Collinsia bicolor | Convallaria majalis |

Convolvulus mauritanicus

(Convolvulus sabatius)
- **Sheltered sunny situation**
- **Light dry soil**
- **Herbaceous**

This relative of the bindweed is superb in a rock garden. It has a tufted, mat-forming nature, with a woody rootstock.

C. mauritanicus comes from North Africa and benefits from being planted in a warm sunny corner, where some protection can be added in winter. It is spreading, with trailing stems up to 60cm (24in) long, which produce a succession of clear blue, white-throated trumpet flowers in late summer and early autumn.

Seed can be sown in spring, but a good method of keeping the plant over the winter is by taking cuttings of non-flowering wood in summer and keeping them under glass in heat, stopping the rooted plants to ensure a good growth for the following year.

Below: Convolvulus mauritanicus is low and spreading, ideal for planting in a rock garden.

Convolvulus tricolor 'Rainbow Flash'

(Dwarf morning glory, Morning glory)
- **Sow in spring**
- **Light well-drained soil**
- **Sunny position**

This hardy annual is well known, growing up to 38cm (15in) high. There are many varieties, and the hybrid 'Rainbow Flash' is only 15cm (6in) high, in a range of colours including blue, purple, pink and rose. The centre of each flower is marked by a star-like form of white or yellow. Because of their dwarf habit, these plants are

Above: Convolvulus tricolor is a hardy annual with a wealth of bright flowers during summer.

invaluable for the front of the border or bed, but try a colourful selection of them in window boxes as well.

Sow seeds under glass in the normal way during spring. It may help germination if you soak the seeds in water for 24 hours before sowing. Keep in a temperature of 18°C (65°F). Keep the temperature constant in the young stages. Harden off and plant out in final positions at the end of spring, 20cm (8in) apart. Water freely during dry weather.

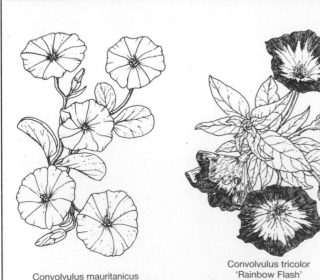

Convolvulus mauritanicus

Convolvulus tricolor 'Rainbow Flash'

Coreopsis tinctoria 'Dwarf Dazzler'

Coreopsis verticillata

Coreopsis tinctoria 'Dwarf Dazzler'

(Calliopsis bicolor)

(Calliopsis, Tickseed)

● **Sow in spring to early summer**
● **Fertile, well-drained soil**
● **Sunny location**

This hardy annual, also known as *Calliopsis bicolor*, is represented by many varieties. 'Dwarf Dazzler'

has beautiful daisy-shaped flowers of deep crimson, and each flower is edged with golden yellow, making a vivid contrast. Only 30cm (12in) in height and tending to spread, it is ideally suited to the front of a border or bed in a sunny position. It can also be useful in containers on a patio. Long-lasting and very free-flowering, it should be planted in bold groups to get maximum effect.

Wherever you choose to grow these plants, they come readily from seed. Sow in spring to early summer where they are to flower, take out shallow drills and cover seed lightly. If you make later sowings and the weather is dry, then water regularly. Thin out seedlings to 30cm (12in) when large enough to handle.

Coreopsis verticillata

(Tickseed)

● **Full sun**
● **Fertile soil**
● **Summer and autumn flowering**

This hardy herbaceous perennial from the eastern United States is one of the best plants for the front of the border. It makes a dense bushy plant. The deep green foliage is finely divided, on stiff needle-like stems that support bright yellow starry flowers as much as 4cm (1.6in) across, and the blooms have a very long season. Coreopsis must not be left in the same place too long without being lifted and divided, or the plants will become starved. Do not let this plant dry out in warm weather and water in the evening. This species does not require support.

Today there is also an improved and larger-flowered variety called *C. verticillata* 'Grandiflora', which has warmer yellow flowers than the species. Propagate this plant by division in spring.

Above: Coreopsis verticillata is an herbaceous perennial that bears bright, starry flowers amid fern-like leaves in summer.

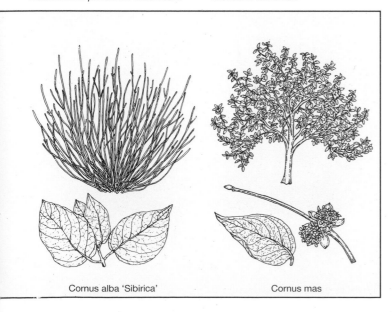

Cornus alba 'Sibirica'   Cornus mas

Cornus alba 'Sibirica'

(Siberian dogwood, Westonbirt dogwood)

● **Sun, but tolerates a little shade**
● **Any soil; damp conditions best**
● **Colourful bark and fruit**

Cornus alba is a hardy deciduous shrub that makes a thicket of erect stems. The cultivar 'Sibirica' is less rampant than the species, but the young shoots are a brighter red. The small yellowish flowers are followed by bluish pea-sized fruits. The oval leaves are opposite, fresh green above and bluish grey below. Flowers and foliage are of less importance than the richly coloured stems. Bushes reach a height of 2-2.7m (6.5-9ft) with a spread of 2.5-3m (8-10ft).

For good colour during the autumn and winter, cut all stems close to the base in late spring. The result will be plenty of young stems; there will be no flowers or berries, but the coloured stems are the main attraction. The cultivar 'Spaethii' has golden-yellow variegated foliage, but its stems are a less brilliant red. Propagate by hardwood cuttings in autumn, inserting them in open ground.

Cornus mas

(Cornelian cherry, Sorbet)

● **Sun; will tolerate some shade**
● **Any good soil, including clay**
● **Flowers in late winter to early spring; fruit in autumn**

This deciduous large shrub or small tree grows 4.5-6m (15-20ft) tall. It is not a cherry, although in autumn it has bright red oblong fruit which are the size of a small plum, but with an acid flavour. In late winter to early spring, clusters of yellow flowers are produced, borne on the previous year's naked wood.

The branches spread almost to ground level, which makes it difficult to grow other plants beneath. However, if a leading shoot is selected from a young plant, a main stem eventually develops, which will let the tree display its handsome bark. Normally little or no pruning is needed, apart from keeping the main trunk of a standard tree clean. Propagate by seeds sown out of doors in spring, but they may take two years to germinate.

Above: Cornus mas becomes smothered with yellow flowers in late winter and early spring.

Cornus stolonifera 'Flaviramea'
(Golden-twig dogwood, Red osier dogwood)
- **Sunny position**
- **Any soil; moist or wet sites**
- **Winter bark**

The species *Cornus stolonifera* is a hardy deciduous shrub, known as the red osier dogwood. It reaches a height of 2.5m (8ft) and suckers freely by underground stems. The young shoots have purple-red bark. The leaves are dark green above and bluish grey beneath, and the white flowers in spring are followed later by white fruits.

The cultivar 'Flaviramea' grows 2-2.5m (6.5-8ft) high. The young shoots are olive to greenish yellow (some describe this dogwood as having butter-yellow bark). When it is planted alongside a red-stemmed cultivar such as *Cornus alba* 'Sibirica', the colour combination is most striking in winter sunshine. To produce good coloured stems, cut bushes hard back each year during spring.

Propagate by hardwood cuttings about 30cm (12in) long inserted in open ground out of doors, or by suckers (both in autumn), or by layering in spring.

Cortaderia selloana
(Pampas grass)
- **Full sun**
- **Light retentive fertile soil**
- **Late summer and early autumn flowering**

Pampas grass is a perennial evergreen plant with masses of gracefully arching leaves that form a good base for the erect stems to carry their silky silvery white plumes. For indoor decoration, gather plumes as soon as they are fully developed .

Varieties include: 'Monstrosa', creamy white plumes and 2.75m (9ft) stems; the compact 'Pumila', with short foliage, creamy white plumes and erect 1.5m (5ft) stems; 'Sunningdale Silver', creamy white open plumes and 2.1m (7ft) stems; 'Rendatleri', with silver-pink plumes and 1.8-2.4m (6-8ft) stems.

They are not fussy over soil but are happiest in light soils enriched with humus or well-rotted farmyard manure or good garden compost. Give ample moisture during very

hot weather. Plant in either autumn or spring. Winter care entails allowing the grass to die down. Never cut it with shears; wear stout leather gloves to pull the leaves out of established clumps.

Propagate by seed under glass in spring, or by division in spring.

Corylopsis spicata
(Spike winter hazel)
- **Half shade**
- **Acid or neutral fertile soil**
- **Early spring flowers; autumn foliage colour**

An attractive early-flowering deciduous hardy shrub that does best in half shade, preferably in a situation that prevents the sun shining on the bush until frost has gone, as frost can damage the flowers. It makes a bush 1.5-2.1m (5-7ft) tall and equally wide. The heart-shaped leaves, 8-10cm (3.2-4in) long and 5-8cm (2-3.2in) wide, are pale green above and

bluish grey below. Drooping spikes of six to 12 yellow cowslip-scented flowers, on a 4cm (1.6in) raceme, are borne on the naked shoots of the previous year's growth in early spring. In autumn the bush displays bright yellow foliage.

As a rule no pruning is needed. Should a bush become too large for its site, it is better to prune back the shrubs around it.

Propagate by half-ripe side shoots taken with a heel during the summer. Insert them in a sand and peat mixture in a warm propagating frame.

Corylus maxima 'Purpurea'
(Purple giant filbert, Purple leaf filbert)
- **Sunny location**
- **Good loamy or chalk soil**
- **Summer and autumn foliage**

All species of the hazel genus are attractive deciduous shrubs grown for their foliage and catkins. The lambs'-tails are the male flowers, and the female flowers are small and red. 'Purpurea' has outstanding purple foliage, akin in colour to that of the purple beech. The toothed leaves are roundish with a heart-shaped base, 5-13cm (2-5in) long and 4-10cm (1.6-4in) wide. The male catkins are also purple. This handsome purple-leaved shrub will reach 2.5-3m (8-10ft) tall. Used as a screen it is very effective.

Above: Cortaderia selloana 'Pumila' has erect, fluffy heads of white flowers during late summer and into early autumn.

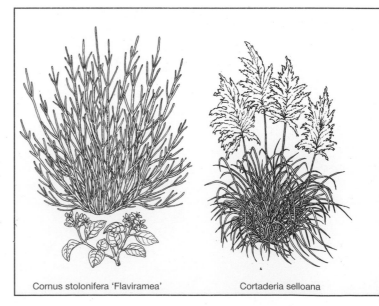

Cornus stolonifera 'Flaviramea'   Cortaderia selloana

To obtain plenty of new growth, cut out all weaker wood during the winter, retaining the more mature, sound and healthy growth.

Propagate by rooted suckers, which can be lifted in autumn or winter and transplanted, or by layering in autumn.

Cosmos bipinnatus 'Candy Stripe'

(Mexican aster)
- **Sow in early spring**
- **Light, and also poor soils**
- **Full sun**

This half-hardy annual, *Cosmos bipinnatus* 'Candy Stripe', has flowers that are up to 7.5cm (3in)

wide and striped rose-red and white. The leaves are intricately cut and formed on branching stems. Attaining a height of 80cm (32in) and very free flowering, 'Candy Stripe' is most suited to the middle of a border. It is a good idea to stake tall plants.

Sow seeds under glass in early spring. Sow in boxes or trays at a temperature of 16°C (60°F). Prick off into small pots and move on into 13cm (5in) pots of loam-based medium when the small pots have filled with roots. Harden off and plant out in late spring.

Below: Cosmos bipinnatus 'Candy Stripe' is a hardy annual, crowned in summer with rose-red and white flowers.

Cotinus coggygria 'Notcutt's Variety'

(Smokebush, Smoke plant, Smoke tree, Venetian sumac, Wig tree)
- **Sunny position**
- **Any type of soil**
- **Summer flowers; spring and autumn foliage**

For many years this deciduous shrub was known as *Rhus cotinus*. It makes a large shrub, 3.6-4.5m (12-15ft) high, with a similar width. The smoke-like inflorescences are a mixture of pink and purple. When the striking purple foliage first unfolds in spring, it is a shade of crimson, then becomes purple, and finally is semi-translucent.

This shrub does not need a rich soil, and indeed flowers more freely on a poor one. The leaves are oval, slightly notched at the apex, and 4-8cm (1.6-3.2in) long. Provided only foliage is wanted, prune annually in spring; cut down young wood, but not too severely, just before new growth starts. If you want the pink and purple smoke-like flowers, however, avoid pruning except to keep the bush in good shape.

Propagate by half-ripe cuttings of the current year's wood, in mid-to late summer.

Below: Cotinus coggygria is a hardy deciduous shrub and is famed for its dominantly-coloured leaves. This is a dark purple type.

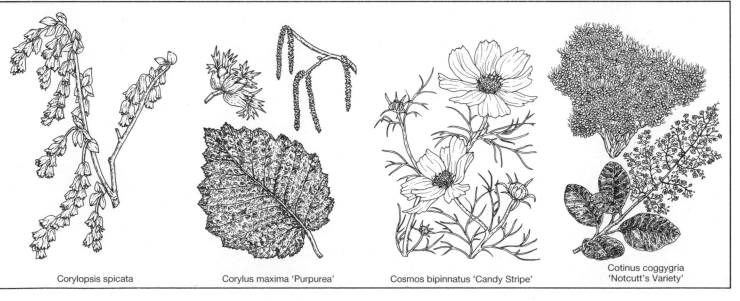

Corylopsis spicata

Corylus maxima 'Purpurea'

Cosmos bipinnatus 'Candy Stripe'

Cotinus coggygria 'Notcutt's Variety'

Cotoneaster horizontalis

(Fishbone cotoneaster, Herringbone cotoneaster, Rock cotoneaster)
- **Sun or partial shade**
- **Any good soil, including chalk**
- **Spring flowers; autumn colour**

This low-growing deciduous cotoneaster gets its common names of fishbone or herringbone because the bare horizontal branches look rather like the bones of a fish. It has dark glossy green leaves above, mostly smooth beneath through sometimes with a few scattered hairs. The leaves are 6-12mm (0.25-0.5in) long, and 2cm (0.8in) wide. In spring the white flowers suffused with pink are a great attraction to bees seeking nectar. In autumn there are bright red berries, and the dark green foliage changes to shades of orange and red before it finally falls. This is an excellent low-growing shrub for ground cover or to clothe banks. Bushes reach a height of 60-90cm (2-3ft). The cultivar 'Variegatus' has leaves attractively edged with white.

Propagate by seed which should be stratified (stored damp to soften the seed coat) and sown in spring, or by half-ripe cuttings in summer or hardwood cuttings in autumn.

Below: *Cotoneaster horizontalis flowers during spring, followed in autumn by bright red berries.*

Crambe cordifolia

(Colewort, Flowering sea kale)
- **Full sun**
- **Good rich soil**
- **Early summer flowering**

To many people the common name of sea kale will conjure up that most delectable blanched vegetable, but *Crambe cordifolia* is a dramatic herbaceous perennial. This magnificent species has large deep unequally lobed and toothed heart-shaped leaves, 60-90cm (2-3ft) long. From a mound of foliage arise 1.5-1.8m (5-6ft) flower spikes on which massive branching sprays of hundreds of small white flowers appear. The width of one plant can be as much as its height.

Propagate by root cuttings taken off after flowering has ceased, or by seed sown out of doors in spring, but it will be three years before seedling plants will flower. As a perennial it is not long lasting; therefore regularly restock.

Crataegus laevigata

(Crataegus oxyacantha)

(English hawthorn, Hawthorn, May, Quick, Quick-set, White thorn)
- **Sunny location**
- **Any good soil, including chalk**
- **Spring flowering**

The leaves of this deciduous tree are mostly oval, wedge-shaped at the base, with three to five lobes, rounded or slightly pointed, and dark glossy green. The flowers, 2cm (0.8in) wide, are produced in flat-topped clusters of six to 12 flowers.

The cultivars worthy of mention are 'Paul's Scarlet' and 'Rosea Flore Pleno', both double-flowered and without berries. 'Paul's Scarlet' has double scarlet flowers; it makes a rounded, bushy head, about 6-7.6m (20-25ft) tall and as wide. 'Rosea Flore Pleno' is similar to 'Paul's Scarlet', except that it has double pink flowers. Both trees are superb for a small garden. Stake securely after planting, until well established. By careful pruning after flowering has finished, they can be kept within bounds.

Propagate by budding or grafting in spring.

Crinum × powellii

(Cape lily, Crinum lily)
- **Warm sheltered site**
- **Rich well-drained soil**
- **Plant up to 30cm (12in) deep**

Crinums are tender bulbous plants, and unless you have a sheltered border they are best grown as pot plants. They have mid-green sword-like leaves, and form clumps up to 45cm (18in) tall. The trumpet-like flowers are borne in late summer, 15cm (6in) long, in white or pink or striped with both.

The bulbs should be planted in a warm border in late spring. Cover

Cotoneaster horizontalis

Crambe cordifolia

Crataegus laevigata

Crinum x powellii

them with ashes, bracken or garden compost to protect from late frosts. If you prefer to grow one as a pot plant, place the bulb in a large pot of rich soil and keep in the greenhouse or indoors until late spring; then it can be moved outside until mid-autumn, when it should be brought indoors again for the winter. Crinums grown from seed can take five years to flower; it is quicker to propagate with offsets from the bulbs, which are removed in spring, potted up and kept moist, and will reach flowering size in three years.

Below: Crinum × powellii 'Album' reveals trumpet-like white flowers in late summer.

Crocosmia × crocosmiiflora

(Montbretia, Montebretia)
● **Sunny position**
● **Light sandy soil**
● **Plant 7.5cm (3in) deep**

This well-known cormous plant has sword-like leaves and small but profuse flowers borne on 90cm (3ft) stems. The trumpet-shaped blooms, up to 10cm (4in) long, in yellow, orange or deep red, appear throughout the summer.

The plants are hardy and quite invasive. Corms should be planted 7.5cm (3in) deep in a well-drained soil that will retain moisture in the summer, preferably in full sun. The leaves should be cut off in spring before the new growth begins to sprout. Every few years, lift, divide and replant the bulbs with more space around them. Seeds sown in autumn in pots, and kept in a cold frame, germinate in the spring, and should flower in one or two years. This plant is generally free from pests and diseases.

Below: Crocosmia masonorum reveals flame-coloured flowers at the tops of arching stems.

Crocosmia masonorum

(Montbretia, Montebretia)
● **Sun or partial shade**
● **Light sandy fertile well-drained soil**
● **Summer flowering**

Crocosmia masonorum is a rather special montbretia. There are two main differences between this one and *C. × crocosmiiflora*: the broad ribbed, strap-like foliage is broader in *C. masonorum*, and the flame-orange flowers are carried on top of arching stems, instead of being arranged beneath the stems as in *C. × crocosimia*.

When this crocosmia became popular around 1953, it was considered not to be fully hardy. However, its survival through some severe winters has proved otherwise.

The corms are small, and the first year after planting they are shy to flower. However, if planted 15cm (6in) apart and left alone for three or four years, they will soon create a splendid clump. Divide the corms in early spring. Take care not to lift and replant while the corms are doing well.

Crocosmia x crocosmiiflora   Crocosmia masonorum

Crocus aureus 'Dutch Yellow'
- **Sunny position**
- **Well-drained soil**
- **Plant 7.5cm (3in) deep – more in a light soil**

This yellow flowering crocus has fine grass-like leaves, and produces its bright blooms in early spring, growing to 10cm (4in) long. It prefers well-drained soil and a sunny situation, and is recommended for rock gardens. It also thrives in short grass, provided no mowing occurs before the leaves turn yellow in late spring.

Corms should be planted in autumn to flower the following spring, in groups or drifts. Plant them 7.5cm (3in) apart. Crocuses multiply by cormlets produced around the parent corm, or by seeding. Cormlets can be removed in early summer and grown on to flower in two years' time. Seed takes up to four years to flower, and should be sown in summer and transplanted into nursery beds when large enough to handle. A general pesticide will keep most trouble at bay. Also use a fungicide.

Crocus chrysanthus 'Blue Bird'
- **Sheltered sunny position**
- **Well-drained soil**
- **Plant 7.5cm (3in) deep**

This spring-flowering crocus has a bloom with a mauve-blue exterior edged with white, a creamy white inside and a deep orange centre, and it flowers profusely. The short narrow leaves of pale green have a paler stripe along the spine.

These crocuses are ideal for the border or rockery, and do well in pots in a cold greenhouse. Corms can be planted in any free-draining soil. Keep the corms from becoming waterlogged. If the soil is very light, they can be planted 15cm (6in) deep, but otherwise 7.5cm (3in) is recommended. If crocuses are grown in grass, delay mowing until the leaves turn yellow and die back. If you cut sooner, the corms will produce very poor blooms the next season. Treat the soil with a general pesticide and fungicide.

Below: Crocus chrysanthus 'Blue Bird' is dwarf, forming bright splashes of colour in rock gardens in early spring.

Above: Crocus tomasinianus is an early-flowering corm that's ideal for naturalizing in grass and sunny, sheltered borders.

Crocus tomasinianus
- **Sunny site sheltered against cold winds**
- **Ordinary well-drained soil**
- **Plant 7.5cm (3in) deep**

This winter-flowering crocus has smaller flowers than the spring crocus, up to 7.5cm (3in) long. The delicate blue-lavender flowers bud in winter and open in very early spring. They naturalize well in grass and sunny borders, given a sheltered position, and do well also in groups under deciduous trees or on rockeries. The varieties available are mostly deep purples such as 'Bar's Purple' and 'Whitewell Purple', but a white variety called 'Albus' is for sale from some specialists.

Corms should be planted 7.5cm (3in) deep, but if the soil is very light and summer cultivation is likely to disturb the roots, they can be planted as deep as 15cm (6in). Do not remove flowers as they die, and leave foliage until it can be pulled off. Increase stock by growing the cormlets, which should flower in two years. Treat soil with a pesticide and fungicide.

Crocus aureus 'Dutch Yellow'   Crocus chrysanthus 'Blue Bird'

Crocus vernus 'Striped Beauty'
- **Sheltered but sunny place**
- **Well-drained soil**
- **Plant 7.5cm (3in) deep**

Crocus vernus is the parent of the large Dutch crocuses, which over several centuries have resulted in blooms of great variety, up to 13cm (5in) long. 'Striped Beauty' has a large flower of silver white with dark purple-blue stripes and a violet-purple base to the petals.

Corms should be planted 7.5cm (3in) deep, or more if the soil is light and sandy, and not less than 10cm (4in) apart. Over the years the corms will muliltply naturally to form dense mats of flowers, which are spectacular in grass under deciduous trees. The grass-like

Above: *Crocus vernus 'Pickwick' produces large flowers in spring. Ideal for naturalizing.*

leaves should pull off easily when they turn yellow after flowering. At this time the corms can be lifted and divided; remove the cormlets and keep in a nursery area, where they will mature in two years. Do not dead-head or cut leaves until the leaves die back. Treat the soil with a general pesticide and fungicide.

Cryptomeria japonica 'Spiralis'
(Granny's ringlets)
- **Open or lightly shaded site**
- **Slightly acid, moist soil**
- **Slow-growing bush**

This variety of *Cryptomeria japonica* was brought out of Japan in 1860. It normally forms an evergreen conifer about 50cm (20in) in height and width in ten years, with dense bright green leaves twisted around the branches to give a ringlet look. Sometimes, however, the plant forms a large tree, and if this occurs it can drown the surrounding planting. The cones are borne on the tips of the branches and take over a year to ripen from green to brown.

If the seed is sown, keep only the dwarf slow-growing seedlings to grow on to maturity. The best method is to grow from cuttings, using the less vigorous side shoots and setting them in a half peat, half sand mixture. When they are rooted, plant in pots for a year and

then set out in nursery beds for two years. Select the best forms and plant them out in the final positions, using a deep moist soil that is slightly acid.

Cryptomeria japonica 'Vilmoriniana'
- **Open or lightly shaded site**
- **Well-drained but moist soil**
- **Slow-growing dwarf bush**

This popular dwarf bush for the rockery has little in common with its Japanese ancestors. It has very small crowded evergreen foliage on tiny branches that form into a globe. In ten years it will reach only 40cm (16in) tall with a spread of 50cm (20in). In 30 years it should grow to 60cm (2ft) tall and 1m

(3.3ft) wide. The foliage is a rich green for most of the year, but turns reddish purple in winter. Cones form at the ends of the branches, and ripen the following year, turning from green to brown.

Propagate this bush from cuttings to keep plants true to type. They should be set into a half peat, half sand mixture, and the rooted cuttings put into pots for a year, then set out into nursery beds for a further year or two before being transplanted into their final situations. An open site or one with light shade is suitable. It is necessary to keep young plants moist.

Below: *Cryptomeria japonica 'Spiralis' is an unusual small conifer, with shoots having the appearance of twisted ringlets.*

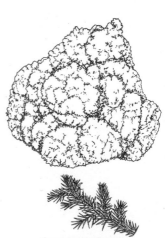

Crocus tomasinianus

Crocus vernus 'Striped Beauty'

Cryptomeria japonica 'Spiralis'

Cryptomeria japonica 'Vilmoriniana'

Cuphea miniata 'Firefly'
- **Sow in very early spring**
- **Ordinary soil**
- **Sun or partial shade**

Grown as a half-hardy annual this sub-shrub will do well in most gardens.

It spreads to 60cm (2ft) and the height is similar. The stems carry green lanceolate leaves, which may be covered with very distinct white hairs.

Flowers are formed from the axils of the leaves near the terminals of the stems. Tubular scarlet blooms, 4cm (1.6in) long, will begin to show colour from early summer and it will flower freely throughout that season.

Treat it as a half-hardy annual for propagation purposes. Sow seed under glass in very early spring, using a soil-based growing medium. Cover the seed lightly in boxes or pots and keep in a temperature of 16°C (60°F). Pot off the seedlings into individual small pots and grow on until early summer, when they should be planted out in flowering positions. Give a weak liquid feed once a week in the seedling stages, starting a month after potting on.

Below: Cuphea miniata 'Firefly', grown as a half-hardy annual, is profuse with summer flowers.

Above: Cyclamen hederifolium is hardy and ideal for naturalizing in woodland or grass under trees.

Cyclamen hederifolium
(Alpine violet, Persian violet, Sowbread)
- **Shade**
- **Soil with added leaf-mould**
- **Plant just under the surface**

This Mediterranean cormous plant is hardy and will grow in poor soil, but it thrives if covered with a 2.5cm (1in) layer of leaf-mould in late spring, after the leaves have died down. The plant grows to only 10cm (4in), often much less. The silvery leaves have dark green markings on the upper surface, and underneath they are red.

Plant the corms 10-15cm (4-6in) apart in a light soil that is rich in leaf-mould. Grow cyclamen from seed: sow in pots or trays in late summer and leave the container outside on its side to prevent it becoming waterlogged. Germination will occur the following spring, and seedlings can be potted on, planting out when they are large enough to handle easily, in either late spring or late summer. Treat with a pesticide; disease is mainly due to wet conditions, so treat the area also with a fungicide.

Cytisus × beanii
(Broom)
- **Sunny situation**
- **Light soil**
- **Deciduous shrub**

This is a deciduous semi-prostrate shrub, with a spread of 60cm. It is essential for the larger rock garden, where it can spread to its full 90cm (3ft). The 12mm (0.5in) long yellow pea-like flowers are borne in late spring or early summer along the previous year's growths.

This is a hybrid of garden origin and it is a sun-loving plant that grows easily in well-drained soil.

Propagation is by taking cuttings, with or without a heel, in early summer. Select shoots that are beginning to harden, and a minimum of 5cm (2in) long. Insert in a sandy frame and when potting on take care not to damage the roots. Once planted out, *C. × beanii* should never be disturbed. It is good in alkaline conditions.

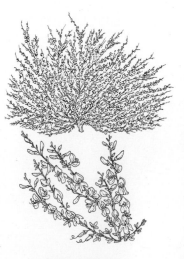

Cuphea miniata 'Firefly'   Cyclamen hederifolium   Cytisus x beanii   Cytisus x praecox

Cytisus × praecox

(Broom, Warminster broom)
- **Sunny location**
- **Any good soil**
- **Spring flowering**

This free-flowering deciduous broom of a dense rounded habit reaches a height about 1-1.5m (3.3-5ft).

It produces arching sprays packed with masses of beautiful creamy-yellow flowers during the spring. Its simple grey-green single leaves are about 1cm (0.4in) long, and borne on silky shoots. The shrub's only fault is that it has a slightly disagreeable odour when in flower.

Warminster broom sets good fertile seed, but does not come true from seed; nevertheless, worthwhile varieties have been raised. One of Dutch origin, 'Allgold', bears deep yellow flowers on slightly taller bushes. Another raised in Germany, called 'Golden Spear', has bright golden-yellow flowers and is of a more compact habit. Both these varieties remain in flower for almost a month.

Propagate by seed sown out of doors in spring, or by heel or nodal cuttings during the summer.

Below: Cytisus × beanii creates a dazzling display of pea-like flowers in late spring.

Above: Cytisus scoparius 'Golden Sunlight' is an eye-catching spring-flowering shrub.

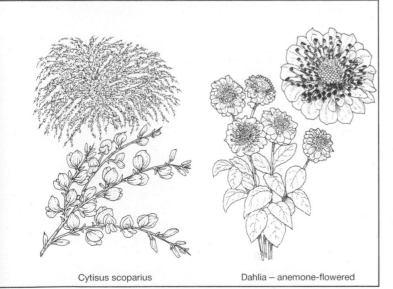

Cytisus scoparius

(Broom, Common broom, Scotch broom)
- **Full sun**
- **Any good deep soil, but avoid chalky soils**
- **Spring flowering**

The common broom is a free-flowering deciduous shrub, but when the foliage has fallen the green stems give an evergreen appearance. The shrub reaches a height of 1.5-2m (5-6.5ft).

The hybrids prefer a deep soil, neutral or slightly acid, but not poor shallow soils. They like plenty of sun. The variety 'Golden Sunlight' grows 60cm (2ft) high and 90cm (3ft) wide. Above the dark, dull green foliage, orange-yellow flowers (singly or in pairs) appear on 30-45cm (12-18in) inflorescences in spring. The many varieties also include the yellow and crimson flowered 'Andreanus'; the cream and yellow 'Cornish Cream'; and the lovely 1.5m (5ft) tall 'Burkwoodii' in shades of maroon, purple and red.

The only pruning required is to cut off roughly two-thirds of the previous year's shoots, being careful not to cut into old wood.

Propagate by seed sown out of doors during spring, or by heel or nodal cuttings during summer.

Dahlia – Anemone-flowered

- **Open sunny site**
- **Rich well-drained soil**
- **Plant 10cm (4in) deep**

This type of dahlia will grow to slightly over 1m (3.3ft), with blooms some 10cm (4in) in diameter. The flowers are double, with the outer petals flat and the inner ones tubular and much shorter, often in contrasting colours. Blooms appear in summer and continue through to the autumn frosts, giving a brilliant show of red, purple, yellow or white.

Tubers can be started in the warmth but must not be planted out until the danger of frosts has passed. Unsprouted tubers can be planted in late spring; the shoots will not pierce the surface until the frosts have gone. The soil should have plenty of organic material added to it, to feed the roots and to retain moisture during dry periods. Remove dead flowers. Lift the plant in autumn and store the tubers in a frost-free place during winter. Spray with a pesticide and fungicide. If leaves turn yellow and wilt, destroy the plant.

Cytisus scoparius

Dahlia – anemone-flowered

Dahlia – Ball
- **Open sunny space**
- **Rich well-drained soil**
- **Plant 10cm (4in) deep**

This group is noted for the ball-shaped blooms. They are fully double; the petals appear to be tubular and open out at the blunt end, and they are arranged in a spiral. The group is split into two sections: the standard ball has blooms over 10cm (4in) in diameter; and the miniature ball has blooms under 10cm (4in). Both will grow to 1.2m (4ft) tall, and spread 75cm (30in). The colours include white, yellow, orange, red, mauve and purple.

Plant tubers in a well-drained soil rich in organic material, in an area that is open to the sun but sheltered from the wind. Mature plants should be staked. Sprouted tubers should not be planted in the open until danger of frost has passed, unsprouted ones can be planted out in spring. Spray plants with a pesticide and fungicide . Wilting plants with yellow leaves must be destroyed at once.

Below: Dahlia 'Alva's Doris' is a dominantly coloured cactus type, ideal for creating summer colour and until the frosts of autumn.

Dahlia – Bedding
- **Open sunny site**
- **Well-drained rich soil**
- **Plant 5-10cm (2-4in) deep**

These small dahlias are normally grown from seed and treated like annuals. They grow 30-50cm (12-20in) tall with a similar spread. The leaves are bright green. Flowers can be single, semi-double or double, in colours from white through yellows and reds to lilac, and 5-7.5cm (2-3in) in diameter. They bloom in midsummer and continue until the autumn frosts.

After the first year, when they are grown from seed, tubers are formed and can be lifted and kept in a frost-free place during winter. If tubers shrivel, soak them in water overnight and then dry them before putting them back into storage. They can be planted the following year in spring unless they have started to sprout, in which case keep them in moist peat until late spring, when they can be planted outside. Seed can be sown in late winter at a temperature of 16°C (60°F), transplanted when large enough to handle, and planted out in late spring in the flowering position. Spray with a pesticide and fungicide.

Dahlia – Cactus
- **Open sunny space**
- **Rich well-drained soil**
- **Plant 10cm (4in) deep**

This group of dahlias can be divided into five sections: miniature, small, medium, large and giant. They are exotic, with the petals rolled back or quilled for over half their length. The largest flowers reach 25cm (10in) in diameter, but the smallest are only 10cm (4in). The colours include white, yellow, orange, red and purple, with some delicate shades of pink and lilac. The larger plants grow to 1.5m (5ft) tall and almost 1.2m (4ft) across; the smaller ones are 90cm (3ft) tall and 75cm (30in) across.

Tubers should preferably be planted in open sun, but will stand some shade. Plant them outdoors in mid-spring or start them off in a greenhouse and plant out in late spring. Winter storage of tubers must be frost-free. Spray with a pesticide and fungicide; destroy wilting plants with yellow leaves.

Dahlia – Collarette
- **Sunny sheltered place**
- **Rich and moist but well-drained soil**
- **Plant 10cm (4in) deep**

This half-hardy plant will grow to 1.2m (4ft) tall, with a spread of 75cm (30in). The leaves are bright

Above: This lovely collarette dahlia is 'Claire de Lune'.

green and make a good setting for the blooms, which are up to 10cm (4in) across in white, yellow, orange, red or pink. The flowers have an outer ring of flat petals with an inner collar of smaller petals around the central disc of stamens. Blooms appear from late summer to the frosts in autumn, when the plant should be lifted and the tuber stored.

The following spring they can be started off in the greenhouse, and the sprouting plant put out in late spring; or the unsprouted tuber can be put out in mid-spring. The soil should be rich in organic material, compost, bonemeal or manure. Plant in full sun. Shelter plants from wind or support the dahlia with a stake. Spray with a general pesticide and fungicide. Destroy plants if the leaves wilt and turn yellow.

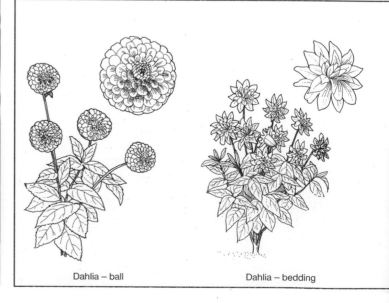

Dahlia – ball

Dahlia – bedding

Above: Dahlia 'Lavendale' is a pretty, pink, decorative type, ideal for planting in mixed borders in sunny gardens.

Dahlia – Decorative
- Open sunny position
- Rich well-drained soil
- Plant 10cm (4in) deep

This group of dahlias is distinguished by the truly double blooms of flat petals, often twisted and normally with blunt points. The group divides into five sections: giant, large, medium, small and miniature. The giants grow to 1.5m (5ft), with blooms up to 25cm (10in) across; the miniatures have a height of 90cm (3ft) with flowers 10cm (4in) in diameter. The colours include white, yellow, orange, red, pink, purple and lavender, with some multicolours.

They all flower from late summer until the autumn frosts. Then the plants should be lifted and the tubers stored in a frost-free place until spring. Support the plants with stakes, particularly the taller varieties. Remove all but one bud from each stem to encourage larger blooms. Remove dead flowers. Treat the plants with a pesticide and fungicide.

Above: Dahlia 'Bishop of Llandaff' is a stunning crimson paeony-flowered dahlia that will accent any garden.

Dahlia – Paeony-flowered
- Open sunny site
- Rich well-drained soil
- Plant 10cm (4in) deep

This type of dahlia grows to 90cm (3ft) tall, with a spread of 60cm (2ft). The flowers, 10cm (4in) across, consist of an outer ring of flat petals and one or more inner rings of flat petals around a central core of stamens, in orange, red or purple. Plant the tubers 10cm (4in) deep in well-drained soil with plenty of organic material mixed in to supply nutrients. The flowers start in late summer and continue until the late autumn frosts.

The tuber should then be lifted and stored free from frost until the following year, when it can be planted out in spring. Alternatively, keep the tuber in a greenhouse to encourage early sprouting, but then it should not be planted out until late spring. Spray with a pesticide and fungicide. If the leaves turn yellow and the plant wilts, destroy it.

Dahlia – cactus

Dahlia – collarette

Dahlia – decorative

Dahlia – paeony-flowered

Dahlia – Pompon

- Open sunny place
- Well-drained rich soil
- Plant 10cm (4in) deep

These dahlias are similar to the ball types, but their blooms are only 5cm (2in) in diameter. Their shape is more ball-like, and the petals are tubular for their whole length. They flower in late summer and continue to the first frosts. Colours include lilac, red, purple and white. They grow to 1.2m (4ft) tall, and 75cm (30in) across.

Plant in a section of the garden that is open but sheltered from the wind. The tubers, if unsprouted, can be planted in mid-spring, but sprouted tubers should be kept in the greenhouse until late spring. Give the plants some support and pinch out the leading shoots one month after planting. When the plants are cut down by frosts, lift and store the tubers in a frost-free place. Plants should be treated with a pesticide and fungicide. Wilting dahlias with yellow leaves should be destroyed.

Dahlia – Single-flowered

- Open sunny site
- Rich well-drained soil
- Plant 10cm (4in) deep

These half-hardy tuberous plants are popular as border specimens. They come into flower in summer and continue until the first frost. The single-flowered varieties have blooms up to 10cm (4in) across, in red, lilac or pink, and consist of a single row of petals around a central disc of stamens. The plants grow up to 75cm (30in) tall.

Plant the tubers outdoors in mid-spring, but if they are already sprouting keep them in a frost-free place until late spring, when they can be planted out. A rich, well-drained soil is needed, with fertilizer or manure added before planting. Place in an open and sunny situation and give the growing plant some support. Remove dead flowers and pinch out leading shoots to encourage larger blooms. Tubers should be lifted and stored each autumn. Spray with a general pesticide and fungicide. If the leaves turn yellow and wilt, destroy the plant to stop the virus.

Below: Dahlia 'Princess Marie Jose' is a single-flowered form that thrives in rich, well-drained soil and in sun.

Daphne × burkwoodii 'Somerset'

- Full sunshine
- A well-drained moist soil
- Flowers late spring to early summer

The semi-evergreen or almost deciduous shrub 'Somerset' is a form of *Daphne × burkwoodii*. It reaches about 1m (3.3ft) in height and makes a sparingly branched bush with 2.5cm (1in) almost lance-shaped leaves. This clone has sweetly scented blush-pink tubular flowers, the outside flushed with rose, and produced in bunches of six on short lateral shoots.

Like most daphnes 'Somerset' likes good drainage, yet it must have an ample supply of moisture. Dryness at the roots must be avoided. 'Somerset' does well on a sandy loam.

As daphnes transplant badly, always obtain young container-grown plants, which should be planted in their permanent positions as soon as possible. Propagate by half-ripe cuttings during the summer.

Daphne cneorum

(Garland flower)
- Fairly open situation
- Well-drained loam with lime
- Evergreen

This small, deciduous shrub seems to do better in cultivation than in

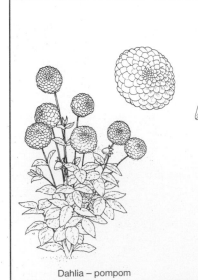

Dahlia – pompom

Dahlia – single-flowered

Daphne x burkwoodii 'Somerset'

Daphne cneorum

the wild, where it often appears scrappy. It is highly scented, and therefore of double value in a garden. Officially it makes a mat 90cm (3ft) across, but may reach up to 1.5m (5ft) across. The many twiggy branches produce clusters of fragrant rosy flowers in spring and possibly again in autumn. It does well in any soil, but benefits from a top-dressing of leaf-mould each year to cover the bare stems.

Propagation is a tease. Cuttings of non-flowering shoots taken in midsummer, dipped in rooting hormone and inserted in a shaded peat frame, have always had a high incidence of losses. Another way is to work sand and peat down between the branches in late spring to encourage them to layer, and then to remove the rooted layers for over-wintering in a cold frame.

Daphne mezereum

(February daphne, Mezereon)
- **Sun, but tolerates some shade**
- **Any good fertile soil**
- **Flowers late winter or early spring**

When *Daphne mezereum* blooms in late winter, it is a good indication that spring is just around the corner. This colourful and fragrant deciduous shrub reaches a height of 1-1.5m (3.3-5ft) and as much in width. Spear-like leaves taper at the base and are either pointed or rounded at the apex; they are 4-9cm (1.6-3.5in) long and 6mm-2cm (0.25-0.8in) wide. The sweetly scented purplish red flowers are produced in twos and threes on erect naked wood. The green berries later become bright red, and these are attractive to blackbirds.

As this is not a long-lived shrub, have a few seedlings or plants from cuttings available in case of losses. Usually a few berries drop to the ground, and some will germinate. Propagate by seed when it is ripe, or by taking nearly ripe cuttings in early autumn. Usually no pruning is needed, but if a shoot needs cutting to improve the shape of the bush, do this in spring.

Left: *Daphne × burkwoodii 'Somerset'* is a semi-evergreen shrub with sweetly-scented flowers in early summer.

Below: *Daphne odora 'Aureomarginata'*, an evergreen shrub, has sweetly scented late winter flowers and light green leaves edged in creamy-white.

Daphne odora 'Aureomarginata'

(Winter daphne)
- **Full sun**
- **Any well-drained soil**
- **Flowers late winter/early spring**

This evergreen shrub has a delicious fragrance. The cultivar 'Aureomarginata' is hardier and more vigorous than the species. Even so, in cold areas choose a sheltered position; otherwise any good open site will suffice. It can be grown successfully in a well-drained clay soil and where there is chalk in the soil, although it does not need it.

The narrow oval leaves, 4-9cm (1.6-3.5in) long, are faintly margined in creamy white. The flowers, reddish purple on the outside and paler within, are sweetly scented. One plant will scent the entire garden in late winter and early spring. This shrub will grow to 1.2-1.8m (4-6ft) tall, and about the same in width. Prune after flowering, but only when really necessary.

Propagate by layering or by taking half-ripe cuttings of the current year's growth during midsummer.

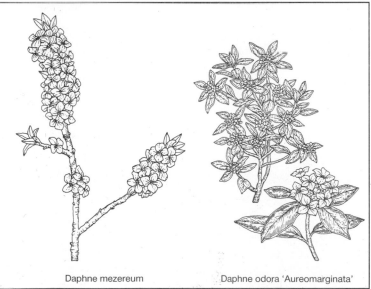

Daphne mezereum

Daphne odora 'Aureomarginata'

Delphinium consolida

(Larkspur)

- Sow in autumn or spring
- Rich, well-cultivated soil
- Sheltered, sunny position

This hardy annual needs a sunny sheltered border. Many individual strains and mixtures are available and all are reliable. Colours include blue, purple, pink, white and red.

Single or double flowers are produced on erect stems up to 1.2m (4ft) tall, in long columns. The plants spread to about 30cm (12in), and need to be planted towards the back of a border. Leaves are mid-green and deeply cut.

As they are very vigorous in growth, make sure you weed through in the early stages on a regular basis. They can be sown in the open ground in spring, but finer results will be obtained if they are planted in the autumn. Take out drills where plants are to flower, about 30cm (12in) apart, sow seed and cover. Thin out to 30cm (12in).

Below: Delphinium consolida 'Extra Choice Mixed' is an easily-grown hardy annual, with lax spires of pink, rose and purple flowers.

Delphinium elatum

- Full sun
- Deep rich well-drained retentive soil
- Summer and autumn flowering

This hardy herbaceous perennial is well known, with deeply-cut, mid-green leaves and large spikes of flowers during midsummer. The true species is seldom cultivated, and it is elatum (large-flowered) and belladonna varieties that are grown.

The elatum types are stiffly erect, rising up to 1.8m (6ft) or more high, and with tall stems tightly packed with flowers. The belladonna types are smaller, to about 1.3m (4.5ft) high and with a graceful and branched nature.

Plant in well-drained but moisture-retentive fertile soil, and in a sunny position. Select a position sheltered from strong winds. Support plants with canes. Cut back to soil-level in autumn.

Propagate these plants by taking 7.5-10cm (3-4in) long basal cuttings in mid-spring, inserting them in equal parts moist peat and sharp sand. Place in a cold frame. When rooted, plant into a nursery bed.

Above: Deutzia × elegantissima 'Fasciculata', a hardy shrub, becomes covered with pale pink flowers early in the year.

Deutzia × elegantissima 'Fasciculata'

- Sunny situation
- Good loamy soil; tolerates lime
- Spring flowering

Deutzias are deciduous shrubs, with clusters of dainty flowers in spring. They need ample moisture and loamy soil; the majority tolerate lime. 'Fasciculata' makes a graceful shrub up to 1.5m (5ft) tall. Deutzias are wiry shrubs, and their oval-shaped foliage is rather wrinkled. The flowers are borne on the previous year's growth. The flowers are almost 2.5cm (1in) wide, bright rosy pink on the outside and paler within. Another equally beautiful deutzia is 'Rosalind', which has deep carmine flowers.

Every two years, thin out old flowering shoots and any dead branches. Although deutzias are winter-hardy, they make rather early growth, and in frost pockets or low-lying districts they can become frosted.

Propagate by half-ripe cuttings inserted where there is gentle bottom heat during early summer to midsummer, or by hardwood cuttings inserted out of doors in autumn.

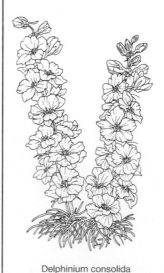

Delphinium consolida

Delphinium elatum – belladonna variety

Dianthus barbatus

(Stinking Billie, Sweet William)
- **Sow in early summer**
- **Avoid very acid soil**
- **Sunny location**

The fragrant Sweet William is a useful and cheerful biennial. The plant ranges in height from 30-60cm (12-24in). The flowers are produced in a compact head up to 13cm (5in) across. Single or double blooms open from late spring to early summer and many colours are available, but red and white predominate. Bicolours are also common.

Stocky plants can be obtained by sowing seeds in a prepared seed-bed during early summer.

Above: *Dianthus barbatus is famed for the fragrance of its brightly coloured flowers.*

Plant out germinated seedlings into nursery rows 15cm (6in) apart. Keep well weeded throughout the summer. Final positioning, 20-25cm (8-10in) apart, should be carried out during the autumn. Alternatively, sow where they are to flower, in early summer, and thin out to correct spacing when they are large enough to handle. Avoid very acid soils and dress with lime before the final planting if your soil is of this type.

Dianthus chinensis 'Telstar'

(Dianthus sinensis)

(Chinese pink, Indian pink, Rainbow pink)
- **Sow in mid-spring**
- **Alkaline to neutral soil**
- **Sunny spot**

The brilliant colours of the 'Telstar' F1 hybrids are a must for the keen enthusiast of annual pinks. This plant is only 20cm (8in) in height. The flowers are produced on short stems in late spring or early summer, earlier than most other cultivars. Blooms may be scarlet, crimson, pink, white, picotee or variable stripes. This very free-flowering strain has great appeal, and is well recommended. Use it in borders, in window boxes and other containers, or alongside a path.

Sow where they are to flower, in mid-spring. Take out shallow drills, and only lightly cover the seed.

Thin out to 15cm (6in) apart. Alternatively, if you have a greenhouse, then – to be sure of a uniform crop of plants – sow seed in a good loam-based growing medium in a temperature of 13°C (55°F) during spring. Prick out the seedlings into boxes, harden off, and plant out in early summer.

Dianthus neglectus
- **Open situation**
- **Lime-free soil**
- **Evergreen**

Pinks usually thrive on alkaline soils, but this is an exception, as it is to be found on lime-free soils in the eastern and southern European Alps. It is a perennial that forms a neat hummock of grey-green linear leaves that varies in height from

Above: *Dianthus chinensis 'Telstar' is diminutive, with delicate red and pink flowers.*

10-20cm (4-8in). It must be admitted that the flowers are variable, and so a good form must be chosen; the flowers are from pale pink to deep crimson, but always with a distinctive buff reverse. At best they are 3cm (1.25in) across, on short stems that hold them just above the foliage, in midsummer.

This species does well in a sunny spot in well-drained soil, but appreciates being moist in summer and less so in winter. Do not plant in chalky or alkaline conditions.

Propagation is by soft cuttings taken in midsummer from non-flowering shoots and inserted in a sandy cutting frame. The plants will be ready by late winter.

Deutzia x elegantissima 'Fasciculata'

Dianthus barbatus

Dianthus chinensis 'Telstar'

Dianthus neglectus

Diascia cordata
- **Warm open situation**
- **Well-drained soil**
- **Evergreen**

Plants from South Africa are usually suspect for hardiness, but this perennial has seemed hardy now for some years. Perhaps its habitat at 2,500m (8,200ft) in the Drakensberg Mountains has built up its resistance to winter cold. It is an attractive plant, producing 15-25cm (6-10in) long racemes of pinky terracotta flowers, 1.5cm (0.6in) wide, from a dense mat of leafy stems.

It relishes a warm position in any well-drained soil, where it will flower in summer.

Propagation is by cuttings of young shoots taken in summer and placed in a sand frame. When rooted these should be over-wintered in a frame before planting out the following spring.

Dicentra spectabilis
(Bleeding heart, Dutchman's breeches)
- **Partial shade or full sun**
- **Rich well-cultivated fertile soil**
- **Late spring and early summer flowering**

This hardy herbaceous perennial has a fragile look. The glaucous, finely divided foliage has attractive arching sprays off the stoutish stems, about 60cm (2ft) high,

sometimes taller, from which dangle crimson and white lockets. When open, the flowers are rosy pink with white tips. It makes a good cut flower, and roots potted in autumn can be forced into flower in an unheated greenhouse.

These delicate-looking plants can be damaged by late spring frosts, and it is advisable to plant them where the sun does not reach the plants before the frost has gone. Plant *D. spectabilis*

where it can be protected by a wall or evergreen shrubs. A mulch of leaf-mould or well-rotted compost should be given each spring.

Propagate in spring by cutting the roots with a sharp knife, or by root cuttings taken in spring and rooted in an unheated frame.

Below: *Diascia cordata creates a bright display in a rock garden, with massed flower heads and nearly prostrate leafy stems.*

Dictamnus albus
(Burning bush, Dittany, Fraxinella, Gas plant)
- **Full sun**
- **Well-drained deep fertile soil**
- **Early summer flowering**

This hardy herbaceous perennial is known as burning bush because on hot dry days, when the seedpods are ripening, it is possible by holding a lighted match to the base of the flower stalk to ignite the volatile oil given off by the plant without doing any damage to the dictamnus itself.

The smooth divided light green leaves are on erect stems that are lemon scented. The erect stems bear white flowers that have very long stamens. The plant usually seen in our gardens is *D. albus purpureus*, which has soft mauve-purple flowers, veined with red. Both are 90cm (3ft) tall. The plants are deep rooted.

Propagate by root cuttings in late autumn or winter, or by division in spring.

Didiscus caeruleus
(Blue lace flower, Queen Anne's lace)
- **Sow in spring**
- **Ordinary well-cultivated soil**
- **Sheltered and sunny position**

This lovely half-hardy annual from Australia has the appearance of the perennial scabious. Clusters of

Diascia cordata

Dicentra spectabilis

Dictamnus albus

Didiscus caeruleus

delicate lavender-blue flowers are carried on stems 45cm (18in) high. The umbel-shaped inflorescence will appear in midsummer and carry on flowering until autumn. Leaves and stems are covered with masses of tiny hairs, and feel rough to the touch. Choose a sheltered position, preferably towards the front of a border.

Sowing should be carried out during spring under glass, in a temperature of 16°C (60°F). Use a loam-based growing medium for both seed and seedlings. When large enough to handle, the latter will respond better if pricked out into small individual pots. After hardening off, plant them out into final positions, 23cm (9in) apart, towards the end of spring.

Below: Didiscus caeruleus, a dainty half-hardy annual, forms a sea of slightly scented flowers from midsummer to late summer.

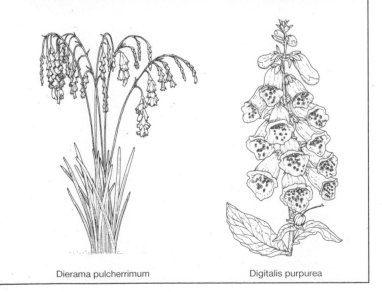

Dierama pulcherrimum

Digitalis purpurea

Above: Digitalis purpurea develops tall stems packed at their tops with tubular flowers.

Dierama pulcherrimum

(Angel's fishing rod, Wand flower)
- **Full sun**
- **Light sandy soil**
- **Late summer flowering**

The stems of this plant are clothed with grassy evergreen leaves 60cm (2ft) long. The bell-shaped purplish red to deep old rose flowers are not unlike inverted crocuses, which hang down from the graceful arching 1.5m (5ft) stems. They open at the tip of the stems first, which is unusual.

This bulbous plant thrives best in a warm position, though it likes to have its root-run in the shade. Choose a suitably sheltered position, if growing in gardens that may be draughty or windswept. Bulbs should be planted in late spring, 8-10cm (3.2-4in) deep, and should be surrounded with sharp sand. Choose well-drained porous moist soil in full sun. Once established, leave them alone until they become overcrowded.

Propagate by lifting the offsets and dividing them. It can also be raised from seed, which germinates very readily, with the seedlings surrounding the older plants.

Digitalis purpurea

(Foxglove)
- **Sow in early summer**
- **Most soils, but slightly acid**
- **Semi-shade**

This hardy biennial has always been a great favourite. Flowering in the year after sowing, it produces the familiar long spikes, 1-1.5m (3.3-5ft), bearing tubular flowers of maroon or purple, and distinctly spotted in the throat of each bloom. The common floxglove has for a long time been associated with medicine, but careful selection and breeding has resulted in the introduction of beautiful garden forms of variable colour and size. Outstanding in this respect are the Excelsior hybrid strains. Flower spikes up to 30cm (12in) long arise from a rosette of grey-green leaves.

Sow seed in well-prepared seed beds in early summer. Sow seed thinly in drills, and plant out seedlings in nursery rows 15-23cm (6-9in) apart. Plant into final flowering positions in autumn, at 60cm (2ft) intervals.

Dimorphotheca aurantiaca 'Dwarf Salmon'

(Cape marigold, Star of the Veldt)
- **Sow in early or late spring**
- **Light well-drained soil**
- **Sunny site**

Flowering from midsummer, this hardy annual needs the sunniest position you can give, otherwise the blooms will not open, especially in shade or dull weather. The cultivar 'Dwarf Salmon' will make a delightful change from the usual range of colours, and its dwarf habit, 23cm (9in), makes it suitable for edging a border, along the side of a pathway, or for an odd gap in the rock garden in full sun. Daisy-like flowers of apricot-pink, about 5cm (2in) across, are formed on short spreading stems carrying pear-shaped leaves, all of which are scented. If possible, plant next to pale blue or white annuals of a similar height, or in front of taller subjects.

Propagation from seed is relatively easy, either under glass during early spring or directly into the open ground in late spring when ground conditions are favourable. Thin out or plant at intervals of 30cm (12in).

Dodecatheon meadia

(Common American cowslip, Shooting star)
- **Damp situation**
- **Leafy soil**
- **Herbaceous**

If your rock garden has a pond, then this is one of the plants that must go by the waterside. Alternatively, it will do nicely in a damp patch. It is a hardy, herbaceous perennial, with a rosette of fresh green linear leaves in spring. The unusual rose-purple flowers follow in late spring or early autumn on stems 30-45cm (12-18in) tall. The 2cm (0.8in) flowers have petals that are twisted and swept back to reveal the protruding yellow anthers. This is an easy-going plant provided it has some shade and moisture.

Propagation is by division in spring, by removing rooted offsets and potting them in a peaty soil, or by sowing seed in winter so that plants will be ready for setting out in autumn.

Doronicum 'Miss Mason'

(Leopard's bane, Plantain doronicum)
- **Full sun or partial shade**
- **Any good fertile soil**
- **Spring flowering**

This is one of the first hardy herbaceous perennials to brighten the garden as spring approaches. The large yellow star-shaped flowers are a good follow-on after the early daffodils are over.

'Miss Mason' has bright yellow daisy-like flowers which are in bloom for several weeks. The smooth heart-shaped leaves have scalloped edges, and are bright green. The flowers are carried at the top of wiry stems 45cm (18in) high. This variety makes an excellent cut flower. When flowering is over, the leaves of 'Miss Mason' do not die down as this hybrid is evergreen.

Remove faded blooms so that plants produce a further crop of flowers in the autumn.

Propagate by division in early autumn or spring. Plants should be divided every third or fourth year.

Above: Dimorphotheca aurantiaca 'Dwarf Salmon' is a superb hardy annual, with bright-faced flowers from midsummer to late summer.

Right: Doronicum 'Miss Mason' is one of the earliest flowering herbaceous perennials.

Dryas octopetala

(Mountain avens)
- **Open situation**
- **Any well-drained soil**
- **Evergreen ground cover**

A native of the European Alps and North America, this hardy, evergreen plant is a valuable asset to any rock garden. In spring, it shows creamy white flowers which are 4cm (1.6in) wide. In summer, it has feathery seed heads.

It is a mat-forming plant with small, dark green crinkled oak-like

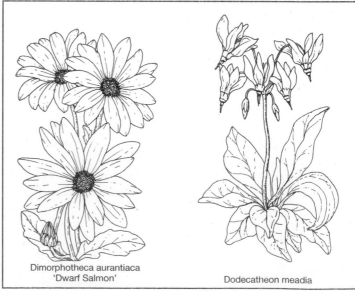

Dimorphotheca aurantiaca 'Dwarf Salmon'

Dodecatheon meadia

leaves, silver on the reverse, and trailing stems that normally spread to about 60cm (2ft). The single flowers rise no more than 10cm (4in) above the foliage, with the seed head slightly taller.

Any soil will do, although the richer it is the less likelihood there is of flowers being produced. Sunshine is also an encouragement to flower.

Propagation is from 8cm (3.2in) long heel cuttings, taken in spring or summer and placed around the edge of a pot in sandy soil. Seed is slow to germinate.

Echinacea purpurea
(Rudbeckia purpurea)
(Purple cone flower)
- **Sunny location**
- **Well-drained soil**
- **Summer flowering**

For many years this strong-growing, hardy herbaceous perennial was known as *Rudbeckia purpurea*. It is a stately plant with rough dark green foliage on stiff stout stems.

The rich reddish-purple flowers have a central boss of orange-brown which makes them quite outstanding. An early flowering variety is the broad-petalled erect carmine-purple flowered 'Robert Bloom', which is 90cm (3ft) tall. If you want a variety of colours, the Bressingham Hybrids, also 90cm (3ft) tall, are well worth planting. For a white-flowered version, try 'White Lustre'.

The echinaceas are best planted in spring. Add leaf-mould or well-

Below: Echinacea purpurea is an herbaceous perennial, bearing flowers in summer.

rotted compost to the soil at the time of planting. Propagate by seed sown in spring, by root cuttings in autumn, or by division in spring.

Echinops ritro 'Taplow blue'
(Globe thistle)
- **Full sun**
- **Not fussy over soil**
- **Late summer flowering**

This hardy herbaceous perennial develops round, drumstick heads in varying tones of blue. They are coarse growing. Attached to the stout rough wiry stems is deeply cut greyish spiny foliage, woolly beneath. Bees are especially attracted to the globular flowers. The flower heads can be dried for winter decoration.

The variety 'Taplow Blue' is 1.5m (5ft) tall, with dark blue globular flowers that have a metallic steely lustre. A variety with a slightly richer blue is 'Veitch's Blue'. There is also the white species *Echinops nivalis (E. niveus)*.

These hardy herbaceous perennials can be grown successfully in the poorest of soils, whether sand or chalk, but should be well drained. Also, provide a good depth of soil, as the thong-like roots of this plant are very penetrating.

Propagate by root cuttings in late autumn or winter, or by division in autumn or spring.

Doronicum 'Miss Mason'

Dryas octopetala

Echinacea purpurea

Echinops ritro 'Taplow Blue'

Echium plantagineum 'Monarch Dwarf Hybrids'

(Echium lycopsis)

(Purple viper's bugloss)

- **Sow in spring or autumn**
- **Light, dry soil**
- **Open, sunny location**

This bushy, hardy annual produces flowers of an upturned bell shape on the end of light green branching stems. The common species is predominantly blue, but 'Monarch Dwarf Hybrids' have blue, lavender, pink, white and carmine shades. And, at only 30cm (12in) tall, they require no staking and can be used near the front of a border. The mixture is highly recommended. Choose an open sunny site to ensure free-flowering plants, which will open at the end of spring in mild areas.

In spring sow seeds where plants are to flower. Take out shallow drills and lightly cover the seeds. Thin out to 15cm (6in) apart. Alternatively, sow in autumn in the usual way but wait until spring before thinning out to final distances. Do not overwater when plants are established.

Below: *Echium plantagineum 'Monarch Dwarf Hybrids' are hardy annuals that attract bees.*

Edraianthus pumilio

(Grassy bells)

- **A sunny open position**
- **Well-drained soil**
- **Herbaceous**

This small, clump-forming, hardy herbaceous perennial is related to the campanulas and produces similar flowers. Because of its size and neatness it is suitable for screes or troughs. It forms a small tuft of narrow grey-green leaves from which in summer emerges the upturned funnel-shaped flowers of lavender blue. The whole plant does not exceed 5-8cm (2-3.2in). It is hardy, although reputed to be short-lived; however, plants have been known to live in troughs for five years.

Propagation is by sowing seed in winter in a gritty compost, potting on into a limy soil, with limestone chippings incorporated. Water carefully. Soft cuttings of non-flowering wood can be taken in midsummer and inserted in sand, making sure they are stopped from flowering.

Above: *Edraianthus pumilio is a dwarf, clump-forming herbaceous perennial, ideal for rock gardens, scree beds and troughs. Plant in full sun.*

Elaeagnus pungens 'Maculata'

(Thorny elaeagnus)

- **Full sunlight**
- **Any soil, including chalk**
- **Year-round foliage**

The cultivar 'Maculata' is an evergreen spreading shrub which can reach 2.7-3.6m (9-12ft) high and 3-4.5m (10-15ft) wide. The striking foliage is marked with a rich yellow patch in the centre of each leaf. The leaves are often as much as 11.5cm (4.5in) long by 6.5cm (2.5in) wide. The foliage lights up any part of the garden, especially when backed by dark evergreen shrubs, such as *Prunus lusitanica* (Portugal laurel).

From time to time green shoots may appear. When this happens, such shoots must be cut out to preserve the variegated foliage.

Propagate by half-ripe cuttings inserted in gentle heat during midsummer, or by hardwood cuttings taken in late autumn.

Echium plantagineum 'Monarch Dwarf Hybrid'

Edraianthus pumilio

Elaeagnus pungens 'Maculata'

Embothrium coccineum

Left: Elaeagnus pungens 'Maculata' has eye-catching variegated foliage that brightens gardens throughout the year.

Embothrium coccineum

(Chilean firebush, Chilean fire tree)
- **Shade**
- **Moist loamy lime-free soil**
- **Flowers in spring and early summer**

This showy evergreen shrub or small tree is sometimes, though rarely, semi-deciduous. It must have a cool root run, which can be achieved where there is a moist loamy soil free of lime or chalk. Also it must have shelter from cold drying winds. Provided it has shelter, and a modicum of shade from surrounding trees, it should eventually give a spectacular display of brilliant orange-scarlet flowers in spring and early summer. The dark glossy green leaves are greyish green above and paler beneath. As a bush it will reach a height of 3.6-4.5m (12-15ft), and as a tree 7.6-9m (25-30ft) high. No pruning is necessary.

Propagate by seeds sown in late winter under glass, or by root cuttings taken in winter and inserted in small pots where there is moderate bottom heat.

Endymion hispanicus

(Giant bluebell, Spanish bluebell, Spanish jacinth)
- **Open or lightly shaded position**
- **Moist but not boggy soil**
- **Plant 10-15cm (4-6in) deep**

This bulbous plant was once included in the genus *Scilla* but now has its own genus. It grows to a height of 30cm (12in), with broad strap-like leaves and bell-shaped white, blue or pink flowers from spring to midsummer. It thrives on neglect and is ideal for growing in the open.

Bulbs should be planted 10-15cm (4-6in) deep, in a moist soil with plenty of organic matter. The bulbs have no outer skin, and should be out of the soil as little as possible. Do not store bulbs, as they shrivel when dry or go mouldy if too wet.

Propagate by lifting the bulbs and removing offsets, which can then be replanted with more space around them. Seed sown on leaf-mould may take six years to flower. Yellow spots that turn to dark brown blotches indicate rust; remove and destroy infected leaves, and spray with a fungicide.

Endymion non-scriptus

(Common bluebell, English bluebell, Wild hyacinth)
- **Open sun or light shade**
- **Moist but not waterlogged soil**
- **Plant 10-15cm (4-6in) deep**

This bulbous plant, widespread throughout western Europe, gives spectacular shows of blue in light woodland and open ground. In Scotland, it is called the wild hyacinth. The strap-like leaves are a glossy mid-green. Purple-blue, white or pink bell-shaped flowers appear in spring. The plant grows to 30cm (12in) and has a spread of 10cm (4in), although the mature leaves will spread further as they become less erect.

The bulbs should be planted 10-15cm (4-6in) deep. They have no outer skin, so the less time they spend out of soil the better. Choose a moist soil with plenty of leaf-mould in it. Plants are increased by lifting and dividing the bulbs after the foliage has died down in autumn. Seed can take up to six years to flower. Endymions are normally free of pests and diseases.

Below: Endymion hispanicus forms a dominant display of bell-shaped flowers.

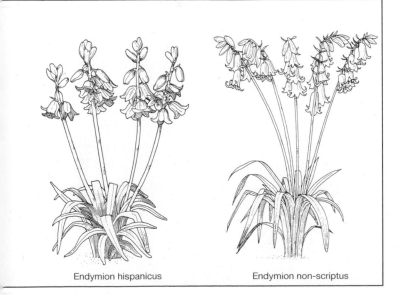

Endymion hispanicus   Endymion non-scriptus

Enkianthus campanulatus

- **Full sun**
- **Moist loamy lime-free soil**
- **Spring flowers, autumn foliage**

When young this hardy deciduous shrub has a slightly erect habit, but as it develops it becomes a densely branched bushy shrub, which normally requires no pruning. It can reach a height of 1.5-2.7m (5-9ft) and almost as much in width. The finely toothed dull green leaves are 2.5-6.5cm (1-2.5in) long and 1.2-3.5cm (0.5-1.4in) wide. The bell-shaped creamy yellow pendulous flowers, veined and red-tipped, form pretty clusters, each flower on an 8mm (0.3in) stalk. The flowers are produced in spring on the terminal buds of the previous year's shoots. In autumn, the foliage changes to attractive shades of yellow and red.

Enkianthus needs a cool moist peaty soil. When bushes become overgrown or misshapen, cut them hard back. Provided new growth appears from the base, all is well.

Propagate by seed under glass in late winter, by softwood cuttings in summer, or by layering in spring.

Above: *Enkianthus campanulatus, a hardy shrub, produces bell-shaped, pendulous flowers in late spring. In autumn, the dull green leaves turn brilliant red.*

Epimedium alpinum

(Barrenwort)
- **Shady corner**
- **Any soil**
- **Semi-evergreen**

A widely distributed genus from the northern temperate regions of Europe and Asia, including Japan. They are particularly useful for ground cover in a semi-woodland or particularly shaded situation. The newly produced leaves in spring are an attractive fresh green, and colour nicely towards the autumn. *Epimedium alpinum*, from the woodlands of Europe, has slightly toothed leaves, turning colour at the edges. It produces attractive racemes of flowers, the outer petals of which are pinky red and the inner bright yellow.

Theoretically the plant is herbaceous, but the old leaves hang on over winter. Old leaves should be removed in spring to reveal the flowers before the new leaves grow up to hide them.

Propagation is by division in spring or autumn and potting into a leafy soil. Keep the pots in shade and the young plants will be ready for planting out in four to eight weeks.

Eranthis hyemalis

(Winter aconite)
- **Sun or partial shade**
- **Well-drained heavy soil**
- **Plant 2.5cm (1in) deep**

This European tuberous-rooted plant grows to a height of 10cm (4in) with a spread of 7.5cm (3in). The leaves are pale green and deeply cut, and the bright yellow flowers appear in late winter. In mild winters it may start blooming in midwinter. The flowers are about 2.5cm (1in) across and look like buttercups but with a collar of pale green leaves just below the flower.

Plant tubers in a well-drained soil that is moist throughout the year – a heavy loam is ideal. Grow them in either sun or light shade. To propagate, lift the eranthis when the leaves die down, break or cut the tubers into sections, and replant these immediately, at least 7.5cm (3in) apart. Seed can be sown in spring and kept in a cold frame; transplant in two years, and flowering will start after another year. Watch for bird attack. If sooty eruptions occur on the plant, destroy it to stop the spread of smut disease.

Below: *Eranthis hyemalis 'Guinea Gold' brightens late winter with deep yellow, fragrant flowers.*

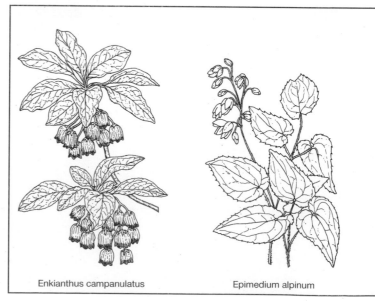

Enkianthus campanulatus

Epimedium alpinum

Eremurus robustus

(Desert candle, Foxtail lily, King's spear)
- **Sunny sheltered border**
- **Well-drained soil**
- **Plant 1.25cm (0.5in) deep**

This hardy herbaceous perennial reaches 3m (10ft) high, with bright sword-like leaves 1.2m (4ft) in length. The flowers, which have the appearance of bushy foxtails,

Above: Erica herbacea 'December Red' brings colour during winter months with a carpet of bright red flowers.

are 1.2m (4ft) spikes of star-like blooms, peach-buff to pink in colour. They appear in summer.

The plants should be kept in a sheltered border, with an aspect to catch midday to evening sun, and the soil should be well drained with plenty of fibre. The crown of the

tuber should have only 1.25cm (0.5in) of soil over it, although some growers recommend planting as deep as 15cm (6in) in light soils. Leave undisturbed until tubers become crowded, then lift, divide and replant in autumn. The flower stems should be cut down when blooming stops, unless seed is needed. Spread well-rotted manure or compost over the area in autumn. Seeds are slow to germinate.

Erica herbacea

(Erica carnea)
(Snow heather, winter heather)
- **Open sunny situation**
- **Light soil; tolerates lime**
- **Autumn to spring flowers**

This hardy, evergreen shrub was known as *Erica carnea*, but it is now *Erica herbacea*. There is a wide variety of colours, from white, pink, red and rosy purple to dark carmine red. The cultivar 'December Red', is 15-23cm (6-9in) high, has bright rose-pink flowers above a mat of dark green leaves from early winter. 'Springwood White' is the same height with light green foliage and long white spikes.

Choose an open situation and avoid rich soils. Plant deeply, with the lowest foliage resting on the soil, in early spring. The tufted shrubs produce tight hummocks 15-30cm (6-12in) high, forming prostrate spreading plants. The

small dark glossy green foliage is usually arranged in whorls of four. Flowers are produced singly or in pairs, in the leaf axils of the previous year's growth. With shears trim all faded blooms after flowering has finished.

Propagate by heel or nodal cuttings in late summer, or by layering in spring.

Erigeron mucronatus

(Erigeron karvinskianus)
(Fleabane)
- **Dry sunny position**
- **Enjoys a poor soil**
- **Evergreen**

This is one of those delightful alpine weeds that seed themselves unobtrusively and do not create a nuisance. Native to Mexico, it is useful for producing its daisy flowers in summer. It enjoys being starved, among paving or in a stone wall, where the white to deep rose-pink flowers (according to age) provide a dainty show. The whole plant appears delicate, with fragile-looking leaves and wiry stems, but although hit hard by a frost in a bad winter, it will recover. The total height is about 15cm (6in) and the flowers are produced over a long period, well into the autumn.

Propagation is by seed sown in late winter, and the young plants are set out in early summer. It is claimed that no one sows this species more than once, as it seeds itself for ever afterwards!

Eranthis hyemalis

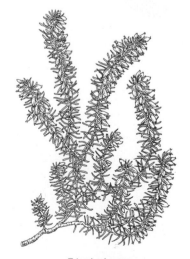

Eremurus robustus

Erica herbacea

Erigeron mucronatus

Erinus alpinus

- **Sun or shade**
- **Enjoys growing in crevices**
- **Evergreen**

This hardy, evergreen perennial is superb in a rock garden and by seeding itself creates a mass of short-lived plants. It is a plant for paving and dry walls, where it will produce a profusion of 7-8cm (2.75-3.2in) wiry stems that bear terminal clusters of small bright pink flowers in summer. There is also a white form, and some named forms with deep crimson or clear pink flowers. Its self-sown seedlings are modest in their behaviour. Seeded into a piece of tufa rock, it makes an attractive show.

Propagation is by seed sown in winter and pricked out into boxes, ready for planting in late spring. Both the species and the colour forms come true from seed, although if they all grow together there may be some variation.

Eryngium bourgatii

(Eryngo)

- **Sunny location**
- **Fertile well-drained soil**
- **Summer and late summer flowering**

This herbaceous perennial has spiny holly-like foliage which is especially attractive, and thistle-like flower heads in varying shades of blue. They are hardy, and flourish by the sea coast. *Eryngium bourgatii* is a native of the Pyrenees. Grey-green foliage and blue-green thistle-like flowers are borne on wiry branching stems. A beautiful plant from Morocco is *E. variifolium*. The spiny-toothed rounded leaves are small compared with many eryngiums, and each leaf has distinctive white veins. The flowers, which are not striking, are borne in late summer and carried on erect stems. The British *Eryngium maritimum* has glaucous leaves and charming blue flowers.

Do not allow these plants to become waterlogged.

Propagate eryngiums by taking root cuttings in late winter or by sowing seed during early spring.

Below: Erinus alpinus is ideal for a rock garden, bright with small pink flowers in summer.

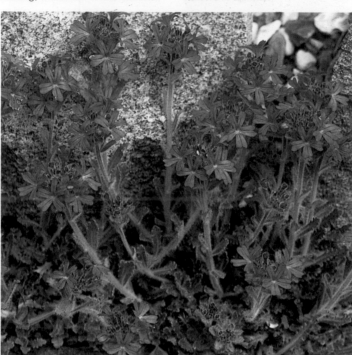

Above: Erysimum 'Jubilee Gold', has short-lived golden flowers in early summer.

Erysimum 'Jubilee Gold'

- **Sunny, open site**
- **Any well-drained soil**
- **Short-lived perennial**

The dwarf wallflowers provide a colourful display on the rock garden in spring, but regrettably are short-lived. The species keeps itself going by self-sown seedlings, but the named varieties have to be propagated by cuttings. There are many varieties, including 'Jubilee

Erinus alpinus

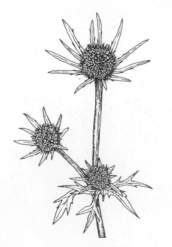

Eryngium bourgatii

Erysimum 'Jubilee Gold'

Erythronium dens-canis

Below: Erythronium dens-canis has spring flowers in white, pink, red and violet amid spotted leaves.

Gold' which forms a low mat of small linear wallflower leaves, which are topped by the golden heads of four-petalled flowers in spring. The parentage of this plant is doubtful, and indeed the whole of this genus and its near relative *Cheiranthus*, with which it has undoubtedly hybridized, is a muddle. Nevertheless these species should not be rejected, as there are some good garden plants to be had from them.

Increase by taking cuttings of non-flowering shoots early in the summer and inserting them in the sand frame. Do not try to raise 'Jubilee Gold' from seed; it will not come true.

Erythronium dens-canis

(Dog's tooth violet)
● **Semi-shade**
● **Moist well-drained soil**
● **Plant 7.5cm (3in) deep**

This cormous plant grows only 15cm (6in) tall. The spotted leaves vary from plant to plant, and some are particularly attractive. The 5cm (2in) flowers appear in spring and the petals are folded back like a cyclamen. They are available in white, pink, red and violet. The leaves are up to 10cm (4in) long.

Corms should be planted in autumn, preferably in groups of at least a dozen for show and in a moist but well-drained soil. Choose a partially shaded site. Here they can be left for many years undisturbed.

Increasing stock by growing from seed can take over five years to reach flowering size. It is quicker to remove offsets in late summer, when the leaves have died down, and to grow them separately in a nursery bed for a year or so. They should take two years to start flowering, and then they can be planted out in autumn. Generally, they are free of pests and diseases.

Erythronium 'Pagoda'

● **Requires semi-shade away from sunshine**
● **Prefers a deep leafy soil**
● **Bulbous**

This is a hybrid between *Erythronium tuolumnense* and one of the species that produces marbled leaves. It is cormous, vigorous and free-flowering, with yellow flowers and mottled leaves. The entire genus is extremely hardy and produces worthwhile subjects for the cooler corners of the rock garden in leafy soil. One authority suggests that they like to be in a damp situation beneath trees, which take up excess moisture. They are certainly subjects for the peat and woodland gardens.

E. tuolumnense has been criticized for its small flowers but recently collected forms from its native California have come with 4cm (1.6in) flowers. 'Pagoda', with flower stems 45cm (18in) long, is more robust than its parent *E. tuolumnense*, which can reach a maximum of only 30cm (12in). Purchase these bulbs from a good dealer, who should pack them in moss or peat to keep moist.

Propagation is by fresh seed, sown no later than early autumn.

Erythronium tuolumnense

● **Shady situation**
● **Moist but not waterlogged soil**
● **Plant 10cm (4in) deep**

This cormous plant grows to 30cm (12in), with a spread of 15cm (6in). It has bright green leaves that are broad and pointed. The spring flowers have six pointed yellow petals and are rather like small lilies.

The corms should be planted 10cm (4in) deep, in a moist but not boggy soil that has plenty of leaf-mould to keep it well-drained, and with some shade. They should be planted in late summer and can be left undisturbed until they become overcrowded. Lift, divide and replant when the leaves die down in summer. Seed takes over five years to reach flowering. It is quicker to increase stock from offsets, which reach flowering in three years. Make sure the soil does not dry out when plants are young, as they need constantly moist soil to thrive. A good layer of well-rotted manure or compost spread over the plants in autumn keeps the organic level high.

Below: Erythronium tuolumnense, ideal in a shady wild garden, reveals yellow flowers in spring.

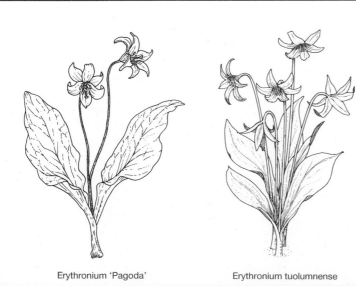

Erythronium 'Pagoda'   Erythronium tuolumnense

Escallonia

- **Sun loving**
- **Well-drained soil; tolerates lime**
- **Summer flowering**

The evergreen escallonias are not considered 100% hardy. In particularly cold areas they go to 'sleep' earlier and 'wake up' later than those in warmer regions, where they flower up to midwinter and then are frosted in late winter.

The following two hybrids are especially recommended. *Escallonia* 'Apple Blossom' is a slow-growing variety with pink and white flowers. It reaches a height of 1.5-2m (5-6.5ft). *Escallonia* 'C.F. Ball' is a free flowering strong-growing escallonia, with large red flowers from summer to early autumn. It reaches 2.1-2.5m (7-8ft) in favoured localities.

Both these escallonias do well by the sea. No regular pruning is required. Cut back after flowering to keep bushes shapely, or do it in spring. Escallonias flower on one-year-old wood.

Propagate by half-ripe cuttings during summer, or by seed sown in late winter under glass.

Eschscholzia californica

(Californian poppy)
- **Sow in autumn or spring**
- **Most soils, including those considered poor**
- **Sunny and dry position**

In mild areas self-seeding of this hardy annual will produce many plants, but kept under control they are an asset to any garden. Nearly always grown as a border plant, they can be used in the rock garden to good advantage. Choose a sunny position for the best results. Flowers are red, yellow, white, pink and orange. Stems carry deeply cut blue-green leaves. The flower buds have a whorled spike effect and when opened the petals are silky in texture. Double hybrids, listed by many seedsmen, are well worth a try and their frilled blooms are an

added attraction. Plants will be 30cm (12in) tall.

Sow in flowering positions in autumn for the best results. The plants that winter through will be stronger and flower earlier. Sow also in spring. In either case thin out the seedlings to 15cm (6in) apart.

Eucomis bicolor

(King's flower, Pineapple flower)
- **Open position or light shade**
- **Rich well-drained soil**
- **Plant 2.5cm (1in) deep**

This bulbous plant reaches 70cm (28in) tall, with a spread of 45cm

Left: *Eschscholzia californica* is a spectacular hardy annual, with flowers in a wide range of bright colours amid finely cut leaves.

Above: *Eucryphia glutinosa* creates a wealth of white flowers, in ones or twos, with yellow centres, in late summer.

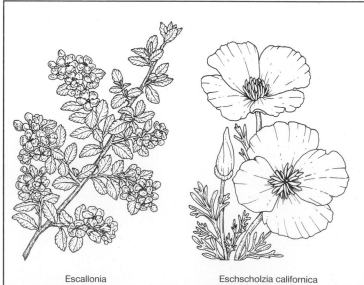

Escallonia   Eschscholzia californica

(18in). It has long, broad, strap-like leaves with pronounced centre spines, and cream flowers in summer borne on fleshy stems crowned with rosettes of petal-like leaves.

It thrives in a rich well-drained soil with plenty of leaf-mould in it. This plant is hardy and needs only a mulch of well-rotted manure each autumn to protect it from hard frosts in winter. Bulbs can be lifted in very early spring, and the offsets separated and replanted. The parent bulbs then have more space to grow, and offsets reach flowering size in two or three years provided they are kept moist all summer and shaded from the sun.

If this species is grown as a pot plant, it should be kept moist in summer but the pot should be rested on its side during winter to allow the soil to dry out. Grown from seed it takes several years to flower.

Eucryphia glutinosa
- **Sunny location; roots in shade**
- **Cool lime-free moist soil**
- **Late summer flowering**

This hardy deciduous, or partially evergreen, small, tree-like shrub has an erect shapely branching habit. It has clusters of pinnate opposite leaves consisting of three or five oval leaflets, 4-6.5cm (1.6-2.5in) long. The flowers, produced either singly or in pairs, each have four petals 6.5cm (2.5in) across,

with a central boss of yellow anthers. The pure white flowers are borne in the leaf axils at the end of the shoot.

This is not the easiest of shrubs to establish, propagate, or transplant. Provide it with moist peaty soil, free of lime or chalk, and keep its roots shaded. Allow eucryphias to grow naturally. Do not prune or train.

Propagate by half-ripe cuttings of side shoots taken with a heel during summer, or by layering in late summer. Whichever is tried, be prepared for losses.

Eupatorium purpureum 'Atropurpureum'
(Joe-pye weed, Purple hemp agrimony, Trumpet weed)
- **Sunny location**
- **Any good fertile soil**
- **Early autumn flowering**

This hardy herbaceous perennial has always attracted attention because of its tall handsome upright purplish stems, bedecked with large fluffy branching heads of flowers in varying shades of pale purple, mauve-pink, cinnamon-pink, purplish rose, and purple-lilac. It grows 1.5-1.8m (5-6ft) high. The variety 'Atropurpureum' has foliage that is purplish, and its fluffy flowers are rosy lilac.

In a large border it needs to be planted well behind shorter-growing plants, or they will be

hidden. This North American plant needs good rich soil if it is to give of its best. A mulch in spring with well-rotted farmyard manure or good garden compost will be welcome. This is an ideal perennial to grow in a wild or semi-wild garden. Propagation is by division in autumn.

Euphorbia griffithii
- **Sun or partial shade**
- **Good fertile soil**
- **Early summer flowering**

This herbaceous perennial has bright yellow flowers 45cm (18in) high. It was introduced from the Himalayas, and was first exhibited in 1954. The flower heads of the

variety 'Fireglow' are a rich burnt orange shade (frequently described as brick red), and carried on erect stems. The 75cm (30in) stems carry the handsome coloured 'flowers', which are in fact bracts.

'Fireglow' does best in an open sunny spot or partial shade. It has slow-spreading shoots, which appear around the base. The dull red asparagus-like shoots soon develop into dark green foliage, reddish beneath. Its roots may become invasive, but if you admire it you will probably not mind.

Propagate this plant by division in spring or autumn.

Below: Eupatorium purpureum 'Atropurpureum' has majestic heads of rosy-lilac flowers.

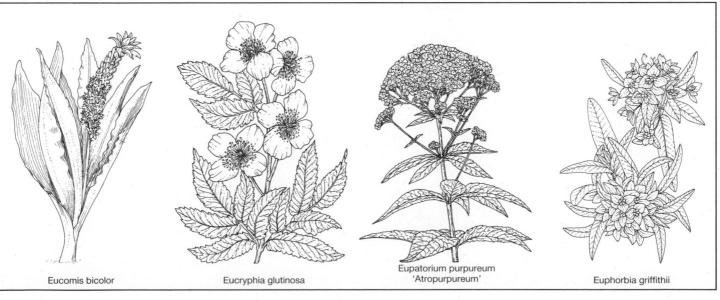

Eucomis bicolor

Eucryphia glutinosa

Eupatorium purpureum 'Atropurpureum'

Euphorbia griffithii

Euphorbia marginata

(Ghost weed, Snow on the mountain)

● **Sow in mid-spring**
● **Ordinary soil, or poor if well-drained**
● **Sun or partial shade**

This hardy annual originates from North America and is grown mainly for its splendid foliage; the flowers are very small, white and insignificant. Stems reach a height of 60cm (24in). The leaves are ovate or oblong, and a pleasant green but with white margins. Bracts beneath the flowers are papery in appearance, and also white. On starved soils the foliage colours are intensified. Use towards the centre of a border.

Sow seed directly where it is to flower, in mid-spring. Thin out the seedlings to 30cm (12in) spacings. Give peastick supports. Avoid damaging plants, as the milky latex can have an irritating effect on the skin. This euphorbia is ideally suited for flower arrangements; when cutting, place the ends of the stems in very hot water, as this will have a cauterizing effect and seal the flow of latex from the stems.

Below: *Euphorbia marginata, a hardy annual, has beautifully coloured variegated leaves.*

Euryops acraeus

● **Sunny situation**
● **Well-drained soil**
● **Evergreen shrub**

This evergreen shrub from South Africa is remarkably hardy in the rock garden. It forms an upright bush, 30cm (12in) high, with bright silver leaves. The pure gold daisy flowers appear on short grey stems in summer.

It was originally thought to be tender, and confined to the alpine house, but it has proved better out of doors by making a neater shaped plant than when under glass. Over the years it forms a compact grey bush when given an open sunny position in a sharply drained soil. Avoid damp situations, and prune the young shrub to a good shape.

Propagation is by cuttings of non-flowering shoots taken in summer and inserted in a sandy frame. However, there is usually a plentiful supply of suckers around the base of the plant, which can be removed with roots attached and potted up. Although the flowers are attractive, this is a plant grown mainly for its grey foliage.

Below: *Euryops acraeus, a dwarf evergreen shrub, is ideal for planting in a rock garden.*

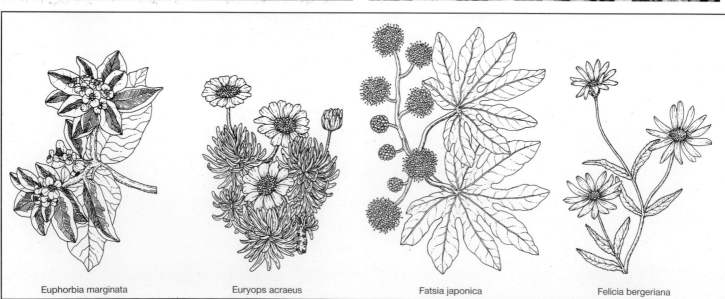

Euphorbia marginata

Euryops acraeus

Fatsia japonica

Felicia bergeriana

Fatsia japonica
(False castor oil plant, Glossy-leaved paper plant, Japanese fatsia)
- **Sun or semi-shade**
- **Good loamy soil**
- **Flowers autumn to early winter**

This magnificent slightly tender evergreen shrub has enormous leaves. It makes a large spreading shrub or small tree up to 4.5m (15ft) high, and equally wide. The leathery, dark green, glossy leaves, of seven to nine lobes, are 30-40cm (12-16in) across, attached to a heart-shaped base and a stalk 30cm (12in) or more long. In late autumn to early winter this shrub produces large clusters of milky-white flowers; these are followed by black fruits.

Fatsia is an ideal shrub to grow in coastal areas and in industrial cities. Plant in a sheltered position.

Below: Festuca glauca, a densely tufted and clump-forming perennial grass, is ideal for planting at the fronts or corners of garden borders.

When *F. japonica* is allowed to grow naturally, it may be necessary to restrict its growth. Do this in spring when branches can be cut down to ground level. Propagate by half-ripe cuttings in late summer, inserting them singly in small pots in a propagator with bottom heat.

Felicia bergeriana
(Kingfisher daisy)
- **Sow in very early spring**
- **Ordinary well-drained soil**
- **Sunny and sheltered position**

The kingfisher part of the common name of this half-hardy annual alludes to the beautiful vivid blue of the flowers. Only 15cm (6in) high, the blooms are carried on short branching stems of a glossy green, as are the narrow grass-like leaves. The single daisy flowers are almost like michaelmas daisies at first glance, about 2cm (0.8in) across, the centre part of the disc being clear yellow. Very compact in habit, they are a choice subject for the front part of a border or rock garden; in either case they need to be sited in full sun.

As this species is a half-hardy annual, propagation will need to be carried out under glass. Sow seed very thinly in pots or boxes of a good loam-based growing medium during very early spring, and keep at a temperature of 16°C (60°F). Prick out the seedlings in the usual way. Reduce the temperature at this time and harden off towards the end of spring, when they should be planted out 15cm (6in) apart.

Festuca glauca
(Sheep's fescue)
- **Sunny location**
- **Well-drained soil**
- **Midsummer flowering**

This useful and accommodating hardy perennial grass is a form of sheep's fescue, *Festuca ovina*. *Festuca glauca* is a densely tufted perennial, with little plumes like miniature pampas grass. The neat clumps have flower spikes 23-25cm (9-10in) tall. It is an ideal plant for the front of a border or as an edging. The foliage is steely blue-grey or a glaucous grey. As it is a slow grower it does not require replanting for several years. Plant in early autumn or spring, and always in light well-drained soil.

Other fescues are *F. amethystina*, which has stems of powder blue 23cm (9in) tall, and *F. punctoria*, which is a steely blue and only 15cm (6in) high.

All these fescues like full sun and are at their best on dry soils. Propagate them by sowing seeds in spring or by division in early autumn or spring.

Filipendula purpurea
(Spiraea palmatum)
(Dropwort, Meadowsweet)
- **Sun or partial shade**
- **Cool moist conditions**
- **Summer flowering**

This Japanese hardy herbaceous perennial is one of half a dozen dropworts. It can still be found in some nursery catalogues and garden centres under its old name, *Spiraea palmatum*. This is a most handsome plant, and if it has moist soil or is growing near the side of a pond, it will not fail to attract attention. It has large lobed leaves and above the elegant leafy crimson stems are large flat heads bearing many tiny carmine-rose flowers, each stem reaching a height of 60-120cm (2-4ft). The pinkish *F. rubra* has large flower heads up to 28cm (11in) across. In damp soil it will form huge clumps, in either sun or shade.

To obtain the best results, grow this plant in partial shade and in rich fertile moist soil. Propagate by seeds sown in pans or boxes under glass in autumn, or by division in autumn.

Above: Filipendula purpurea is a strikingly attractive hardy herbaceous perennial.

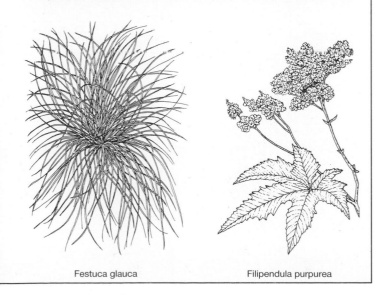

Festuca glauca

Filipendula purpurea

81

Forsythia intermedia 'Spectabilis'

(Golden bells)
- **Full sun**
- **Any good soil, even chalk**
- **Spring flowering**

This hardy deciduous shrub, 2.5-3m (8-10ft) tall and almost as wide, is known to most gardeners for its colourful display in spring. The bright yellow flowers are borne singly or in twos and threes in the axils of the broad lance-shaped leaves.

F. intermedia 'Spectabilis' has large rich yellow flowers. The variety 'Lynwood' has even larger broad-petalled flowers.

Forsythias do not seem to mind how much they are pruned, but if cut hard back every year they will not produce many flowers. New shoots, made after the flowers have faded, will bud up during the year and flower the following spring.

Each year cut out a few of the oldest growths to encourage new wood from the base; if this is not done, a mass of twiggy growth accumulates in the centre of a bush, which causes non- or poor flowering wood. Cut newly planted bushes back to within 30cm (12in) of ground level.

Propagate by softwood cuttings in summer with heat, or take hardwood cuttings in autumn.

Above: Forsythia intermedia 'Spectabilis' is a widely grown, spring-flowering deciduous shrub with bell-shaped flowers.

Freesia × hybrida
- **Sheltered sunny situation**
- **Light sandy soil**
- **Plant 5cm (2in) deep**

These cormous plants grow to 45cm (18in) tall, with a spread of 15cm (6in). The leaves are narrow and sword-like, and the flower stems have spikes of scented trumpet-shaped 5cm (2in) blooms in summer. Although most are suitable for the greenhouse only, some are available for growing out of doors, being planted in spring to flower in the summer of the first season only. A wide variety of exquisite colours is available, from white through yellow to pink, red, magenta and violet.

Freesias need a light sandy soil and a position that is sunny and sheltered from cold winds. Plant the corms in spring unless you have a frost-free area, where they can be planted in late summer to flower the following spring. After flowering the corms can be lifted and treated as greenhouse bulbs where they can provide flowers in early spring, but they need a minimum temperature of 5°C (41°F). Offsets removed in late summer flower the following year.

Fritillaria imperialis

(Crown imperial)
- **Full or partial shade**
- **Well-drained soil**
- **Plant 20cm (8in) deep**

This hardy bulbous plant grows up to 90cm (3ft) tall, with a centre stem on which is carried a series of narrow pointed glossy leaves to half the total height. The top half of this stem carries a circle of large beautiful drooping flowers about 5cm (2in) long, which is topped with a green crown of leaves. The range of bloom colour is yellow, orange and red.

The bulb should be planted in autumn in a rich well-drained soil in shade, preferably where it can be left undisturbed. Handle bulbs carefully and do not let them dry out. Plant the bulb on its side to stop water getting into the hollow crown and rotting the bulb. In heavy soil a handful of coarse sand around the bulb will speed drainage. Cut the stems down when they die off in summer. Seed will not produce flowering bulbs for six years. It is quicker to use offsets taken from the parent bulb in late summer; plant them out in a nursery bed for two years, then transplant to final position.

Below: Fritillaria imperialis has crown-like flower heads, on long, upright stems, in spring.

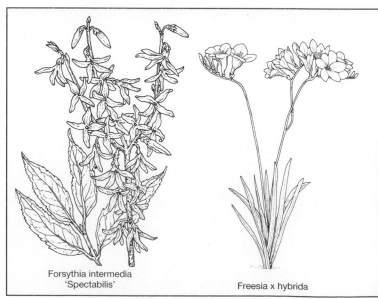

Forsythia intermedia 'Spectabilis'

Freesia × hybrida

Above: Fritillaria meleagris has a dainty and petite nature with its spring flowers. It is ideal for naturalizing in short grass.

Fritillaria meleagris

(Checkered lily, Guinea flower, Snake's-head fritillary)

- **Full or semi-shade**
- **Well-drained fertile soil**
- **Plant 15cm (6in) deep**

This hardy bulbous plant has delicate blooms with a fine chequerboard pattern. They grow to 45cm (10in) tall with fine grass-like leaves mid- to blue-green in colour. The blooms are just under 5cm (2in) in length and hang down like bells, appearing in spring. The flowers are purple, brown, violet-red and white. The white varieties do not have the chequerboard pattern, but some have fine green veining instead.

They should be planted in the autumn, 15cm (6in) deep on their side, in rich fertile soil that is well-drained, and in full or partial shade.

Leave undisturbed for at least four years. Then they can be lifted, and the bulblets removed and replanted in a nursery bed for two years, then transplanted to their final flowering positions. When young, they should be kept moist but not wet. If the soil is too wet, mix in plenty of sharp sand to aid drainage. Fritillarias are generally free of pests and diseases.

Fritillaria pallidiflora

- **Needs moisture when growing**
- **Well-drained peaty sandy soil**
- **Bulbous**

This hardy bulbous plant is becoming very popular in gardens, especially in rock gardens. The 15-50cm (6-20in) stem bears broad lance-shaped grey leaves. Up to four pendent greenish to luminous yellow 4cm (1.6in) bells appear in the axils of the upper leaves in spring.

It does not require the dampness of the snake's-head fritillary (*F. meleagris*) but prefers a good but sharply drained soil in a moderately sunny position, although it will tolerate some shade.

Seed sown in the summer when fresh is a satisfactory method of propagation, and *F. pallidiflora* will flower three years after sowing, which is better than some other species. Fritillaries should be sown thinly, as the seedlings have to remain *in situ* for a time before transplanting. Bulbils may be found around the parent bulb and these can then be detached and grown on.

Fuchsia 'Mrs. Popple'

- **Full sun; roots cool**
- **Most soils, including lime and chalk**
- **Summer flowering**

Fuchsias are herbaceous or shrubby plants and some varieties including 'Mrs. Popple' are hardy. 'Mrs. Popple' has single blooms with scarlet tubes and sepals and deep violet corollas.

Fuchsias are not fussy over soil, but this should be prepared by double digging. Incorporate large quantities of peat moistened before use, well-rotted farmyard manure, leaf-mould or wood ash. Fuchsia roots appreciate a cool root run. Plant in late spring or early summer. When planting, place the top of the ball of soil 8cm (3.2in) below ground level, as a precaution against frosts. In early spring prune back almost to soil level; at the same time apply fertilizer and a dressing of well-rotted manure. In early summer give another application of fertilizer, and yet another during the summer. In the first year, water until established.

Propagate by softwood cuttings in early spring in a greenhouse at 16°C (60°F). Take cuttings below a node (where leaves join the stem).

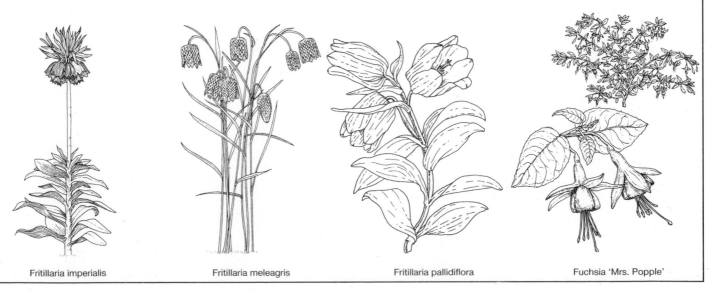

Fritillaria imperialis   Fritillaria meleagris   Fritillaria pallidiflora   Fuchsia 'Mrs. Popple'

Gaillardia aristata
(Gaillardia grandiflora)
(Blanket flower)
- **Sunny location**
- **Light well-drained soil**
- **Summer flowering**

Gaillardias are among the most colourful hardy herbaceous perennials, and the hybrids are chiefly derived from *G. aristata*, better known in the nursery trade as *G. grandiflora*. These vivid flowers can be had in shades of yellow, bronze, orange, flame, brown and maroon-red. Their large daisy-like saucer-shaped flowers are ideal for cutting. The height varies from 60-90cm (2-3ft). All parts of the plant are sticky, and its leaves have an aromatic scent.

As they are short-lived, gaillardias should be grown in well-drained soil, and they will flourish in calcareous (chalk or lime) soils. As they are rather floppy, support them with a few peasticks. The long flowering season lasts from midsummer to late summer.

Propagate by seeds sown under glass in late winter or out of doors in early summer, or by root cuttings in autumn or softwood cuttings in midsummer.

Below: Gaillardia aristata, an herbaceous perennial, produces large, daisy-like flower heads in the summer.

Galanthus nivalis
(Snowdrop)
- **Partial shade**
- **Rich well-drained soil**
- **Plant 10-15cm (4-6in) deep**

This hardy bulbous plant has leaves that are flat, sword-shaped and often blue-green in colour. The flowers are either single or double, in white with green markings on the inner petals, and can be as long as 2.5cm (1in). Snowdrops' time of flowering depends on the severity or mildness of the winter weather, but normally starts around midwinter. One variety flowers in late autumn, before the leaves appear. They can grow up to 20cm (8in) tall in rich soil and in partial shade.

The bulbs should be planted 10cm (4in) deep in heavy soil, or 15cm (6in) deep in light soil, in autumn. The soil should be moist but well-drained. Move bulbs after they have finished flowering, while the soil is moist. Seed may take five years to bloom, so it is better to split clusters of bulbs and spread them out. Take care when lifting not to damage the roots or to let them dry out. Use a soil insecticide and fungicide.

Below: Galanthus nivalis, the well-known snowdrop, starts to flower during midwinter. Some varieties flower earlier.

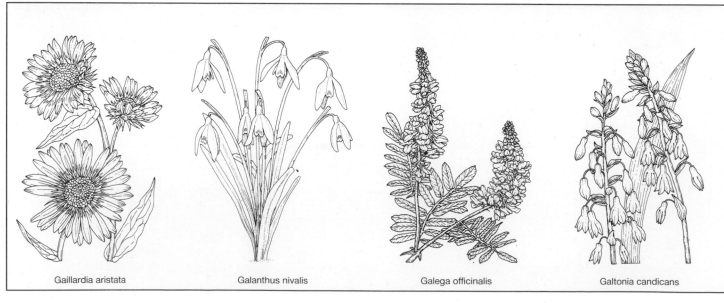

Gaillardia aristata

Galanthus nivalis

Galega officinalis

Galtonia candicans

Galega officinalis
(Goat's rue)
- **Full sun**
- **Any good soil, or even poor soils**
- **Summer flowering**

This hardy herbaceous perennial needs to be planted at the back of the border, as it has a rather sprawling habit. So plant it behind perennials that can shield it when the flowers have faded and the plant is looking a little the worse for wear. Goat's rue will thrive in any sunny corner and in any good soil. The small pea-shaped flowers of *G. officinalis* are mauve, and they are borne on branching stems up to 1.5m (5ft) tall. There is a white variety called 'Candida'.

Plant galegas in autumn or early spring and allow sufficient room for them to develop. Insert a few peasticks in the ground early in the year, so that the plants can grow through to hide them. They will thrive in a sunny location and are generally free of pests and diseases. Propagate by division in autumn or spring.

Above: Galega officinalis is a vigorous herbaceous perennial.

Galtonia candicans
(Summer hyacinth)
- **Full sun**
- **Deep fertile soil**
- **Late summer flowering**

This hardy bulbous plant has fragrant, white, dangling, bell-like flowers carried on 90-120cm (3-4ft) stout tube-like stems. At the base are long glaucous-green leaves.

This bulb has to be planted 15cm (6in) below the soil, which needs to be well drained. Bulbs can be planted in autumn or spring, and in a year or so they will be established. If they are planted behind the violet-flowered liriope, the two may flower together. This bulb needs good fertile soil, as bulbs may deteriorate in poor sandy soil. Add plenty of humus, such as well-rotted farmyard manure or well-rotted garden compost, before planting bulbs. Once established they should be left undisturbed. Propagate by detaching offsets in spring, but not too often. Seeds can be sown as soon as ripe out of doors, or under glass in spring. Galtonia will readily produce self-sown seedlings.

Above: Gaultheria procumbens, a hardy, low-growing, evergreen shrub, ideal for smothering the soil with leaves and shoots.

Garrya elliptica
(Silk tassel bush)
- **Sunny location**
- **Ordinary soil, but moisture-holding**
- **Catkins early to late winter**

This is a striking evergreen catkin-bearing shrub that thrives in the protection of a wall where it can receive good light. In favoured areas, bushes reach as much as 5m (16.4ft) tall. The oval wavy-margined leathery leaves, 4-8cm (1.6-3.2in) long, are matt grey-green above and woolly underneath. In winter the bush has attractive pendent greyish-green catkins 15-25cm (6-10in) long.

This shrub does not require a rich soil, but should have plenty of sun and moisture. Choose pot-grown plants, as it is not a good transplanter, so small plants are preferable to large ones. Little or no pruning is needed.

Propagate by seeds sown in spring in a cool greenhouse. For male plants grafting is necessary during late winter under glass in heat. Layering is possible in summer.

Gaultheria procumbens
(Checkerberry, Mountain tea, Partridgeberry, Wintergreen)
- **Partial sunshine**
- **Leafy lime-free soil**
- **Evergreen ground cover**

This hardy, evergreen, prostrate sub-shrub from North America forms a mat of shiny dark evergreen oval leaves, 2.5cm (1in) long and slightly toothed, which can spread to 1m (3.3ft) or more. Small white or pinkish bell-shaped flowers, about 5-6mm (0.19-0.23in) long, appear at the tips of the shoots in late summer, followed by attractive bright red berries in autumn. The whole plant is not taller than 15cm (6in). It spreads by means of underground stems, and could be termed moderately invasive, although it is easy to control.

Gaultheria procumbens is happier in a situation with some but not total sunshine, and appreciates a cool moist leafy soil that is never allowed to dry out.

Propagation is by cuttings taken in early summer and inserted in the peat and sand frame, where they root easily. Pot up into peaty soil during the summer, and overwinter in a frame before planting in spring.

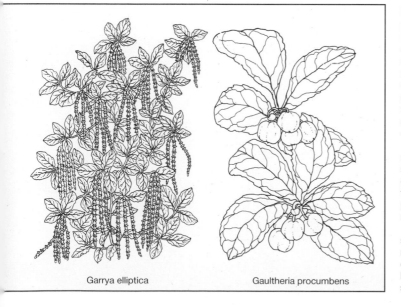

Garrya elliptica

Gaultheria procumbens

Gazania × hybrida 'Chansonette'

(Treasure flower)
- Sow in midwinter
- Ordinary well-drained soil
- Sunny site

Without doubt this tender herbaceous perennial plant is one of the finest border or rock garden plants, of an almost exotic nature. However only in the mildest parts will they survive winter as a perennial, so they are usually treated as an annual.

Hybrid types carry large daisy flowers, and the 'Chansonette' mixture has a colour range including red, bronze and bicolours. Blooms are carried on short stems 20cm (8in) long and backed by glossy green leaves, but the undersides of white or silver ensure a contrast.

Most useful planted in full sun on the rock garden, they will give an abundance of flower from early summer onwards.

Sow seed under glass in midwinter in a temperature of 16°C (60°F). Use a loam-based compost for sowing, and prick off into individual small pots. Make sure ground is free draining to avoid stem and root rots. Harden off and plant out in early summer, or in late spring in milder districts.

Above: Gazania × hybrida 'Chansonette' has bright, large, daisy-like flowers from mid-summer to the frosts of autumn.

Genista hispanica

(Gorse, Spanish gorse)
- Sunny position
- Well-drained ordinary soil
- Flowers in late spring and early summer

This is a hardy deciduous shrub, up to 80cm (32in) high and 2.5m (8ft) wide, with an almost evergreen appearance because of the deep green of its dense tangle of twigs and spines. Mounds of this delightful ground-hugging shrub become a cushion of pea-shaped, golden-yellow flowers.

This gorse does not like rich heavily manured soil; if given such liberal treatment, plants become soft and growth will be rank. As a result, winter frosts will damage them and spoil the flowers.

Pruning consists of a light clipping as soon as flowering is over. If bushes are damaged by frost, remove all dead wood. Peg down living growth, covering it with leaf-mould, to encourage rooting of the base stems.

Propagate by seeds sown out of doors in early spring, or by heel cuttings in summer.

Genista lydia

- Full sun
- Well-drained soil; tolerates lime
- Flowers in late spring to early summer

This hummock-forming hardy deciduous shrub will reach a height of 80cm (32in). The bright golden-yellow flowers are usually produced in clusters of four at the end of leafy twigs on pendulous green five-angled branches during late spring and early summer.

It will tolerate lime, but this is by no means essential. What it does need is a well-drained, sunny position. Although hardy, plants may succumb after a mild wet autumn followed by early winter frosts or late spring frosts. When this happens, scrap the plant and start afresh. Where more compact plants are needed, light pruning can be given when flowers fade.

Propagate by seeds sown under glass in late winter or out of doors in early spring. Heel cuttings can be taken during the summer.

Genista pilosa

- Full sunshine
- Light soil
- Deciduous shrub

There are two forms of this hardy, deciduous dwarf shrub from southern Europe: the species itself, which can be as tall as 45cm

(18in); and the form 'Prostrata', which is virtually prostrate and will not rise much above 7.5cm (3in). Both produce masses of small yellow pea-like flowers that almost obscure the foliage, and both do well on a sunny bank in the rock garden. *G. pilosa* spreads to about 45cm (18in), but 'Prostrata' will reach 1.2m (4ft) across, contouring over rocks in its path.

Propagation is not too easy, as seed is not plentiful and cuttings

Gazania x hybrida 'Chansonette'

Genista hispanica

are slow to root. The most proven method is to insert soft cuttings in late spring around the edge of a clay pot, in a mixture of four parts of sand to one of peat. Young plants should not be kept too long in pots as they form a tap root, which may be damaged when the pot is removed.

Below: Genista sagittalis is a superb ground-covering miniature shrub with yellow summer flowers.

Genista sagittalis

- **Full sun**
- **Fairly light soil, good drainage**
- **Deciduous shrub**

This hardy, deciduous, dwarf shrub comes from central and southern Europe. It is a curious miniature broom, with branched flowering stems, between 10 and 15cm (4-6in), depending on the richness of the soil. These branched stems have wings, which look like leaves. The actual leaves are small and hairy when young. The small yellow pea-like flowers appear in summer. This plant can spread up to 60cm (2ft).

A much smaller plant, which goes under the name of *Genista delphinensis*, is similar in flower and behaviour; this comes from southern France and is only about 5cm (2in) tall.

Propagation is by taking soft cuttings in summer and inserting them round the edge of a clay pot, in a 4:1 mixture of sand and peat.

Gentiana acaulis

(Stemless gentian)
- **Sunny but moist situation**
- **Prefers heavy soils**
- **Evergreen**

Of all the botanical names that are suspect, this is the classic. For years the experts have decreed this herbaceous perennial to have an invalid name, but everyone

continues to use it. *Gentiana acaulis* is the name for the large blue trumpets on the grassy slopes of the Alps.

In gardens, however, these plants evoke a degree of frustration: either they will flower or they will not, for no apparent reason. They are happiest in a heavy loam and planted firmly. In desperation it has been suggested that they need to be trodden upon deliberately to encourage them to

flower, as this emulates the treatment given them by cows in their native habitat. The 5-7.5cm (2-3in) long trumpets appear above mid-green ovate leaves that can form a mat 45cm (18in) across.

Propagation is by division in midsummer, potting into a good loam on the heavy side.

Below: Gentiana acaulis smothers rock gardens with trumpet-shaped blue flowers in early summer.

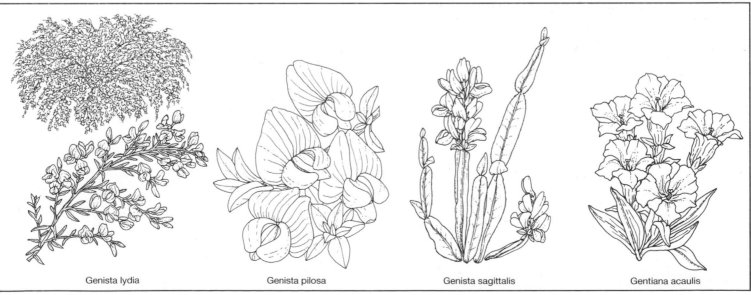

Genista lydia

Genista pilosa

Genista sagittalis

Gentiana acaulis

Ginkgo biloba
(Maidenhair tree)
- **Warm sunny position**
- **Ordinary garden soil**
- **Medium to large tree with medium rate of growth**

This curious deciduous conifer grows wild in eastern China, but fossils of its leaves have been found in various parts of the world, showing that it was widespread in prehistoric times. The ginkgo forms a medium to large tree, a 200-year-old specimen reaching over 30m (98ft). But the rate of growth is erratic, being quite rapid in hot summers but slowing down when the temperature is lower. It is one of the few conifers that is not evergreen. The flat fan-shaped yellow-green leaves turn to yellow in autumn. There are male and female trees, and the cones (borne on the female plant) form a fruit enclosing an edible nut.

The ginkgo is normally grown from imported seed sown in autumn in a seed compost. Pot on when 10cm (4in) tall, and grow on for four years before planting in the final site in ordinary garden soil. Do not prune, as cut stems will die back further. Choose a warm and sunny situation.

Gladiolus byzantinus
- **Full sun**
- **Ordinary rich garden soil**
- **Plant 10cm (4in) deep**

This hardy cormous plant, up to 60cm (24in) tall, has a flower spike about 40cm (16in) long. A succession of wine-red blooms, 5-7.5cm (2-3in) across, appear along the spike in midsummer. The leaves are sword-shaped with pointed tips.

Plant in full sun in ordinary garden soil fed with manure, in either autumn or spring. Plant a little deeper in light soil, to give more anchorage. In heavy soil a base of sharp sand under the corm will help drainage and prevent rot. Avoid waterlogged soil. Keep the young plants weeded, and after 10 weeks of growth start watering well. In the autumn the leaves will die back; remove them when they virtually fall off. After a few years lift them and remove the cormlets to increase the stock; these take up to three years to flower. Treat

Above: Ginkgo biloba has fan-shaped leaves that turn beautiful shades of yellow in autumn.

the plant with a pesticide and fungicide to prevent trouble. If a plant looks sick and turns yellow, destroy it to stop the virus.

Gladiolus – Miniature Hybrids
- **Sunny position**
- **Good well-drained garden soil**
- **Plant 10-15cm (4-6in) deep**

These hardy cormous plants grow to 45-90cm (18-36in) tall, and the flower spikes are about 35cm (14in) long, with each flower about 5cm (2in) across. They bloom after midsummer, and flowers are often frilled or fluted. The colours are bright, and varied with blotches, spots and stripes.

These corms are best grown in a sunny part of the garden in a good

well-drained soil. They should be planted 10-15cm (4-6in) deep, depending on the soil – plant deeper in light soil to give better anchorage. In heavy soil, add plenty of sharp sand under and around the corm to aid drainage, keep the young plant weeded, and water well once the flower spike starts to open. However, do not grow in waterlogged soil. Lift the plant in autumn, remove the young corm and store it in a frost-free place for the following year.

Keep the plant free from disease with a fungicide. If the plant wilts and turns yellow, destroy it to stop the virus disease spreading to others.

Right: Gladiolus byzantinus creates midsummer spikes of wine-red flowers.

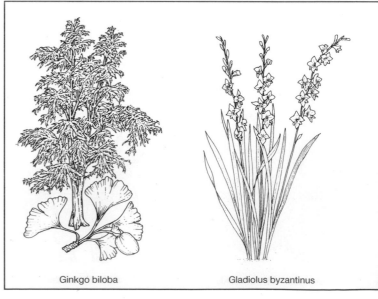

Ginkgo biloba

Gladiolus byzantinus

Gladiolus – Primulinus Hybrids

- Full sun
- Ordinary garden soil enriched with manure
- Plant 10-15cm (4-6in) deep

These hardy cormous plants are not as vigorous or as big as the large-flowered gladiolus but they are free flowering and decorative. The plants grow to a height of 45-90cm (18-36in), with the flower spike almost 40cm (16in) long. The flowers themselves, up to 7.5cm (3in) across, are placed alternately on the stem, and bloom after midsummer. A variety of colours is available, some with stripes and contrasting throats. The leaves are long, slender and sword-shaped.

The plant is half-hardy, surviving in some winters underground, but normally the corm is lifted in autumn. A new corm is found above the old one, which is discarded. Store the young corm in a frost-free place during the winter. Grow in a well-drained soil, keeping it moist in the summer at flowering time. Treat with a fungicide to keep rot and fungus at bay. Destroy diseased corms to prevent spread.

Below: Gypsophila paniculata, commonly known as baby's breath, produces masses of feathery flowers.

Godetia grandiflora 'Azalea-flowered'

- Sow in autumn or spring
- Light, moist soil
- Sunny location

Godetias are popular hardy annuals. The exotically coloured azalea-flowered types are semi-double and have wavy edged petals of pink, salmon, crimson, cerise and white. Almost silky in texture the blooms are produced on branching stems forming a compact plant of about 30cm (12in). The leaves are oblong at the base, narrowing towards the tip, with age they tend to take on a reddish tinge. If these plants are grown next to their near cousins, the clarkias, a riot of colour can be expected.

As hardy annuals they are very easy to grow from seed. Sow where they are to flower, in either autumn or spring. Plants raised from the autumn sowings will be stronger and will flower slightly earlier, about the end of spring onwards. In either case take out drills, sow seed very thinly, and cover lightly. Thin out the seedlings to 15cm (6in) apart, and water if necessary.

Gypsophila paniculata

(Baby's breath, Chalk plant)
- Sunny location
- Well-drained, preferably limy, soil
- Summer flowering

The flower heads of the hardy perennial *Gypsophila paniculata* are a mass of small feathery flowers, white or pink. The glaucous leaves are also small. The branching flower heads are used by flower arrangers to add a light cloud effect to arrangements of other flowers. *G. paniculata* 'Bristol Fairy' is the best double form, 90cm (3ft) tall.

As gypsophilas are deep-rooted, the ground must be well prepared before planting; it should be double dug. To do this, take out the first spit or spade's depth of soil, break up the bottom spit with a fork and fill up with the next top spit. Also enrich the ground with well-rotted farmyard manure or well-rotted garden compost. You may want to insert a few peasticks for support. Provided they have full sun and well-drained soil, gypsophilas should be no trouble.

Propagate 'Bristol Fairy' by taking softwood cuttings in late spring to very early summer.

Gladiolus – miniature hybrid

Gladiolus – primulinus hybrid

Godetia grandiflora 'Azalea-flowered'

Gypsophila paniculata

Hedychium gardnerianum

(Gingerwort, Kahili ginger)
- **Sun or light shade**
- **Rich potting mixture**
- **Plant just below the surface**

This tender, rhizomatous-rooted, herbaceous perennial will grow outdoors only in very mild areas, and is usually grown as a pot plant. It grows 1.8m (6ft) tall and 1.5m (5ft) across. The leaves are often 30cm (12in) long and as broad. In summer it has spikes of scented yellow flowers 5cm (2in) wide, with brilliant scarlet stamens.

Due to its size, this plant needs a tub. Use a potting mixture supplemented with a liquid feed every two weeks during the growing period. In autumn the stems should be cut down almost to the rhizome. Let the plant rest in winter, keeping it dry. In early spring water it a little, increasing the amount as it grows. The plant can be repotted in spring when it starts to shoot; at this stage divide and replant the rhizomes to increase your stock. If grown outdoors, plant it in a sheltered place in summer and lift before the first frost.

Helenium autumnale 'Wyndley'

(Sneezeweed)
- **Full sun**
- **Prefers heavy soil**
- **Late summer flowering**

The North American helenium is one of those hardy herbaceous perennials with daisy-like flowers, chiefly in late summer and autumn. The variety 'Wyndley' has large coppery yellow, flecked flowers, 60cm (24in) tall and fairly rigid. Like all helenium flowers, they have a prominent central disc. The 90cm (3ft) high 'Coppelia' has coppery-orange flowers.

Although these plants will grow in almost any type of soil, they prefer a fairly stiff loam. The fact that their stems are fairly rigid can make plants flop over in heavy rain so push in a few peasticks around the plant at an early stage; then the stems will grow through and cover the sticks. Their pleasing branching stems make heleniums useful as cut flowers, and they last well in water. Keep them moist during hot dry spells in summer.

Propagate heleniums by softwood cuttings in early summer, or by division in autumn or spring.

Above: Helianthemum nummularium 'Ben Dearg' has deep copper-orange flowers.

Helianthemum nummularium 'Ben Dearg'

(Rock rose, Sun rose)
- **Thrives in sunshine**
- **Any well-drained soil**
- **Evergreen**

Rock roses are dwarf, low-growing, hardy evergreen shrubs, producing a wide range of colours from yellow to deep orange and from pink to deep red. The foliage is grey or green, and the combination of pink flowers and grey foliage, as in the variety 'Wisley Pink', is charming. 'Ben Dearg' flowers are deep copper orange with dark centres.

This group of plants is easy-going and sun-loving, and provides a brilliant display in midsummer. They are, however, rampant, and spread to 60cm (24in), so care should be taken in siting them; cut back hard after flowering. They seem to thrive well on both acid and alkaline soils.

Propagation is easy: take cuttings of non-flowering shoots, from midsummer to late summer, and insert in a peat and sand frame. Pinch out the tips of the plants when they are established in pots.

Above: Helenium autumnale 'Wyndley' creates a wealth of coppery-yellow, daisy-like flowers in late summer.

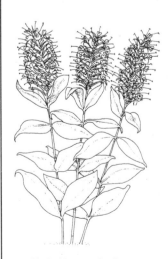

Hedychium gardnerianum

Helenium autumnale 'Wyndley'

Helianthus annuus 'Sungold'

(Sunflower)
- **Sow in spring**
- **Ordinary soil**
- **Sunny position**

So many people grow the giant exhibition types of this hardy annual that it is often forgotten that a number of the same sunflowers have dwarf counterparts that are easier to manage.

'Sungold', only 60cm (24in) tall, can have a worthy place in any border as long as it can benefit from a sunny position. The beautiful, double, golden-yellow blooms can be up to 15cm (6in) across, and almost ball-shaped. The short stems and longish

leaves feel coarse to the touch. These sunflowers are best suited to the front of a bed.

Sow seed directly into the ground where they are to flower, putting three seeds to a station. When germination is complete, discard the two weakest seedlings, leaving only the strongest. Check carefully for slug damage at germination time. Spacing should be 30cm (12in). In mild areas sow in spring; for other districts, late spring.

Right: Helichrysum beilidioides has bright, star-like flowers and attractive leaves.

Below: Helianthus decapetalus reveals bright yellow flowers from midsummer.

Helianthus decapetalus

(Sunflower)
- **Full sun**
- **Well-drained stiff loam**
- **Late summer flowering**

This is a hardy herbaceous perennial from North America, and the parent of several good hybrid sunflowers. All have coarse, rough foliage. The double-flowered 'Loddon Gold' bears rich yellow blossoms on 1.5m (5ft) stout stems. The semi-double 'Triomphe de Gand' has large golden-yellow flowers with ball-shaped centres, 1.2-1.5m (4-5ft) high. Another rich yellow variety, 'Morning Sun', has anemone-centred flowers, and this erect and sturdy grower is 1.2m (4ft) tall. The graceful, lemon-yellow, single-flowered *H. orgyalis*

'Lemon Queen', reaches 1.5m (5ft) high.

Grow these plants in a well-drained loamy soil and ensure that they receive plenty of sunshine. Do not let perennial sunflowers starve.

Propagate perennial sunflowers by division in autumn or spring. Divide and replant every three or four years.

Helichrysum bellidioides

- **Sunny exposure**
- **Light, well-drained soil**
- **Evergreen**

This helichrysum is a half-hardy shrub that comes from the southern hemisphere. It loves to roam around the crevices or rocks and wander through stony ground. It has a degree of aggressiveness in the garden, where it may spread over less uninhibited subjects. It is prostrate, spreading to between 30cm and 60cm (12-24in), with 2cm (0.8in) wide clusters of everlasting flowers appearing in summer. The leaves are an attractive dark green above and woolly-white beneath. It likes a well-drained sunny situation and is hardier than most authorities suggest.

Propagation is by 1.5cm (0.6in) soft cuttings taken in summer and put in a sand frame. These are ready to plant out in autumn or the following spring. Plants can be divided during the summer.

Helianthemum nummularium 'Ben Dearg'

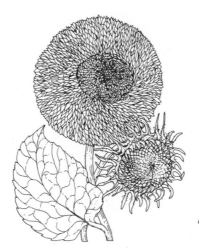

Helianthus annuus 'Sungold'

Helianthus decapetalus

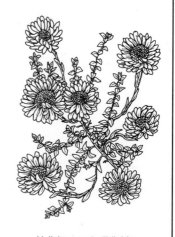

Helichrysum bellidioides

Helichrysum bracteatum

(Everlasting flower, Immortelle)
- **Sow in very early spring**
- **Light but well-drained soil**
- **Sunny location**

This half-hardy perennial, which invariably is grown as a half-hardy annual or hardy annual, produces a wide range of colourful flowers. Stems may be up to 90cm (3ft), fairly stiff and branching. Flowers are produced terminally on the stems in shades of red, yellow, pink, orange and white, up to 5cm (2in) across. The centre of each bloom is surrounded by a mass of coloured bracts of a papery texture.

Cut stems for drying before the flower centres are fully open and hang them upside down in a cool airy place away from strong sunlight, which may bleach the colours.

Sow seed under glass in very early spring at a temperature of 18°C (65°F); use a loam-based growing medium for sowing and subsequent pricking off. Harden off carefully and plant out at the end of spring. Blooms appear from early summer onwards. Use brushwood supports around the groups of plants.

Below: Heliopsis scabra, an herbaceous perennial, creates a bright display from midsummer to early autumn.

Heliopsis scabra

(Orange sunflower, Oxeye)
- **Full sun**
- **Good fertile soil**
- **Late summer flowering**

This hardy herbaceous perennial is a stiff upright plant. It has strong woody branching stems, and the spear-shaped foliage is dark green. Several single or double, yellow or orange flowers, 7.5-10cm (3-4in) across, are carried on each stem. They are very resistant to drought, but will grow in moist or rich soil and become very lush. They flower from midsummer to early autumn. Cut down flowering stems to ground level in late autumn.

The variety 'Summer Sun' develops large, golden-yellow, double flowers. It is ideal as a cut flower, and grows to about 1m (3.3ft) high.

Propagate by division, or by basal cuttings in spring.

Helichrysum bracteatum

Heliopsis scabra

Helipterum manglesii

Helleborus orientalis

Left: Helipterum manglesii, a hardy annual, is famed for its bright, 'everlasting' flowers during summer.

Helipterum manglesii
(Rhodanthe manglesii)
(Everlasting flower, Swan River everlasting)
- **Sow in spring**
- **Poor or ordinary but free-draining soil**
- **Sunny position**

This 'everlasting' hardy annual is also known as *Rhodanthe manglesii*. Growing 30-60cm (12-24in) high, it is an ideal subject for a single small bed. Use a few spot plants through the bed to give extra height. Flowers are mainly pink, white and shades of red, about 2.5cm (1in) in diameter. The dainty bracts supporting the blooms terminate on single glaucous stems. Cut the stems for future use before the bracts are fully open; in this way they will keep their colour longer. Avoid strong sunlight in storage.

Sow directly where they are to flower, during spring, lightly covering the seed. Free-draining soil is essential. Thin out to 15cm (6in) apart.

Alternatively raise under glass in the usual way during early spring at a temperature of 16°C (60°F). Plant out carefully at the end of spring. Losses may occur when transplanting, as helipterums do not take kindly to disturbance.

Helleborus orientalis
(Lenten rose)
- **Partial or full shade**
- **Not fussy over soil, provided it is not bog**
- **Winter and spring flowering**

This native of Greece and Asia Minor has produced a large number of good garden varieties in many colours, including pure white, cream, pink, rose, purple, plum-colour or almost black, and prettily spotted maroon or crimson. They are 45cm (18in) tall, and have large open cup-like flowers. The foliage is evergreen, and is a useful ground cover.

Above: Helleborus orientalis brings colour to gardens in late winter and early spring. It has evergreen, dark green leaves.

The variety 'Kochii' is a little shorter than *Helleborus orientalis* and blooms a little earlier, having large coarsely toothed foliage. In bud it is yellowish green, later opening its nodding primrose-yellow flowers.

Provided the soil is fertile and the plants are growing in partial or full shade, they should give pleasure for many years. Propagate by seeds sown in spring or autumn, or by division of the roots in spring.

Hemerocallis
(Day lily)
- **Sun or partial shade**
- **Any soil but avoid dry ones**
- **Summer flowering**

These hardy herbaceous perennials create large clumps of bright green arching foliage and a display of scented lily-like flowers over a long period. The flowers of early day lilies lasted for only one day, but modern varieties last two or sometimes three days. The lily-like flowers are carried at the top of stout 90cm (3ft) stems.

Three modern varieties are: 'Pink Damask', with pretty pink flowers, 75cm (30in); 'Nashville', large, creamy yellow with streaked orange-red throat markings, 90cm (3ft); and the glowing bright red 'Stafford' 75cm (30in).

Propagate day lilies by division in spring. Plants can be left undisturbed for many years; lift

and divide them only when clumps become overcrowded. In very hot dry weather, give plants a thorough soaking.

Hesperis matronalis
(Damask violet, Dame's violet, Sweet rocket)
- **Sun or partial shade**
- **Well-drained moist soil**
- **Summer flowering**

The single hesperis is not a long-lived herbaceous perennial, and it is therefore necessary to raise fresh stock. Single seed is available in shades of lilac, purple and white. As a cut flower choose the double white. The singles are easier to grow than the doubles. Plants are about 1-1.2m (3.3-4ft) in height. The cross-shaped blooms develop on spikes up to 45cm (18in) long in midsummer and are sweetly fragrant during the evening. Once they have finished flowering it is best to cut the flower spikes down.

To be successful, hesperis needs good drainage and a moist sandy loam. Propagate the singles as biennials, sowing seed out of doors in spring. The double varieties can be divided in spring, or cuttings of basal growth taken in midsummer or early autumn.

Below: Hesperis matronalis is a well-known, sweetly scented, short lived herbaceous perennial with a wealth of summer flowers.

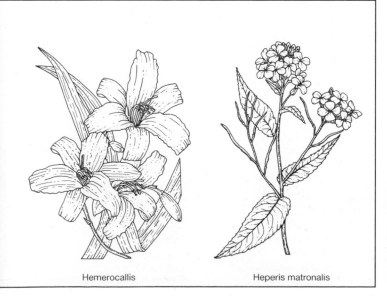

Hemerocallis   Heperis matronalis

Heuchera sanguinea 'Red Spangles'

(Alum root, Coral bells, Coral flower)

- **Sun or partial shade**
- **Well-drained fertile soil**
- **Early summer flowering**

Heucheras have evergreen heart-shaped leaves and their pretty tiny bell-shaped flowers hang down from slender wiry stems. The foliage comes in various shades of green, sometimes with zonal markings marbled like pelargoniums. 'Red Spangles' has crimson-scarlet flowers and is 50cm (20in) tall.

Heucheras make bold clumps as much as 30cm (12in) wide, but deteriorate if not divided and transplanted every few years. Throw out woody pieces, keeping only the young vigorous ones. Work in well-rotted garden compost or well-rotted manure before planting. Heucheras prefer a light, well-drained fertile soil, but dislike cold clay, wet or very acid soils. Given good feeding, flowers will be produced from spring to early autumn. Keep moist during hot dry days in the summer. Propagate by division in late summer or early autumn.

Hibiscus syriacus 'Woodbridge'

(Rose of Sharon, Shrubby mallow)

- **Full sun**
- **Any good well-drained soil**
- **Flowers summer to autumn**

This hibiscus is a hardy deciduous flowering shrub with a stiff, erect growing habit. The stems are greyish white and bear smooth, coarsely toothed green leaves up to 10cm (4in) long. The large trumpet-shaped flowers are 6.5-10cm (2.5-4in) across, with a distinctive yellow stamial column (like an erect clapper in a bell). The flowers are produced singly on short stalks in the axils of the leaves. 'Woodbridge' has deep rose to rich pink flowers, blotched with carmine at the base of the petals; the single flowers are 10cm (4in) across.

For hibiscus to flourish they like hot dry soil and full sun. In a hot dry summer and autumn they are in their element. Little pruning is necessary apart from cutting out dead wood during spring or summer, and shortening the young shoots to keep bushes balanced.

Propagate by taking half-ripe cuttings of short side shoots with a slight heel during the summer.

Hibiscus trionum

(Flower of an hour)

- **Sow in spring**
- **Ordinary well-drained soil**
- **Sunny location**

This exquisite half-hardy annual from Africa blooms continuously from midsummer through to the end of autumn. The delicate exotic flowers are up to 7.5cm (3in) across, white to pale yellow with a chocolate-maroon centre. Stems,

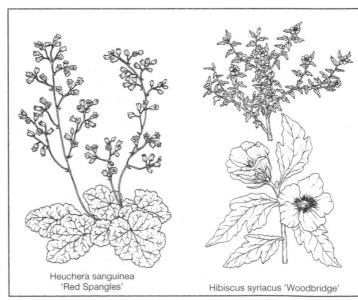

Left: *Heuchera sanguinea 'Red Spangles' creates a sea of tiny, scarlet flowers on thin stems.*

Above: *Hibiscus syriacus 'Woodbridge' produces superb trumpet-shaped flowers.*

Heuchera sanguinea 'Red Spangles'

Hibiscus syriacus 'Woodbridge'

up to 75cm (30in) long, are dark green, with ovate leaves. Individual flowers usually last for only one day, but they are eventually followed by an inflated bladder-shaped calyx.

To obtain early-flowering plants, sow seed in pots or boxes in spring; use any good growing medium. When seeds have germinated, prick off seedlings into individual small pots, harden off in a cold frame and plant out at the end of spring. Plants produced in this way will flower earlier than those directly sown in mid-spring. For both methods space the young plants 30cm (12in) apart.

Hosta fortunei 'Albopicta'
(Day lily, Plantain lily)
- **Dense or partial shade**
- **Rich fertile soil**
- **Summer flowering**

These hardy herbaceous perennials have large and beautiful foliage. The variety 'Albopicta' has large scrolled leaves exquisitely marbled in shades of golden yellow and edged with pale green. As summer advances the golden yellow becomes primrose coloured and the pale green turns darker. Above this magnificent foliage are 45-60cm (18-24in) stems carrying bell-like flowers. A recent introduction is *Hosta rectifolia* 'Tall Boy' with green leaves and violet-mauve flowers.

Provided hostas are not allowed to become dry during summer, and are well laced with rotted farmyard manure or well-rotted garden compost, the gardener will be rewarded handsomely for his labours. Propagate these plants by division in spring.

Houttuynia cordata
- **Requires very damp situation**
- **Any soil**
- **Herbaceous ground cover**

This hardy herbaceous perennial comes from Eastern Asia and is useful for ground cover in damp or waterlogged conditions. It will also thrive under 5cm (2in) of water, so it is useful for the side of a pool. Given the right conditions it can spread rapidly by underground stems and has been described as a 'pretty nuisance'.

Erect 30-45cm (12-18in) stems spring from the ground and have heart-shaped leaves with an almost metallic sheen. At the tip of these appear pure white flowers in midsummer. There is also a double form that is most attractive. The whole plant has a tangy aroma.

Propagation is by division in spring or autumn; place pieces of the underground stem, with growing shoots, in a pot of compost until rooted.

Right: Hyacinthus orientalis 'Ostara' produces soldier-like flower heads during spring.

Hyacinthus orientalis
(Garden hyacinth)
- **Full sun or light shade**
- **Ordinary garden soil**
- **Plant 12.5-15cm (5-6in) deep**

This bulbous plant flowers in spring with bright scented blooms on a stem over 30cm (12in) long, and 15cm (6in) of the stem is covered in flowers. They are ideal bedding plants either in formal arrangements with other plants or in clumps to give patches of colour. They can be propagated from seed but may take six years to reach the flowering stage; it is far better to obtain specially prepared bulbs produced by professional bulb growers. These are planted in ordinary garden soil in autumn. Choose a site in full sun or light shade. After flowering they can be lifted and moved to another part of the garden to recuperate, leaving space for other plants to provide summer colour.

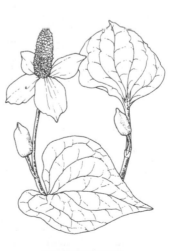

Hibiscus trionum

Hosta fortunei 'Albopicta'

Houttuynia cordata

Hyacinthus orientalis

Hydrangea macrophylla

● Light shade
● Acid soil
● Flowers all summer

This is a well-known deciduous shrub. There are two types: Lacecaps and mop-heads. Lacecaps have flat heads up to 15cm (6in) wide, while the mop-head types have dome-shaped heads up to 20cm (8in) wide.

The variety 'Blue Wave' is a particularly good Lacecap type and has pink to blue flowers. It forms a bush up to 2m (6.5ft) tall and as wide. The large ray flowers have attractive waved edges.

To obtain a really good colour, give 'Blue Wave' very acid conditions and gradual feeding with aluminium. No pruning should be carried out before mid-spring.

Propagate by nodal cuttings, taken from late spring to midsummer.

Hydrangea paniculata 'Grandiflora'

● Sun or very light shade
● Rich loamy soil
● Summer and autumn flowers

Hydrangea paniculata is a deciduous shrub, or sometimes almost a small tree up to 4.5m (15ft) tall. The cultivar 'Grandiflora', as its name suggests, has even more dramatic-looking flowers

than the species *Hydrangea paniculata*. Its closely packed cone-like blossoms are at first white, later turning a purplish pink, and finally becoming brown.

To make a first-class bush and superb flowers, this hydrangea needs to be planted in rich loamy soil. Strict pruning gives the best

Below: *Hydrangea macrophylla serrata 'Rosalba' blooms in summer with pinkish-white flowers with blue centres.*

blooms; in spring prune back shoots before new growth starts, and once there are several young shoots, remove the weakest. Finally reduce the bush to about six to ten shoots when they reach 30-71cm (12-28in) high. Mulch with well-rotted farmyard manure after growth has started. Do not overprune by too much thinning, or you will shorten the life of this elegant hydrangea.

Propagate by half-ripe cuttings during midsummer to late summer.

Hymenocallis × festalis

(Spider lily)

● Full sun, sheltered from frost
● Rich well-drained soil
● Plant with top just level with surface

This bulbous-rooted plant is susceptible to frost; unless your garden has a near frost-free climate, treat it as a pot plant. The white scented flowers, 10cm (4in)

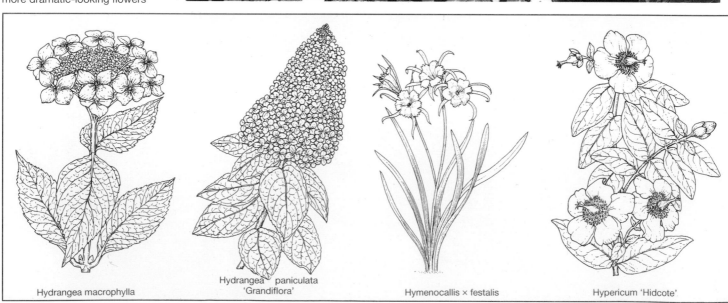

Hydrangea macrophylla

Hydrangea paniculata 'Grandiflora'

Hymenocallis × festalis

Hypericum 'Hidcote'

across, have a centre not unlike a daffodil trumpet, but the outer petals are long and slender. The strap-like leaves are 30cm (12in) long. The plant grows to 45cm (18in) tall, and blooms in spring if grown as a pot plant; out of doors it flowers in summer.

When growing this as a pot plant, use a medium or large pot with a general potting mixture. For early blooms keep it at 16°C (60°F), but for later flowers keep the greenhouse just frost-free. In spring give a mild liquid feed every two weeks. Keep it in shade, and water well in hot weather; repot every two or three years. For outdoors grow it in a pot and plant out in late spring in a well-drained soil in full sun. Generally this plant is trouble-free.

Hypericum 'Hidcote'
- **Full sun**
- **Well-drained loamy soil; tolerates alkaline soils**
- **Flowers midsummer to autumn**

This hardy, semi-evergreen shrub is a superb garden plant. From midsummer to autumn its saucer-shaped golden-yellow flowers, up to 8cm (3.2in) across and each with a central boss of orange anthers, are a lovely sight. The lance-shaped leaves, 4cm (1.6in) long, are pointed at the apex, dark green above and pale grey-green beneath, barely stalked and

oppositely arranged around reddish stems. Bushes will reach a height of 1.5m (5ft) and 1.5-2.1m (5-7ft) wide.

Although this bush is quite hardy in cold areas, the young wood may become damaged by frost. If it does not flower very well, prune it hard each spring; cut back last year's growth to its base and remove any weak shoots. Propagate by softwood cuttings in summer, or by hardwood cuttings in autumn inserted out of doors.

Above: *Hypericum olympicum 'Citrinum', with pale yellow flowers during summer, is ideal for a large rock garden.*

Hypericum olympicum 'Citrinum'
- **Open situation**
- **Light well-drained soil**
- **Evergreen**

This small, evergreen shrub comes from SE Europe, Syria and Asia Minor, and puts on a good display in summer. Upright slender stems with grey-green leaves form a low mounded bush, and at the end of these 20-25cm (8-10in) stems are

borne large (5cm/2in) lemon-yellow flowers with a central boss of similarly coloured stamens. It is said to spread to 60cm (24in), but it can seed to cover 90cm (3ft).

Unfortunately, seed is variable, so soft cuttings of good forms should be taken in late spring; insert them in a peat and sand frame. Young plants will be ready the following spring.

Iberis sempervirens
(Edging candytuft, Perennial candytuft)
- **Full sun**
- **Any soil**
- **Spring and early summer flowering**

This slightly shrubby, hardy, perennial evergreen is superb as an edging to a path or as a bold clump. In spring and early summer the mounds of evergreen foliage are covered with dense wreaths of snowy white flowers; the hummocks of green are about 30cm (12in) high.

Provided they grow in good soil, plants will flourish for a number of years. The ground where iberis is to be planted should be free of perennial weeds. After flowering has finished, cut off the old flower heads; this encourages new growth and keeps the tufts neat and tidy. Propagate by taking half-ripe cuttings during early summer, inserting them in a cold frame or under a large glass jar.

Below: *Iberis sempervirens smothers banks and path edges with snowy-white flowers during spring and early summer.*

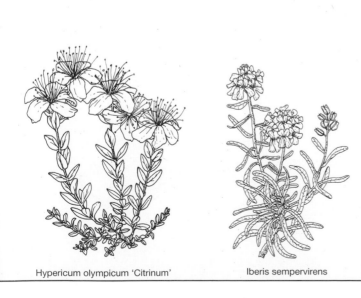

Hypericum olympicum 'Citrinum'   Iberis sempervirens

Above: Iberis umbellata creates clusters of white and pale purple flowers from early to late summer. There are many varieties.

Iberis umbellata

(Globe candytuft)
- **Sow from spring onwards**
- **Ordinary or poor soil**
- **Sunny situation**

Iberis umbellata is a hardy annual. It is strongly aromatic and looks good along the edge of a well-used pathway where its scent can be appreciated. Use it also in bold drifts towards the front of a border.

Umbel-shaped flowers form in clusters up to 5cm (2in) across, on stems 15-38cm (6-15in) high, from early summer to the autumn. The colours are purple, rose-red and white. Leaves are green, lanceolate and slender-pointed, and may be smothered by the profusion of blooms. As flowering is quick from seed, successive sowings will help to prolong the season of flowering. Keep removing dead flowers.

Sow thinly where they are to flower, in spring. Seedlings should be thinned to 15cm (6in) spacing. It is essential to carry out this process correctly if overcrowding and losses are to be avoided.

Impatiens 'Novette F1 Mixed'

(Busy Lizzie, Touch-me-not)
- **Sow in mid-spring**
- **Ordinary but fertile soil**
- **Shade, semi-shade or sunshine**

During recent years these half-hardy annuals have been developed to suit almost any position and conditions. They are very versatile, and can be safely used in difficult shady parts of the garden or in full sunshine. Not many half-hardy annuals can tolerate both.

So many cultivars or hybrids are available that it is difficult to make a choice, but the very dwarf 'Novette' mixture, with plants only 10cm (4in) high, is worth growing.

As a tender half-hardy annual, it will need to be raised under glass. Sow seed in spring on a peat-based growing medium and lightly cover. Keep at a temperature of 18°C (65°F); if it falls below this, then germination will be difficult and uneven. When they are large enough to handle, prick out the seedlings into boxes of a peat-based growing medium. Harden off gradually and plant out in final positions in early summer.

Incarvillea mairei

(Incarvillea grandiflora brevipes)
(Trumpet flower)
- **Full sun**
- **Light fertile soil**
- **Early summer flowering**

This handsome herbaceous perennial, sometimes known as *Incarvillea grandiflora brevipes*, is 30cm (12in) tall, with deeply pinnate foliage. The flowers, held well above the foliage, are a rich pinkish purple, with a yellow throat.

The fleshy root needs to be planted 7.5cm (3in) deep. Incarvilleas need a light sandy well-drained soil in full sun. As this species is only 30cm (12in) high, it needs to be planted near the front of the border. In gardens where frost could cause damage, put a covering of bracken or a pane of glass over these plants during the winter. As slugs are attracted by incarvilleas, put down slug pellets.

Propagate by sowing seed as soon as possible after ripening. Although division can be done in spring, the crowns may be too tough to split easily and so seed is a wiser way to increase them.

Below: Impatiens 'Novette F1 Mixed' is very floriferous, with flowers in many colours.

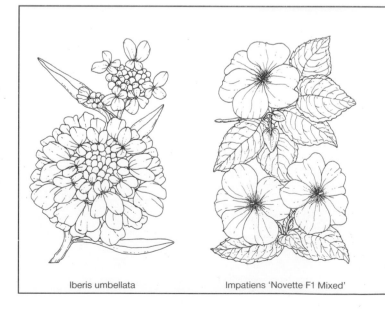

Iberis umbellata   Impatiens 'Novette F1 Mixed'

Ipheion uniflorum
(Spring starflower)
- **Full sun**
- **Ordinary soil with good drainage**
- **Plant 5cm (2in) deep**

This bulbous plant is noted for its grass-like sea-green leaves and star-shaped flowers. The plants grow only 20cm (8in) tall, with spring flowers 5cm (2in) wide. The white to deep lavender-blue blooms are scented.

Bulbs should be planted in autumn. Plants should be kept weeded, and when leaves and flower stems die back in summer

Above: *Ipheion uniflorum 'Violaceum' is a bulb with scented flowers in spring. Colours range from white to deep lavender.*

they should be removed. Position plants in full sun in well-drained soil. The bulbs are increased by bulblets; the plants should be lifted in autumn, divided, and replanted at once. Do this every two or three years to keep the plants free-flowering and healthy. Make sure bulbs do not dry out or become wet during transplanting, and keep the time out of the soil to the minimum. Ipheions are generally trouble-free.

Iris – Apogon/ Laevigatae
(Beardless iris)
- **Full sun**
- **Grow in moist soil and water**
- **Just below surface of soil, or 7.5-15cm (3-6in) under water**

This group of irises thrives on the banks of streams, rivers, ponds and lakes. *Iris laevigata, Iris pseudacorus* and *Iris versicolor* are water irises for the garden pool, but *Iris kaempferi* should be planted in moist soil but not directly into water. The blooms of the kaempferi irises are particularly beautiful in both colouring and form. The flowers may grow up to 20cm (8in) across, in either single or double form.

All these irises have the characteristic sword-shaped leaves, and all of them will grow up to 60cm (24in) tall except *Iris pseudacorus*, which reaches 1.2m (4ft) in water.

Plant rhizomes just under the soil, or between 7.5-15cm (3-6in) under water. Lift the plants every three years, and divide and replant.

Iris – Apogon/Sibirica
(Beardless iris)
- **Sunny position**
- **Moist garden soil**
- **Plant 2.5cm (1in) deep**

This group of irises grows well both in the border and by water. They are noted for their grass-like leaves, their hardiness and their summer flowers. Plants can reach 90cm (3ft) tall, but most grow to only 60cm (2ft). The flowers come in various colours and shadings and can measure up to 10cm (4in)

across. The variety 'Tropic Night' is particularly attractive.

Hybrids are readily available from nurseries in autumn. Plant them in moist soil, but if next to water the rhizome must be at least 15cm (6in) above the water level to prevent rot. If the soil is dry, give it a good watering, and add humus to conserve moisture. Plant rhizomes 2.5cm (1in) deep in a sunny situation and avoid hoeing around the plant as the root system is very near the surface. Mulch well in spring to deter weed growth. The plants can be lifted in late autumn or early spring and divided and replanted; do this every four years or so.

Below: *Iris sibirica 'Tropic Night' has deep purple flowers with golden-brown blotches.*

Incarvillea mairei

Ipheion uniflorum

Iris – apogon/laevigatae

Iris – apogon/sibirica

Iris – Pogoniris/ Eupogon

(Bearded iris)
- **Full sun**
- **Ordinary garden soil**
- **Plant with the top of the rhizome exposed**

This lovely group of irises is distinguished by the rhizomes that lie on the surface, by the scented flowers and by the blue-green sword-like leaves. Size varies from 7.5cm (3in) to 1.5m (5ft) according to the variety. The dwarf members will thrive in rock gardens, and the taller varieties are suitable for the herbaceous border. Blooms appear from early to late spring in a wide range of colours and sizes. Many of the flowers are heavily veined, and up to 15cm (6in) across. These are delightful plants that help to fill the gap between spring and summer flowering plants.

Give them a sunny place with ordinary garden soil. Rhizomes should be planted either at midsummer or in early autumn. Keep them moist until established. Cut leaves back in winter to stop slug attack. Plants can be divided to increase stock.

Below: Iris reticulata 'Jeanine' is popular in rock gardens and on scree beds, where it flowers in late winter and early spring.

Iris – Reticulata

(Iris reticulata var.)
- **Light shade or sun**
- **Light well-drained limy soil**
- **Plant 5-7.5cm (2-3in) deep**

These hardy Asian bulbous plants have a net of fibres around the outside of the bulb and grass-like tubular leaves that are dark green with a paler tip. They are early flowering; some start at midwinter and others follow successively through to spring. The flowers are often 7.5cm (3in) wide, in lemon-yellow and blue. These plants are small, and ideal for the rock garden; they rarely grow more than 15cm (6in) tall.

Plant them in a light well-drained chalky soil. If the ground is heavy, the bulb may not shoot after the first year. Give each bulb a covering of 5-7.5cm (2-3in) of soil. They do best when planted in autumn. After flowering give a liquid feed every four weeks until the bulb dies back. If grown for indoor decoration, plant in pots, keep in the cool until flower buds show, then bring indoors.

Juniperus communis 'Depressa Aurea'
- **Full sun**
- **Most well-drained soils**
- **Slow-growing prostrate shrub**

This is a dwarf, wide-spreading, evergreen conifer. The branches grow just above the soil with the tips curving downwards. It reaches 1.2m (4ft) wide and 30cm (12in) tall in ten years, and an ultimate width of over 3m (10ft). This plant has needle-like leaves. In spring the young foliage is bright yellow, dulling to bronze by autumn. It makes a fine plant for a rockery or sunny border. The cones are berry-like and very small, 6mm (02.in) wide, and turn black as they ripen during their second or even third year on the tree.

Iris – pogoniris/eupogon

Iris – reticulata

Juniperus communis 'Depressa Aurea'

Juniperus communis 'Hibernica'

This conifer is best propagated from cuttings, which will keep the colour and habit of the parent. Set them into an equal peat and sand mixture until they have rooted, and then move to nursery beds (allowing for them to spread horizontally). After two years plant them out to their final site.

Below: Juniperus communis 'Depressa Aurea' is a low and spreading dwarf conifer with yellow-green foliage.

Juniperus communis 'Hibernica'
(Irish juniper)
- **Full sun or light shade**
- **Most garden soils**
- **Slow-growing large shrub**

This superb, narrow, column-like evergreen conifer makes a fine plant for a formal arrangement. Its very upright form needs no training or trimming to keep its shape. It grows to a height of 2m (6.5ft) with

Above: Juniperus communis 'Hibernica' forms a narrow column and is ideal for bringing height to a large garden.

a width of 40cm (16in) after ten years, and the final height is almost 6m (20ft). This is too large for the average rockery, but it is a good plant for a border or a focal point in the garden. The needle-like leaves are closely positioned on the branches. The cones are berry-like, turning black as they ripen during the second or third year.

Grow from cuttings to keep the form true. These should be set into a half peat, half sand mix. When rooted, transplant into pots or a nursery bed to grow on for two years before moving to their final situations. Choose a well-drained soil in sun or light shade.

Juniperus communis 'Hornibrookii'
- **Full sun or light shade**
- **Most garden soils**
- **Slow-growing dwarf spreading shrub**

This small, evergreen conifer forms a low creeping plant that follows the contours of the ground. It will spread to over 1.2m (4ft) across with a height of 25cm (10in) in the first ten years, but as it grows older it will slow down its spread and increase in height. The sharply pointed needles are grey-green with a silvery underside.

It can be grown from cuttings taken in the autumn. Set them into a half peat and half sand mixture, and when rooted plant out into nursery beds with at least 20cm

(8in) between the cuttings to allow for spread. Leave them to grow for two years before planting out into their permanent positions. Choose a site that is open and sunny or in light shade, with ordinary well-drained soil. Add some peat, leaf-mould and bonemeal to give the plants a good start.

Juniperus × media 'Old Gold'
- **Full sun**
- **Ordinary well-drained soil**
- **Slow-growing wide-spreading medium shrub**

This slow-growing, evergreen conifer forms a shrub as high as it is wide, with ascending branches, giving it the look of a golden explosion. It will grow to 1.5m (5ft) wide by 70cm (28in) tall in ten years (although it can form plants of 1m (3.3ft) wide and high in the same period), with a final size of some 2.4m (8ft) wide and 2m (6.5ft) tall. The golden scale-like leaves stay bright during winter.

Grow from cuttings taken in autumn and set in a half peat and half sand mix; the rooted cuttings are then grown on in a nursery bed for two years before being planted out in their permanent situations. Select the best for colour and form. Use an open site with plenty of sun to keep a bright gold colour. An ordinary well-drained soil fortified with peat, leaf-mould and bonemeal will suit the plants well.

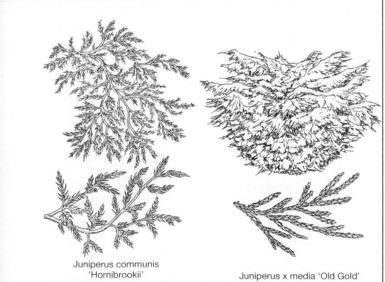

Juniperus communis 'Hornibrookii'

Juniperus x media 'Old Gold'

Above: Juniperis communis 'Hornibrookii' hugs the ground, forming a sea of beautiful grey-green foliage.

Juniperus × media 'Pfitzerana'

(Pfitzer juniper)
- **Full sun or light shade**
- **Well-drained garden soil**
- **Wide-spreading medium bush**

This is a well-known, slow-growing, evergreen conifer. It is an excellent plant for formal or informal gardens, with its wide-spreading habit that can reach 2m (6.5ft) across by 1m (3.3ft) high in ten years. The branches rise at an angle with a drooping tip. The whole bush has an irregular shape, with scale-like leaves. Although on the large size for the average rockery, it can be used there as a centre point around which other plants are grouped.

Grow it from cuttings taken in autumn, and set into a half peat and half sand mixture. When rooted, the best specimens should be planted out into a nursery bed for two years and then moved into their final situations. Grow in a well-drained soil, in sun or shade; peat, leaf-mould and bonemeal are helpful to the young plants.

Juniperus squamata 'Blue Star'
- **Sunny situation**
- **Well-drained soil**
- **Slow-growing dwarf bush**

This slow-growing, evergreen conifer forms a small low shrub with quite large needle-like leaves packed on the short stems; the intense silvery blue colour gives it great impact. After ten years' growth it makes a globe 40cm (16in) in diameter. Its ultimate size is still a matter for conjecture, but some experts estimate 1m (3.3ft) tall with a slightly greater spread. The berry-like cones are just over 6mm (0.2in) wide.

Grow from cuttings taken in autumn and set into a half peat and half sand mixture. Overwinter in a cold frame, then set out in a nursery bed to grow on for two years. Plant out in final positions in a well-drained soil in full sun, keeping the young plants weeded and clear of over-shadowing plants. Give peat, leaf-mould and bonemeal to encourage good growth.

Juniperus virginiana 'Skyrocket'
- **Sunny position**
- **Well-drained garden soil**
- **Medium- to slow-growing small tree**

This is probably the most narrow of the upright conifers in cultivation, being only 30cm (12in)

wide and 2m (6.5ft) tall after ten years, and 5m (16.4ft) tall but still only 30cm (12in) wide after 20 years. It is very popular as a vertical plant for use as a contrast where there is a flat horizontal scheme, such as a heather garden or a large paved area. The evergreen scale-like foliage is a silvery blue-green.

To get the best plants, propagate from cuttings. These are taken in autumn and put into a mixture of half peat and half sand. Overwinter in a cold frame, and then transplant the rooted cuttings into a nursery bed, keeping the soil well weeded. After two years move them into their final situations. Pick a sunny position with a well-drained soil, improved by digging in peat, leaf-mould and bonemeal to encourage good roots.

Kalmia latifolia

(Calico bush, Ivy bush, Mountain laurel, Spoonwood)
- **Full sun or light shade**
- **Moist fertile peaty soil; not chalk or lime**
- **Early summer flowering**

Surely one of the most beautiful evergreen shrubs, with an affinity to a rhododendron, and a lover of acid peaty soil. A single specimen can reach a height of 3m (10ft) with a similar width. Its large oval leathery leaves are a rich glossy green. A well-grown bush forms dense thickets. The pink ten-

Above: Juniperus virginiana 'Skyrocket' develops pencil-like spires of silvery, bluish-green scale-like leaves. Plant in a heather or dwarf conifer garden.

Left: Juniperus squamata 'Blue Star' creates a carpet of blue-green, needle-like leaves that smothers all weeds.

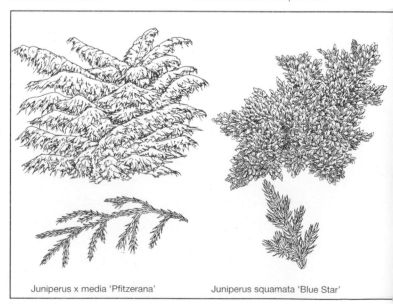

Juniperus x media 'Pfitzerana'   Juniperus squamata 'Blue Star'

ribbed flowers, each one like the inside of a parasol, are borne in superbly delicate clusters in early summer.

To flourish, this shrub needs moist well-drained peaty soil, above all lime-free – in full sun or light shade. When it fails, the fault is usually unsuitable growing conditions. No regular pruning is needed. Should a bush grow out of hand it will have to be cut hard back in spring, but it then takes time to regenerate new growth.

Propagate by seed sown in spring under glass, but this is not an easy plant to propagate. Half-ripe cuttings taken in late summer can sometimes be successful.

Above: Kerria japonica 'Pleniflora' has bright yellow flowers amid slender, apple-green shoots during spring.

Kerria japonica 'Pleniflora'

(Japanese rose, Jew's mallow)
- **Full sun**
- **Any good garden soil, including chalk**
- **Spring flowering**

Kerria is a useful deciduous hardy shrub, which has apple-green, bamboo-like branches and shoots that bear bright orange-yellow double pompom flowers, 4cm

(1.6in) across or sometimes more. It will reach a height of 2.5-3m (8-10ft). It spreads very freely by underground stoloniferous roots, which in turn send up new shoots. This vigorous shrub not only has attractive flowers and apple-green branches, but in autumn its leaves turn an attractive light yellow.

Prune after flowering by cutting flowering wood, and reduce unwanted shoots. Propagate by hardwood cuttings in autumn, or by division of sucker growths in spring. Take care to remove all unwanted sucker shoots that appear.

Kniphofia

(Red hot poker, Torch lily)
- **Full sun**
- **Rich retentive well-drained soil**
- **Early summer to autumn flowering**

Kniphofias are hardy herbaceous perennials that survive most winters. To ensure their safety, tie the foliage into a kind of wigwam in winter, to keep the crowns dry. The flowers are carried on stout stems. One beauty is 'Little Maid' about 60cm (24in) tall, with attractive creamy flower spikes. *Kniphofia galpinii* 'Bressingham Seedlings' produce graceful spikes in orange shades, 45-90cm (18-36in) tall, through summer to autumn. *Kniphofia praecox* has brilliant scarlet flowers on 1.8-2.1m (6-7ft) stems.

Above: Kniphofia uvaria 'Maxima' produces torch-like heads of orange flowers, yellow at their bases, during summer.

Kniphofias require a fairly rich soil with ample humus such as rotted manure or garden compost. After clumps have been divided, do not allow them to dry out before or after planting. A mulch of rotted manure or garden compost should be given annually in spring; otherwise they can remain untouched for several years. Protect crowns during winter. Plant them three or four to the square metre (square yard). Propagate by division in spring.

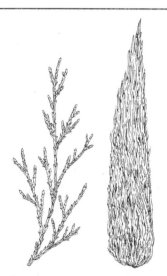

Juniperus virginiana 'Skyrocket'

Kalmia latifolia

Kerria japonica 'Pleniflora'

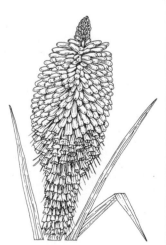

Kniphofia

Kochia trichophylla 'Childsii'

(Burning bush, Red summer cypress)
- **Sow in spring**
- **Fairly light, open soil**
- **Sunny location**

Fine foliage is always welcomed in the garden and kochias are excellent for providing it. Half-hardy in habit, these plants will reach 1m (3.3ft) in height in the one season. Each plant consists of a multitude of fine narrow pointed light green leaves. The flowers are also green, but small and inconspicuous. The whole plant will change its colour to a beautiful deep rich red towards autumn.

Above: Kochia trichophylla creates beacons of narrow, pointed, light green leaves.

Propagation is fairly easy and should be carried out in spring. Sow seeds in pots or boxes of a good growing medium, in a temperature of 16°C (60°F). Pot seedlings into individual medium-size pots and grow on at a reduced temperature. Harden off in the usual way and plant out into final positions at the end of spring at 60cm (24in) intervals.

Kolkwitzia amabilis 'Pink Cloud'

(Beauty bush)
- **Sunny position**
- **Any good soil, including chalk**
- **Flowers in spring and early summer**

This handsome, deciduous, hardy shrub, 2-2.5m (6.5-8ft) high, forms a dense twiggy bush, most suitable for a medium-sized garden. The opposite leaves are roughly oval, and rounded at the base, dull green above and paler beneath. In spring and early summer the arching branches are covered with dense clusters of bell-shaped flowers; the roundish lobes are pink, the throat a delicate yellow. One of the best clones is 'Pink Cloud', with the same colouring as the species.

The only pruning needed is to remove old or weak wood as soon as the bushes have finished flowering, but always bear in mind that kolkwitzias should be allowed to grow naturally.

Propagate by taking half-ripe cuttings in summer; insert them in a propagating frame with some bottom heat.

Laburnum × watereri

(Golden rain)
- **Sunny location**
- **Any garden soil**
- **Early summer flowering**

This hardy deciduous flowering tree is a hybrid between *Laburnum alpinum* and *Laburnum anagyroides*, and it makes a small compact tree with glossy green trifoliate leaves. It has slender 30cm (12in) racemes of yellow fragrant flowers in early summer.

The seeds of laburnum species are poisonous, but *L.* × *watereri* has the advantage that seed does not set so freely on this hybrid as it does on the common laburnum. Another equally beautiful cross with the same parent as *L.* × *watereri* is the cultivar 'Vossii', which has even longer racemes of golden-yellow flowers, up to 70cm (28in) long. Trees will reach a height of 9-10.7m (30-35ft).

Like all laburnums, in the early stages of their life they must be given secure staking.

Propagate by grafting on to *L. anagyroides* in spring.

Below: Laburnum × watereri is famed for drooping clusters of yellow flowers in early summer.

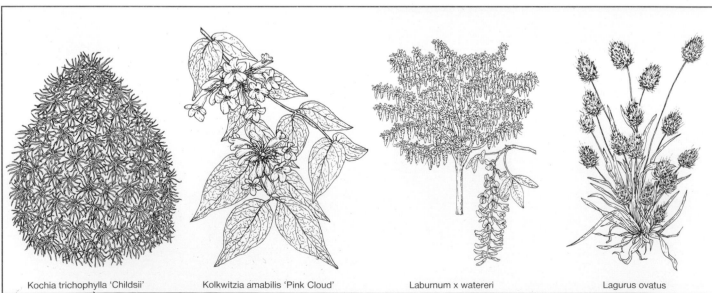

Kochia trichophylla 'Childsii'   Kolkwitzia amabilis 'Pink Cloud'   Laburnum x watereri   Lagurus ovatus

Lagurus ovatus

(Hare's-tail grass, Rabbit tail grass)
- **Sow in late summer or early autumn**
- **Ordinary well-drained soil**
- **Sunny position**

This beautiful annual grass is of medium height, 30cm (12in), with a very attractive inflorescence. The almost white ovate flower heads appear from early summer through until autumn. As the common name implies, its shape is somewhat like that of a hare's woolly tail. The greenish grey foliage is linear, and gives a good contrast to the fine flowers. Grow near the front of a bed or border where the plants will be admired at their best. As with all grasses, avoid over-rich soils, which can lead to fungal diseases.

Best results will be obtained if seed is sown into boxes during late summer or early autumn in a cool greenhouse. Prick out the seedlings into clumps in boxes of loam-based growing medium. Grow on through the winter and keep protected only from the severest weather. Plant out in mid-spring 15cm (6in) apart.

Right: Lathyrus odoratus 'Sheila McQueen' has orangish rose-coloured flowers in summer.

Below: Lamium maculatum 'Beacon Silver' has beautiful leaves, ideal for ground-cover.

Lamium maculatum 'Beacon Silver'

(Spotted dead nettle)
- **Sunny or shady situation**
- **Any soil**
- **Ground cover**

This beautiful, hardy, herbaceous perennial is of relatively recent introduction, and could be considered a degree too coarse for the more orderly rock garden. However, it has most attractive silver foliage, edged with green, with interesting – but not important – blue-mauve, dead-nettle flowers. It thrives on well-drained acid soil, and makes a carpet some 1.5m (5ft) across. In late summer the leaves have small blotches of colour to match the flowers.

This is obviously a plant to be put in a carefully chosen site, where its invasive tendencies can be either curbed or given full rein. It is happy in either sun or shade, but gives a better foliage colour in full sun. A starvation diet would curb this plant's zest for life, but it would still require moisture. Never plant near anything of value and watch out for slugs.

Propagation is by division in spring when growth is just starting; pull the clump apart and replant.

Lathyrus odoratus 'Sheila McQueen'

(Sweet pea)
- **Sow in autumn or spring**
- **Well-drained, medium loam**
- **Sunny but sheltered location**

'Sheila McQueen' is a variety of this hardy annual climber. It is a lovely shade of salmony orange with a pink tint showing through; a creamy base is also apparent. For ordinary garden purposes let them ramble over trellis work or arches, or provide a wigwam of peasticks in the annual or mixed border.

Dig in plenty of organic material before planting, to provide for a cool root run by retaining moisture at the hottest times of the year. Sow the seed (peas) in autumn or spring; those sown in autumn will flower earlier. To help the seed to germinate, nick the hard outer casing of the seed or soak it in water for 24 hours before sowing in a loam-based growing medium. Use pots or boxes for sowing and then place the seedlings singly in small pots. Autumn sowings need to be placed in a cold frame; those sown in spring must be kept in a temperature of 16°C (60°F). Plant out in early spring, 15cm (6in) apart.

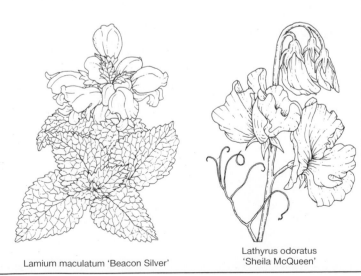

Lamium maculatum 'Beacon Silver'

Lathyrus odoratus 'Sheila McQueen'

Lavandula 'Hidcote'

(Lavender)
- **Full sun**
- **Light, not too rich soil, including chalky soils**
- **Early summer flowering**

The evergreen, low-growing, fragrant-foliaged, early-flowering lavenders, such as 'Hidcote' and 'Munstead', are very useful for a small garden, either as a clump of three or four plants, or as a low edging or hedge by a flower border. 'Hidcote' will reach a height of 25-38cm (10-15in), forming a compact small bush. It has narrow grey-green foliage, and stems which produce close spikes of violet-coloured flowers.

Lavenders thrive best on a light, not-too-rich soil and grow well in chalk or lime soils. The best time to prune lavender is in the spring, but do not prune immediately after flowering, because the old growth protects the young growth, which will produce the next year's crop of flowers.

Propagate by taking heel or nodal cuttings of ripened wood; insert them in sandy soil in a cold frame in late summer.

Lavandula stoechas

(French lavender, Spanish lavender)
- **Well-drained open situation**
- **Warm, light soil**
- **Almost hardy shrublet**

Common lavender is far too large for any rock garden, but its miniature cousin from the Mediterranean region – which forms a small, hardy, evergreen shrub up to 30cm (12in) tall in gardens, although taller in the wild – is a most suitable subject. Its slightly curious four-angled spikes of deep purple flowers, topped by a tuft of ovate purple bracts that persist after the plant has faded, appear in summer.

Coming from the Mediterranean area, it does possess a degree of tenderness, but this can be overcome by keeping a supply of young plants. Either sow seed in winter in a seed compost, or take cuttings of non-flowering shoots in early autumn and overwinter them in a frame.

Below: Lavandula stoechas with spikes of deep purple flowers is ideal for well-drained soil.

Lavatera trimestris 'Silver Cup'

- **Sow in autumn or spring**
- **Ordinary soil**
- **Sunny and sheltered spot**

Lavateras have long been grown for their attractive free-flowering effects. The hardy annual 'Silver Cup' recommended here is one of a number of new varieties. Glowing pink blooms 7.5-10cm (3-4in) in diameter are freely produced on stems 60-70cm (24-28in) high and spreading to 75cm (30in). This plant is a member of the hollyhock family, and its leaves are a good

Above: Leontopodium alpinum is distinctive, with white, spiky, ray-like flower heads.

green, ovate and lobed. Flowers grow from the leaf axils and are trumpet-shaped, almost satin in texture, and very pleasing to the eye. Apart from their use in the perennial border, try them towards the back of an annual border.

Sow seed directly where plants are to flower, in autumn or spring, and cover lightly. Thin out the seedlings of either sowing during late spring to 45cm (18in) intervals. The strong low branching habit of this plant requires no staking.

Lavandula 'Hidcote'   Lavandula stoechas

Leontopodium alpinum

(Edelweiss)
- **Well-drained situation**
- **Light soil**
- **Herbaceous**

To many, the beginning and end of alpines is the edelweiss: stories are told of the impossible locations on steep cliffs in which this species grows, but in fact it is a hardy herbaceous perennial that is easily found in meadows at no great height in the Alps.

A clump of narrow grey basal leaves is formed on this alpine, which puts forth a 15cm (6in) flower stem at the top of which is borne a flat head of what can best be described as rayless daisies. The whole plant is covered with white woolly hairs. It is undoubtedly a unique plant, and it grows very happily in any well-drained sunny situation.

Propagation is by seed sown in winter, ready for pricking out in spring and planting in autumn.

Leucojum aestivum 'Gravetye Giant'

(Giant snowflake, Snowflake, Summer snowflake)
- **Light shade**
- **Moist soil**
- **Plant 7.5cm (3in) deep**

These hardy, bulbous plants have sword-like leaves. The large drooping bell flowers are produced in spring, 2.5cm (1in) long, in white with the petals tipped with green. 'Gravetye Giant' is an improved form, growing 50cm (20in) tall.

These plants prefer a moist soil, in which they should be planted 7.5cm (3in) deep and positioned so that they can enjoy some shade. They should be planted in late summer or early autumn, and left undisturbed for several years until they become too crowded, with too few blooms. Then, when the leaves have turned yellow they can be lifted, divided and replanted immediately, 20cm (8in) apart. This is a better way to increase your stock than by growing from seed, which can take six years to reach flowering size. These leucojums do not like drying off in summer so it is important to keep them moist.

Lewisia cotyledon
- **Requires moisture in summer**
- **Prefers acid soil**
- **Evergreen**

This valuable plant family from North America produces many showy evergreen perennials that are essential for the rock garden. When plants hybridize, they sometimes produce inferior seedlings, but not so the lewisias, which produce some wonderful colour forms in the pink, peach and apricot to orange range. The plant forms a thick caudex (root stock), which produces almost succulent fleshy leaves, and 15-30cm (6-12in) tall flower spikes of many blooms in early summer.

This plant thrives on a rich diet, but in well-drained gritty soil. It prefers to be planted on its side in the garden and only just tolerates chalk. *Lewisia cotyledon* and its many colour forms and variations are excellent for the alpine house, where they enjoy a drying-off period after flowering.

Propagation is by seed.

Below: *Lewisia cotyledon hybrid, ideal for rock gardens, has bright pink flowers.*

Lavatera trimestris 'Silver Cup'

Leontopodium alpinum

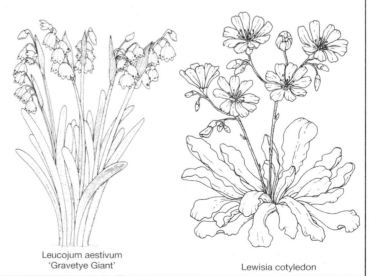

Leucojum aestivum 'Gravetye Giant'

Lewisia cotyledon

Leycesteria formosa

(Flowering nutmeg, Granny's curls, Himalayan honeysuckle, Pheasant berry)

- **Full sun or partial shade**
- **Any rich fertile soil**
- **Flowers from early summer to early autumn**

This hardy deciduous shrub has pinkish white pendent flowers surrounded by claret-coloured

bracts, which are produced from early summer to early autumn. They are followed by clusters of reddish purple berries like small gooseberries, in autumn. The hollow green bamboo-like stems are enhanced by opposite leaves, which are green above and paler beneath, attached to wine-red stalks. It is a native of the shady forests of the Himalayas and Tibet.

Provided it has a rich soil, this shrub will reach a height of 2m (6.5ft) at least, and 1.2m (4ft) in width. The only pruning needed is to thin out the older and weaker shoots down to ground level in spring. Also cut back any shoots that have been frosted.

Propagate by seeds sown in spring, or by hardwood cuttings in autumn.

Liatris spicata 'Kobold'

(Blazing star, Gay feather, Spike gay feather)

- **Full sun**
- **Ordinary well-drained soil**
- **Summer flowering**

The flowers of this hardy, tuberous-rooted, herbaceous perennial open at the top first, whereas most plants that have spike-like flowers open from the base and those at the top open last. The small strap-like leaves form a rosette near the ground. The flower stems also have small leaves. The flower heads are closely packed and look not unlike a paint brush. The variety 'Kobold' has brilliant pinky mauve flowers, 60cm (24in) tall. Also recommended is *L. pycnostachya*, the Kansas feather, with pinky purple crowded flower heads, 15-20cm (6-8in) long, on rather floppy 1.2m (4ft) stems. It makes a fine

Left: Leycesteria formosa has pinkish-white flowers surrounded by claret-coloured bracts.

display in late summer and early autumn. Liatris are useful as cut flowers and ideal for drying for winter flower arrangements.

The species is better in poor soil, and prefers firm ground. Propagate by seed sown in pans in early spring, or by division in late spring.

Lilium – American Cultivars

- **Light shade**
- **Well-drained acid soil**
- **Plant 15cm (6in) deep**

These varieties, grown from crossing American lilies, produce a range of plants that can reach 2.1m (7ft), with 7.5cm (3in) blooms in yellow, orange and reds, some in two-colour forms with markings and spots.

Plant bulbs 15cm (6in) deep in a well-drained neutral to acid soil with plenty of peat, leaf-mould or compost. These cultivars give best results if grown in light shade. The bulbs should be left undisturbed, with a mulch of leaf-mould and bracken each winter. They can be lifted in late autumn, divided and replanted to give the bulbs more room, but treat only a few each year, as they take a season to recover. You may want to stake plants to prevent wind damage. Give the plants a general pesticide and fungicide to keep them free from trouble. Use a slug bait to stop slug or snail damage.

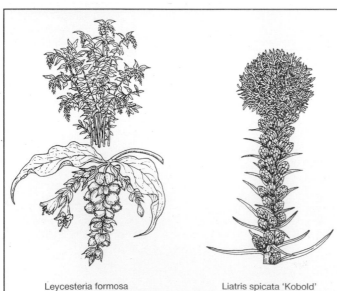

Leycesteria formosa

Liatris spicata 'Kobold'

Lilium – American cultivar

Lilium – Asiatic cultivar

Lilium – Asiatic Cultivars

- **Full sun or semi-shade**
- **Well-drained garden soil**
- **Plant 10-15cm (4-6in) deep**

These are early-flowering lilies with blooms growing either singly or in groups springing from the same point on the stem. These cultivars grow up to 1.5m (5ft) tall, with some flowers reaching 15cm (6in) across. Some forms have hanging flowers with petals curled back to form a 'Turk's cap'. Blooms appear at midsummer with a variety of colours, shapes and markings.

The bulbs should be planted 10-15cm (4-6in) deep in well-drained garden soil, in full sun or semi-shade, during the winter months. During the growing season they should be kept moist with plenty of water and mulching with peat, compost or leaf-mould. Every few years the plants can be lifted in the winter months, divided and replanted with more space around them. Seed will take up to three years to reach flowering.

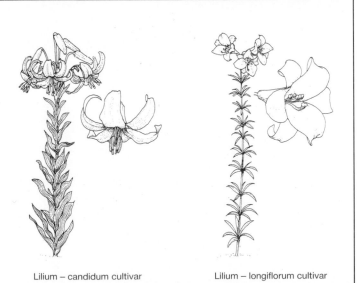

Left: Liatris spicata 'Kobold' displays eye-catching pinky-mauve flowers in late summer. Ideal in flower arrangements.

Above: Lilium Asiatic cultivars have attractive flowers, many with Turk's-cap type heads. Plant in well-drained soil.

Lilium – Candidum Cultivars

- **Full sun**
- **Ordinary well-drained soil**
- **Plant 10cm (4in) deep**

These lilies grow to 1.8m (6ft) tall, and in summer they have flowers 7.5cm (3in) long, with very curved petals. These blooms are scented, in yellow, orange and white with bright red pollen. The original parent, *Lilium candidum*, has been cultivated for over 3,500 years and revered by many civilizations.

Bulbs should be planted 10cm (4in) deep in autumn in a well-drained garden soil containing plenty of humus. To obtain a succession of flowers over the years, a few plants each year should be lifted, divided and replanted, as they take at least a year to recover. Seeds take up to three years to reach flowering size, so it is quicker to increase your stock by division. If weather conditions are bad for planting, put the bulbs in damp peat until the soil is ready, to stop them drying out. Stake mature plants.

Lilium – Longiflorum Cultivars

- **Full sun**
- **Limy soil**
- **Plant 10cm (4in) deep**

These bulbous plants are crosses of lilies from Japan and Taiwan and are generally half-hardy and often recommended as pot plants, although the variety 'Holland's Glory' is highly regarded for outdoor cultivation as well, with its large white strongly scented blooms. It grows to a height of 1.2m (4ft).

The bulbs should be planted at a depth of 10cm (4in), in soil fortified with leaf-mould or compost to hold moisture during drought periods. They should be left undisturbed for several years; then they should be lifted in the autumn, divided and replanted with more space around each bulb. An autumn mulch of leaf-mould or compost is very beneficial, but do not use fresh manure because this will rot the roots. These lilies are prone to disease and care should be taken to treat them with a fungicide.

Lilium – candidum cultivar

Lilium – longiflorum cultivar

Lilium – Martagon Hybrids
- Partial shade or light woodland
- Well-drained garden soil
- Plant 10-15cm (4-6in) deep

These hybrid lilies flower from late spring onwards. They are easily grown, and reach 1.5m (5ft) tall, with flowers up to 7.5cm (3in) wide in white, cream, yellow, orange or deep red, with spots and markings on the petals.

They thrive in partial shade, tolerate lime, and require a good well-drained soil with plenty of leaf-mould, compost and well-rotted manure mixed into it to retain moisture in dry periods. The bulbs should be planted 10-15cm (4-6in) deep in the winter months, and left undisturbed for several years. During winter they can be lifted, divided and replanted with more space around them to increase stock. Divide in rotation, as they take a year to recover. Seeds take three years to mature to flowering size. Treat plants with a general pesticide and fungicide, and spread some slug bait on the soil.

Above: Lilium regale has white, funnel-shaped flowers with reddish-purple shading on the outside, and yellow centres.

Lilium – Oriental Cultivars
- Full sun
- Rich well-drained gritty soil
- Plant 15cm (6in) deep

These hybrid forms of Oriental lilies are often sub-divided into flower shapes: trumpet, bowl, star or flat and the very curved petal forms. The flowers appear in summer, and sometimes reach 25cm (10in) across; many are scented, and they have very decorative shapes in a wide range of colours, often marked, striped and spotted. The plants grow to a height of 2.1m (7ft) and should be planted at a distance of 30cm (12in) apart and at a depth of 15cm (6in) in a rich, well-drained but gritty soil with plenty of humus.

Place them in full sun and as they grow stake them against being blown over. A mulch of humus in early spring is advisable. The bulbs can be lifted in the late autumn or winter months, divided and replanted with more space around them, but make sure that they do not lose moisture. Seeds take up to three years to flower.

Lilium regale
(Regal lily, Royal lily)
- Full sun
- Well-drained garden soil
- Plant just below the surface

This bulbous lily originates from China, and is probably the best-known of all lilies, with its scented, white, funnel-shaped flowers up to 12.5cm (5in) long, blooming in summer. The centres of the flowers are brilliant yellow, and the backs of the petals have red-purple shading. These lilies can reach 1.8m (6ft) but most grow to 1.2m (4ft) tall.

Regal lilies require to be placed in full sun in a well-drained soil, where they will spread quickly. The bulbs should be planted just below the surface. Bulbs can be lifted, divided and replanted during the winter months. Seeds take up to three years to reach maturity. In exposed areas they should be staked to prevent wind damage.

Lilium tigrinum
(Tiger lily)
- Full sun
- Well-drained lime-free soil
- Plant 15cm (6in) deep

This spectacular bulbous lily is a native of China, Korea and Japan and is grown for its very curved petals that give it a 'Turk's Cap' 10cm (4in) long in late summer. The bright orange or red-orange petals are spotted with black, and have dark red pollen on the anthers. There is a variety that has bright yellow blooms with purple

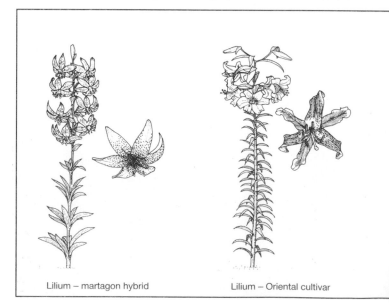

Lilium – martagon hybrid

Lilium – Oriental cultivar

spots, known as *Lilium tigrinum flaviflorum*. The plants can reach 1.8m (6ft).

Bulbs should be planted at a depth of 15cm (6in) in a well-drained lime-free soil, 23cm (9in) apart. Grow this separate from other lilies, because it is prone to virus disease. Keep the soil moist throughout the growing season. Increase by picking off the bulbils. Plant just under the soil surface in pots, for a year, then plant out.

Lilium – Trumpet and Aurelian Cultivars
- **Partial shade**
- **Rich well-drained soil**
- **Plant 15cm (6in) deep**

Grouped in this section are the funnel-shaped, bowl-shaped, pendent and star-like blooms that are mainly crosses from the Aurelian lilies. Some are lime-tolerant, but others are not. They grow to 2.1m (7ft), and should be planted 30cm (12in) apart in a rich well-drained soil in partial shade at a depth of 15cm (6in). Most of this group are hardy, but a mulch of leaf-mould or compost spread over them in autumn will protect the less hardy from frost. The flowers, many of them scented, are often over 12.5cm (5in) across, and some reach 20cm (8in) wide. A wide range of colours is available; some have stripes, others are bicoloured. The flowering period is in late summer. The bulbs can be

lifted in the winter months, divided and replanted, but make sure that they do not dry out.

Limnanthes douglasii
(Meadow foam, Poached egg flower)
- **Sow in spring**
- **Ordinary soil**
- **Sunny position**

This hardy annual is popularly known as poached egg flower because of its blooms, which have yellow centres surrounded by white. Each flower is saucer-shaped, and the blooms are produced on 15cm (6in) stems with deeply cut light green leaves. The blooms open in early summer, and are 2.5cm (1in) across. Bees have a particular liking for the flowers of this plant, which are delicately scented, and they can nearly swamp the plants. Apart from their outdoor use these plants can give a succession of colour in a cool greenhouse or conservatory during

winter or spring; seed for this should be sown in early autumn.

For flowering in the garden, sow seeds where they are to flower, in spring. In milder areas autumn sowings will produce earlier flowering plants. Only just cover the seed with fine soil, and later thin out seedlings in both methods to 10cm (4in) intervals.

Below: Limnanthes douglasii is superb at the edge of a path, creating colour with yellow flowers surrounded by white.

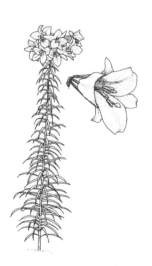
Lilium regale

Lilium tigrinum

Lilium – trumpet and aurelian cultivars

Limnanthes douglasii

Limonium sinuatum 'Gold Coast'
(Statice sinuata)
(Sea lavender, Statice)
- **Sow in very early spring**
- **Ordinary soil**
- **Open, sunny position**

Formerly known as *Statice sinuata*, this 'everlasting' half-hardy annual has long been popular for its papery blooms in white, yellow, rose and blue. The cultivar 'Gold Coast' has bright yellow flowers, which are produced on slightly winged green stems 60cm (24in) high. Formed in clusters up to 10cm (4in) long, the blooms appear in midsummer.

Sow seed under glass in very early spring at a temperature of 16°C (60°F). The seeds will be slightly clustered and will need teasing apart so that individual seeds can be sown. If this task is carried out, patience will be well rewarded by more even germination, and growth will be more rapid. Use a loam-based growing medium for seeds and pricking out. Harden off in the usual way and plant out at 30cm (12in) intervals in early summer.

Below: Limonium sinuatum 'Gold Coast' has papery, bright yellow flowers in summer, borne on green, winged stems. It is an 'everlasting' annual.

Linaria reticulata 'Crimson and Gold'
(Portuguese toadflax, Purple-net toadflax)
- **Sow in mid-spring**
- **Ordinary soil**
- **Sunny position**

This crimson and gold hardy annual has been developed from the very tall Portuguese toadflax. Its reduced height, 30cm (12in), makes it easier to manage in the garden. Gold-splashed scarlet-crimson flowers, resembling snapdragons with a short spur, open from late spring and are 2cm (0.8in) long. The compact plants, made up of pale green, linear leaves holding spiky flower heads, can be put to good use in the

Above: Linaria reticulata 'Crimson and Gold' is a hardy annual with clusters of crimson flowers blotched bright gold, which open from late spring.

annual border. Try also to sow these eye-catching plants directly into containers on a patio in full sunshine. At the end of each season discard any self-sown seedlings.

As a hardy annual and for ordinary garden purposes, sow the seeds in spring in shallow drills where they are to flower, and only lightly cover the seed. Thin out the seedlings to 15cm (6in) apart. Further sowings at monthly intervals to the end of spring will ensure a succession of flowering over a longer period.

Limonium sinuatum 'Gold Coast'

Linaria reticulata 'Crimson and Gold'

Linum grandiflorum 'Rubrum'

Linum narbonense

Linum grandiflorum 'Rubrum'

(Flowering flax, Scarlet flax)
- Sow in autumn or spring
- Ordinary well-drained soil
- Full sun

Waving in a light summer breeze this hardy annual is splendid if you can give it the correct cultural conditions. The scarlet saucer-shaped flowers are up to 5cm (2in) across, on wispy 30cm (12in) stems of a light green. The narrow leaves are in sympathy with the light airy feeling of this plant. The slightest air movement will set the flowers in motion. Use in conjunction with a pale contrasting-coloured annual, towards the front of a border.

Sow directly where they are to flower – during spring in most areas, but milder districts can take advantage by sowing in the autumn, which will produce flowers earlier. Broadcast the seed over the chosen area and rake in lightly. Thin out seedlings to 15cm (6in) apart. Seeds can rot before germination if the site is not well drained.

Other, usually taller, cultivars of *Linum grandiflorum* are available.

Below: Linum grandiflorum 'Rubrum' bears scarlet, saucer-shaped flowers amid narrow leaves during the summer.

Liriope muscari

Lithodora diffusa 'Grace Ward'

Linum narbonense
- Sunny position
- Light soil
- Herbaceous

This hardy perennial is a rather tall plant for the smaller rock garden, but its elegant 50cm (20in) arching stems are thin enough to be accommmodated unobtrusively. It is a native of southern Europe, but is hardy in all but the severest winters and not fussy over soil or situation. The addition of peat or leaf-mould seems to help, although in the wild it is native to calcareous soils.

The 2.5cm (1in) wide rich blue flowers appear at the tips of the graceful stems in summer. It usually dies back in winter, but it may persist as an evergreen.

Propagation is by seed sown in winter, ready for potting up in spring and planting out in midsummer to late summer. If you have a good form, try soft basal cuttings in spring or take firmer cuttings late in the summer.

Above: Liriope muscari has stiffish leaves and lilac-mauve flowers in upright spikes during late summer and autumn.

Liriope muscari

(Big blue liriopes, Turf lily)
- Sunny location
- Fertile soil with moderate drainage
- Late summer or autumn flowering

This hardy, evergreen perennial has foliage that arches over, forming a neat hummock from which the 23-30cm (9-12in) stems arise, bearing lilac-mauve flowers crowded together and looking rather like a bottle brush. Liriope can be used quite effectively as an edging to a border of shrubs. It is always useful to have a few of these evergreen plants in a border during winter.

This plant seems to do better in a light acid soil with a pH of 5 to 5.5 rather than in a more neutral soil. This tuberous-rooted plant also seems to do better in full sun than in shade or partial shade. Propagate it by division in spring.

Lithodora diffusa 'Grace Ward'

(Lithospermum diffusum)
- Well-drained open site
- Acid soil
- Evergreen

This prostrate, sub-shrubby plant has undergone a name change, and may still be found in catalogues as *Lithospermum diffusum*. The type species is rarely seen nowadays, being replaced by named clones of which 'Grace Ward' now seems to have superseded 'Heavenly Blue'. A 60cm (24in) wide mat of rough dark green foliage is formed, which is covered with deep blue flowers in early spring.

Its requirements are particular if it is going to look its best, for it hates lime and prefers a sandy soil with plenty of peat and leaf-mould. It also prefers full sun.

Successful propagation is very precise. In the Northern Hemisphere take soft green cuttings after the first week in July and before the second week in August. (In the Southern Hemisphere this would be January and February respectively.) The percentage of germination is much higher during this time period. Water the plants before and after taking cuttings.

Lithophragma parviflora

(Woodland star)
- **Appreciates woodland conditions**
- **Leafy acid soil**
- **Herbaceous**

Although the flowers of this herbaceous perennial are small, they make up for that disadvantage by producing enough on a flowering stem to make a show.

It is a delightful woodlander from North America and thrives in peaty soil and light shade. Do not plant in alkaline conditions. The root consists of grain-like bulblets and these produce orbicular basal leaves, which are cut into three sections that in themselves are three-lobed, so they end up looking much divided. The 15cm (6in) flower stems have heads of deeply fringed pale pink flowers. It is an attractive plant for the peat garden in partial shade.

Propagation is by division in early spring, when growth is being started; the bulblets transplant well at this stage.

Above: Lobelia cardinalis 'Cherry Ripe' is a superb hybrid, with tall stems bearing small, crimson flowers during late summer.

Lobelia cardinalis

(Cardinal flower)
- **Sunny location**
- **Rich fertile moist soil**
- **Late summer flowering**

This short-lived border plant is very handsome. Above a rosette of green leaves, which also cover the stem, are brilliant scarlet blooms. The stems are 90cm (3ft) high.

Planting is best done in spring; plenty of moistened peat, leaf-mould or well-rotted garden compost should be incorporated. This species likes rich moist soil. Never let the roots suffer from drought during the growing season. If the ground is not forked over or cleaned for the winter, plants will come through unscathed in areas that are more or less frost-free. If doubtful, lift them in autumn and store in a dry frost-proof shed, covering the roots with peat or leaf-mould. Propagate by division in spring.

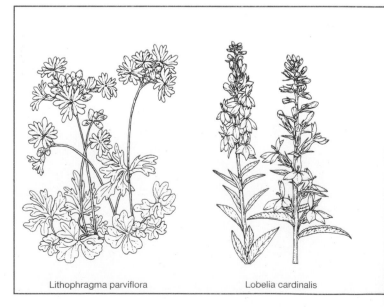

Above: Lobelia erinus 'Colour Parade' displays small flowers in a mixture of colours in summer.

Lobelia erinus 'Colour Cascade Mixed'

- **Sow in late winter or early spring**
- **Ordinary well-cultivated soil**
- **Sun or partial shade**

This half-hardy perennial is usually grown as a half-hardy annual. It includes varieties in many shades of blue, rose, red, mauve and white eyed flowers, which continue to appear until autumn.

Although best results are obtained from planting in sunny positions, lobelias also succeed in partial shade. These tender plants need to be sown in heat in late winter or early spring to obtain maximum results. Sow the small seeds very thinly on the surface of a moistened peat-based seed mixture and do not cover. Germinate in a temperature of 18-21°C (65-70°F). Water carefully to

Lithophragma parviflora

Lobelia cardinalis

avoid disturbance. Prick out as soon as the seedlings can be handled, either singly or in small clumps. Grow on in cooler conditions and plant into the garden when risk of frost has passed. Keep the plants watered in dry weather, and fed at intervals.

Lonicera nitida 'Baggesen's Gold'
- **Full sun**
- **Any good garden soil**
- **Summer and autumn foliage**

This golden-leaved, hardy, evergreen shrub will reach a height of 1.2-1.5m (4-5ft) and just over 1m (3.3ft) wide. The small opposite leaves are almost oval, 1.2cm (0.5in) long, heart-shaped at the base and blunt at the apex. Throughout the summer they are golden-yellow in colour, but during the autumn and winter they turn to a yellowish green.

If three to five plants are grown as a clump they will make a bright addition to the garden in summer and autumn. They are not quite as bright as golden privet in winter, but still worth growing. To keep bushes shapely, trim them when necessary during the summer. Should they become overgrown and ill-shapen, then hard pruning in spring will soon improve their appearance.

Propagate by hardwood cuttings in mid-autumn, inserted out of doors.

Lunaria annua
(Lunaria biennis)
(Bolbanac, Honesty, Penny flower, Silver dollar)
- **Sow in late spring or early summer**
- **Light soil**
- **Partial shade**

This hardy biennial, also known as *Lunaria biennis*, starts to flower quite early, usually from mid-spring onwards. Individual blooms are made up of four petals in a cross shape, in shades of purple and white; some crimson can appear in mixtures. The flowers are followed by flattened disc-like seedpods. Blooms and seedpods are formed on stems up to 75cm (30in) long, carrying heart-shaped leaves of a dark green. Grow towards the back of a border.

Sow seeds in nursery rows during late spring. Thin out the seedlings to 15cm (6in) apart, still in nursery rows. Plant out into final positions in the autumn at 30cm (12in) intervals.

Left: Lupinus polyphyllus creates tall stems packed with mauve, purple, red and white flowers.

If storing the seedpods, cut the stems in late summer when the pods are still slightly green.

Lupinus polyphyllus
(Lupin)
- **Sun or light shade**
- **Light sandy loam**
- **Early summer flowering**

This herbaceous perennial enjoys sun and well-drained soil; avoid lime, and heavy wet clay soils. Before planting, see that the ground is well cultivated, with an ample supply of well-rotted farmyard manure or garden compost. On well-drained soils, plant in autumn; otherwise, wait until spring.

With established plants restrict the number of flower spikes to between five and seven, when stems are about 30cm (12in) high. Remove faded flower heads to prevent them forming seeds, which will take strength from the plant. Give a light spraying of plain water in the evening during dry springs. As a rule staking is not necessary. Named varieties can be obtained, but the Russell hybrids have a good mixture of colours, and vary in height from 90 to 120cm (3-4ft).

Propagate by basal cuttings in early spring, when 7.5-10cm (3-4in) long; insert in a cold frame.

Lobelia erinus 'Colour Cascade Mixed'

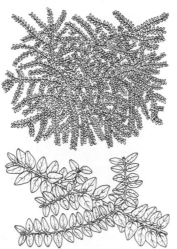

Lonicera nitida 'Baggesen's Gold'

Lunaria annua

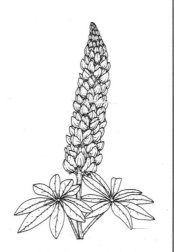

Lupinus polyphyllus

Lychnis coronaria 'Abbotswood Rose'
(Agrostemma coronaria)
(Campion, Catchfly, Mullein pink)
- **Full sun**
- **Fertile well-drained soil**
- **Summer flowering**

This short-lived, hardy, herbaceous perennial has attractive, soft, furry foliage. Its leaves are coated with fine silver hairs, which almost cover the entire plant. The leaves are borne in pairs from a basal clump up the 60cm (24in) stems on which the branching sprays of dianthus-like brilliant rose-crimson flowers of 'Abbotswood Rose' are carried (some call the flowers rose pink). It is a lovely plant, and a clump of five plants to a square metre (square yard) will add charm and colour to any perennial border.

There is also a variety 'Alba' which has white flowers. Apart from the colour, it is similar to the variety 'Abbotswood Rose'.

Propagate by division in autumn, but if the soil is cold and wet, leave it until spring. These plants will need a fertile soil.

Below: *Lychnis coronaria 'Abbotswood Rose' has a lax habit, with small, rose-crimson flowers during summer.*

Lysimachia nummularia 'Aurea'
(Creeping Charlie, Creeping Jennie, Moneywort)
- **Sun or semi-shade**
- **Any soil**
- **Ground cover plant**

This is a trailing, vigorous, prostrate border plant with evergreen stems and leaves. The type species is a native of Europe, including Great Britain, and is found growing by the waterside, but it has adapted to growing in drier conditions in gardens. Although technically evergreen, its foliage can hardly be considered very attractive in winter.

The variety 'Aurea' has yellow leaves, as well as cup-shaped yellow flowers during midsummer.

Propagate by division and replanting in midsummer, taking care to keep the divisions moist.

Lysimachia punctata
(Garden lysimachia, Loosestrife)
- **Sun or semi-shade,**
- **Ordinary garden soil, preferably damp**
- **Summer flowering**

This hardy herbaceous perennial is quite unconnected with the purple loosestrife, *Lythrum salicaria*, but one must admit that both plants have tall and dominating flower spikes. *Lysimachia punctata* has straight stems bearing whorls of

bright yellow five-petalled flowers. Each stem is about 90cm (3ft) high, and it blooms for at least two months during the summer.

Plants can be invasive so it should not be grown near other perennials that could become swamped. It grows in full sun or partial shade, but although it will grow in dryish soil, it is happier where it has damp or moist soil conditions. Grouped in clumps of four plants it can give brightness to an otherwise dull corner in a garden.

Propagate by division in spring or autumn. Cuttings of young shoots can be taken in spring and inserted in sandy soil under glass. Seeds can be sown in pots or boxes in spring in a cold frame.

Lychnis coronaria 'Abbotswood Rose'

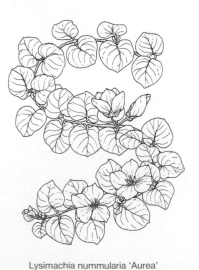

Lysimachia nummularia 'Aurea'

Lysimachia punctata

Lythrum salicaria 'Firecandle'

Above: Lysimachia punctata is an herbaceous perennial that creates an eye-catching display of yellow flowers during the summer.

Above: Lythrum salicaria 'Firecandle' is outstandingly attractive, with tall spikes of deep rose-red flowers.

Lythrum salicaria 'Firecandle'

(Purple loosestrife, Spiked loosestrife)
- Sunny location
- Fertile moist soil
- Late summer flowering

The purple loosestrife is one of the most handsome herbaceous perennials during summer, when it is found growing wild on river banks, ditches and marshes. This indicates the type of soil and situation in which to grow garden varieties. But although they prefer to grow in damp boggy soil, they succeed quite happily in any moist border. The showy spikes of flowers are borne on 1.2m (4ft) wiry stems. They are hardy, long lived and long flowering. The variety 'Firecandle' has deep rosy red flowers borne in the leaf axils on spikes 90cm (3ft) tall. A dwarfer one is the clear pink 'Robert', only 75cm (30in) tall. Plant bold clumps of five in the middle of the border.

Another lythrum is *L. virgatum* 'The Rocket', which is 90cm (3ft) high with erect spikes of rose-red flowers borne in the leaf axils.

Propagate by root cuttings in spring; as the rootstock is very woody, division is difficult.

Magnolia stellata

(Star magnolia)
- Sunny position
- Good loam or peaty soil
- Spring flowering

This is the ideal deciduous shrub for a small garden where a magnolia is desired. It makes a compact rounded shrub, 2.5-3.6m (8-12ft) tall and as much or sometimes more in width. The long narrow oblong leaves are 6.5-10cm (2.5-4in) in length. In spring the bush produces fragrant, pure white strap-like flowers, each flower having 12 to 18 petals.

This plant needs a sunny position and a good loamy soil, with added leaf-mould, peat and sand if the ground is at all wet or inclined to drain badly. Initial preparation prior to planting is essential. Newly planted bushes will take up to two years to establish. This species is easily blackened by frost, so try to plant it in a sheltered position. No pruning is necessary.

Propagate this superb shrub by layering in early spring.

Malope trifida 'Grandiflora'

- Sow in mid-spring
- Light soil
- Sunny position

This hardy annual comes from Spain. Its richly coloured flowers will enhance any sunny border. Once established the plants, up to 1m (3.3ft) tall, will provide wide trumpet flowers of a light purple with internal veins of a deep almost black-purple, up to 7.5cm (3in) across, borne on erect branching stems with lobed green leaves. They make compact plants, and will require no staking despite their height. In large borders use them near a pale yellow or white annual. Container-grown for the patio they will give height to a somewhat flat area.

As this is a hardy annual it is not necessary to propagate it under glass, but simply sow the seeds where they are to flower. Carry out the usual process in mid-spring and thin out seedlings to 15-23cm (6-9in) apart. The flowers will appear from early summer onwards.

Below: Malope trifida 'Grandiflora' is an easily grown hardy annual, with large, pink flowers from early summer.

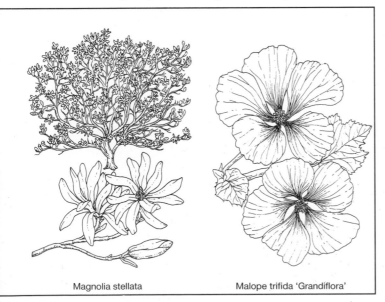

Magnolia stellata

Malope trifida 'Grandiflora'

Malus floribunda
(Japanese crab, Showy crab apple)
- **Full sun**
- **Any fertile soil**
- **Spring flowering**

A deciduous flowering tree with a semi-weeping habit that forms a small rounded spreading tree with arching branches. In spring the bare branches produce small rosy-red buds, which later become pale pink flowers, up to 3-3.5cm (1.2-1.4in) across and carried in clusters of four to seven, on stalks 3-4cm (1.2-1.6in) long. In autumn there are small round red and yellow berry-like fruits. It has oval leaves on the weaker shoots, but on stronger shoots there are three- to five-lobed leaves, dullish green above and paler beneath.

Initial preparation of the soil is very important, and newly planted trees should be securely staked. Once the tree is well-established, little or no pruning is needed. Remove all suckers that arise below the union – where the budding or grafting has been performed. Propagate by budding or grafting.

Malus tschonoskii
- **Full sun**
- **Any fertile soil**
- **Spring flowers, autumn foliage**

An exceptionally colourful deciduous tree of erect pyramidal formation with broadly oval or rounded leaves, 5-13cm (2-5in) long and 4-8cm (1.6-3.2in) wide, and grey-felted beneath. In spring, large white flowers, at first rose-tinted, and 2.5-3.5cm (1-1.4in) across, are produced in clusters of four to six; these are followed in autumn by globose, 2.5cm (1in) wide, fruits of brownish yellow and flushed a purplish crimson. The final glory of the malus is the turning of its foliage in autumn through bronze to brilliant blood-red. Although trees will reach a height of 9-12.2m (30-40ft), their erect conical shape makes them suitable for the smaller garden.

Little, if any, pruning is needed. But remove all suckers that arise below the union – where the budding or grafting has been performed. Propagate by budding in summer, or by grafting in spring, on to the common crab apple.

Matthiola incana 'Giant Imperial Mixed'
- **Sow in early spring**
- **Most soils, preferably alkaline**
- **Sunny position, but tolerates partial shade**

Stocks must be one of the most popular scented annuals. *En masse* this fragrance can be overpowering, however, so do not overplant. The 'Giant Imperial mixture' always provides reliable flowers with a high percentage of doubles. Stems 38-50cm (15-20in) tall carry a profusion of pink, white, lilac, purple and crimson spikes of flowers from early summer onwards. Grey-green soft narrow leaves are formed under the flower heads and give a contrast.

Sow seed for summer flowering during the early spring under glass

Above: Malus floribunda 'Atrosanguinea' is ideal on a lawn, where in spring it bears delicate, pinkish flowers.

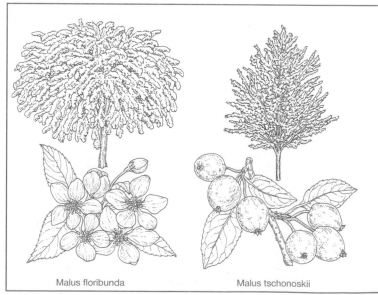

Malus floribunda

Malus tschonoskii

Above: Matthiola incana 'Giant Imperial Mixed' has heavily fragrant, white and purple flowers.

in a temperature of 13°C (55°F). Use a loam-based mixture for sowing and pricking off seedlings. Grow on in a lower temperature, and harden off before planting out 23cm (9in) apart.

Take much care to kill caterpillars at once.

Mentzelia lindleyi
(Bartonia aurea)
- **Sow in early spring**
- **Light and fertile soil**
- **Sunny position**

Known in the past as *Bartonia aurea*, this beautiful hardy annual has lovely golden-yellow flowers resembling the common St John's wort. The masses of stamens in the centre of each bloom are surrounded by five large petals. Fleshy stems carry a profusion of flowers from early summer, up to 45cm (18in) high; the leaves are lovely and somewhat narrow and deep green. The choice of site is

Above: Mesembryanthemum oculatum 'Lunette' is low growing, with clear yellow flowers.

important as mentzelias love the sun; plant them between the front and the centre of an annual or mixed border. Water them well in dry periods. Sweetly scented, they can be used in patio borders.

As they are hardy annuals sow them directly where they are to flower, in early spring. Take out shallow drills and sow the seed, cover over lightly and water if necessary. The resultant seedlings should be thinned to 23cm (9in).

Mesembryanthemum criniflorum
(Dorotheanthus bellidiformus)
(Livingstone daisy)
- **Sow in spring**
- **Most soils, including poor ones**
- **Full sun**

This half-hardy perennial is usually grown as a half-hardy annual, and needs a warm, sunny position. Prostrate in growth but tending to trail, it is an ideal subject for the front of a window box, over a low dry stone wall, or as a drift near the front of a border. Stems are fleshy, green to reddish in colour, with cylindrical leaves. Flowers are up to 4cm (1.5in) across and appear in a multitude of colours including white, orange, red, pink; a number will be bicolours with a white centre.

This tender fleshy annual requires some heat for germination; sow seeds in spring

under glass in a temperature of 16°C (60°F). Prick off seedlings into a good growing medium, harden off in the usual way and plant out at the end of spring at intervals of 23-30cm (9-12in). Alternatively sow in flowering positions at the end of spring, and later thin out.

Mesembryanthemum oculatum 'Lunette'
(Sphalmanthus oculatus)
- **Sow in spring**
- **Ordinary or poor soil**
- **Sunny position**

Also known as *Sphalmanthus oculatus*, this half-hardy annual is very attractive. The variety 'Lunette' is a clear yellow, 8cm (3.2in) high, flowering much earlier than the crinifolium types. Try to plant it near light blue annuals in the border. For formal designs and in window boxes use it along the front edge, or in hanging baskets in a sunny position; in the latter it should be planted before other subjects are included in the design.

Spring sowings are essential if this plant is to flower early. Germination will take two or three weeks if kept at a temperature of 18-21°C (65-70°F). Prick off seedlings into a good growing medium, preferably loam-based. Grow on at a lower temperature and then harden off in the usual way. Plant out at the end of spring at 23cm (9in) intervals.

Matthiola incana 'Giant Imperial Mixed'

Mentzelia lindleyi

Mesembryanthemum criniflorum

Mesembryanthemum oculatum 'Lunette'

Mimulus luteus guttatus

(Mimulus guttatus)
(Monkey flower)

- **Likes moisture**
- **Any soil**
- **Brightly-coloured flowers**

Also known as *Mimulus guttatus*, this short-lived herbaceous perennial is very flamboyant, with brightly coloured flowers from early to late summer. It needs a fair amount of moisture, and the side of a pond or stream would be ideal, otherwise a cool, moist spot on a rock garden. It is definitely not a plant for a hot, sunny situation.

It has 3.6cm (1.5in) wide yellow flowers, blotched with brownish-purple, on 15-20cm (6-8in) long stems. Its leaves are a fresh green. The stems have a tendency to flop, although basically it is not an untidy plant.

Propagation is either by seed in winter, sown under glass and kept at 13-16°C (55-60°F), or more readily by cuttings or division in spring, when new plants are ready within two or three weeks.

Mimulus variegatus

(Monkey flower)

- **Sow in late winter**
- **Ordinary but moist soil**
- **Sunny position or shade**

Nearly all mimulus plants like a moist site and this plant,

raised as a half-hardy annual, is no exception. They are very useful in the bog garden or as a marginal plant along the edge of a waterside planting. They are also at home as ground cover plants in the shade, as long as ground conditions remain moist throughout the growing period. Open trumpet-shaped flowers are produced on stems 30cm (12in) high. Individual blooms are 5cm (2in) long and can be yellow, orange or scarlet, and blotched with brown, maroon or purple. The supporting leaves are obovate to oblong. Dwarf strains are available, but flowers tend to be the same size.

Sow seed in late winter or very early spring under glass in a temperature of 13°C (55°F). Use any good growing medium of a loam-based nature. Pot seedlings into individual small pots, and grow on in cool conditions. Plant in late spring or early summer at 30cm (12in).

Below: Mimulus luteus guttatus displays flamboyant yellow flowers throughout summer.

Monarda didyma 'Cambridge Scarlet'

(Bee balm, Bergamot, Oswego tea)

- **Full sun or partial shade**
- **Moist fertile soil**
- **Summer flowering**

This fragrant hardy herbaceous perennial has nettle-like foliage. It has erect square stems, and at each joint there are pairs of pointed leaves. At its base the leaves form a dense clump. Above the several whorls of leaves, at the top of each stem, there is a

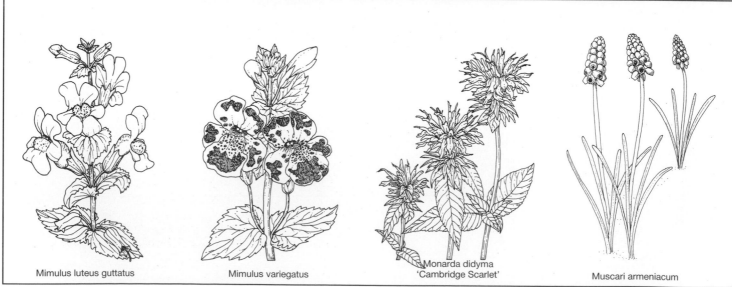

Mimulus luteus guttatus

Mimulus variegatus

Monarda didyma 'Cambridge Scarlet'

Muscari armeniacum

crowded head of hooked scarlet flowers, also in the axil of the pairs of opposite leaves. The flowers have a pleasant fragrance.

The mat-like roots are not as a rule invasive though in well-cultivated soil they can widen, but plants are easily divided in spring, and this should be done about every third year. Be careful to not let the soil dry out. Today, apart from the old favourite 'Cambridge Scarlet', there are several other good varieties: 'Croftway Pink' has clear pink flowers; 'Prairie Night' is a rich violet-purple; 'Snow Maiden'

is white. All are 90cm (3ft) tall, except the bright ruby 'Adam', a showy variety, which is 1m (3.3ft).

Propagate all varieties by division in spring.

Muscari armeniacum
(Grape hyacinth)
- **Full sun**
- **Ordinary well-drained soil**
- **Plant 7.5cm (3in) deep**

This bulbous plant has tight bell-like blue flowers grouped closely together like miniature inverted bunches of grapes on single stems in spring. The plants grow to a height of 25cm (10in), with an equal spread after the leaves separate at flowering time.

Plant the bulbs 7.5cm (3in) deep in a well-drained ordinary garden soil in full sun. After a few years the bulbs will become congested and after the leaves turn yellow the plants need to be lifted, divided and replanted immediately. Sometimes the plants seed themselves; otherwise you can take the seed in summer, sow it in pans, and keep it cool in a cold frame. The seedlings can be transplanted the following year, and will come into flower in another year or so. Occasionally the flowers are spoilt with smut; destroy plants to stop it spreading.

Left: Monarda didyma 'Cambridge Scarlet' has dominantly coloured flowers during summer.

Myosotis alpestris 'Ultramarine'
(Forget-me-not)
- **Sow in late spring**
- **Most soils**
- **Sun or partial shade**

This hardy biennial is strongly recommended for spring bedding, especially in association with wallflowers and tulips. 'Ultramarine' has flowers of a deep indigo blue, produced on very neat compact plants only 15cm (6in) high. The individual flowers are fairly small but have attractive yellow centres. Stems and leaves feel slightly sticky, due to the mass of small hairs. This to some extent has a repellent effect against birds that devastate other spring-flowering plants.

Sow seed in nursery beds in late spring. When seedlings are large enough, plant them in further nursery rows, 15cm (6in) apart. Grow on through the summer, and keep well weeded until the autumn when final planting in flowering positions should be undertaken at 15cm (6in) intervals. Water in as necessary so that wilting is kept to a minimum.

Narcissus bulbocodium
(Hoop petticoat daffodil, Petticoat daffodil)
- **Moist situation**
- **Grows well in grass**
- **Bulbous**

It is surprising that this bulb, which comes from SW France, Spain, Portugal and NW Africa, is so hardy in gardens. Flowering in late winter or early spring, it comes at a thin time of year for flowers. It is excellent value and – given the right conditions – will naturalize in grass. There are many varieties.

The funnel-shaped corona, which gives rise to its common name because of its resemblance to a crinoline, dominates the petals entirely. These 2-5cm (0.8-2in) long trumpets appear on stems up to 15cm (6in) tall. As mentioned, this bulb does well in grass, and will tolerate a peat bank if it is not too shady or too dry.

Propagation is by division every three or four years, digging up and separating the clumps of bulbs. Otherwise the seed can be used, and in many cases it sows itself naturally.

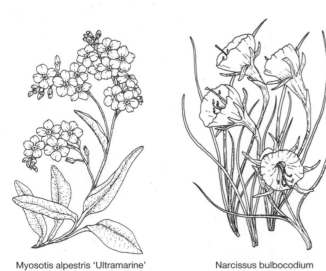

Myosotis alpestris 'Ultramarine'   Narcissus bulbocodium

Above: Muscari armeniacum creates a sea of blue flowers, *resembling spires of tightly packed bunches of grapes, during spring.*

Narcissus cyclamineus

- **Sun or partial shade**
- **Moist well-drained soil**
- **Plant 5cm (2in) deep**

Like all members of the narcissus and daffodil family, this species has the typical cup and petals, but the petals are turned back. This hardy bulb comes from Spain and Portugal, is small, only 20cm (8in) tall, and the trumpets are 5cm (2in) long. This dwarf habit makes it ideal for the rock garden, where its fine delicate form and dark green grass-like leaves keep it in scale with other low-growing plants. The yellow flowers bloom in early spring, and do equally well in the open or in partial shade provided the soil is moist.

Plant the bulbs 5cm (2in) deep and 5cm (2in) apart. They will seed themselves, or in late summer they can be lifted, divided and replanted to allow more space. Treat the plants with a pesticide to keep troubles to a minimum.

Below: Narcissus cyclamineus 'Tête-à-Tête' is bulbous and delicate, ideal for rock gardens.

Narcissus – Large-cupped Types

- **Light shade**
- **Well-drained moist soil**
- **Plant 7.5-10cm (3-4in) deep**

These are large-cupped narcissi, with one flower to each stem, and the cup is more than one third the length of the petals but no longer than them. The group has been sub-divided into three sections: those with the cup darker than the petal colour; those with the cup coloured and the petals white; and those with both the cup and petals white. The cups may be frilled, serrated or plain, and the colours are white, yellow, orange, pink or red. Among the highly prized varieties are 'Fortune', 'Carlton', 'Desdemona', 'Royal Orange', 'Ice Follies', and 'Tudor Minstrel' which has blooms of over 13cm (5in) across. Most of these varieties grow to a height of 45cm (18in).

The mid-green, strap-like leaves should be left to turn yellow and die back without tying them into knots, as this is the period when the bulb takes up nutrition for the next season. Increase by division in the autumn every few years.

Narcissus pseudonarcissus

(Lent lily, Wild daffodil)
- **Sun or light shade**
- **Moist soil**
- **Plant 5cm (2in) deep**

This hardy, bulbous plant has strap-like leaves, and grows to a height of 30cm (12in). The flowers have bright lemon trumpets with very pale yellow petals 5cm (2in) across, and appear in spring. They thrive in a good moist soil, among low grass or in open woodland. They are good for naturalizing where a small daffodil will be in scale with other plants.

This species is easy to grow in a moist soil, and will be happy in either sun or light shade, where it should be planted at a depth of 5cm (2in). If the soil and the situation are to its liking, it will thrive and spread vigorously, forming clumps. After a few years it is advisable to lift the bulbs after the leaves have died back, divide them and replant with 7.5cm (3in) between bulbs. A more natural look is obtained by casting the bulbs over the area and planting them where they have fallen.

Narcissus cyclamineus

Narcissus – large-cupped type

Left: Narcissus pseudonarcissus is suitable for naturalizing in short grass, or in woodland.

Right: Nemesia strumosa, a half-hardy annual, forms a blanket of many-coloured flowers.

Narcissus tazetta

(Bunch-flowered narcissus, Polyanthus narcissus)
- **Sun or semi-shade**
- **Moist soil**
- **Plant 7.5-10cm (3-4in) deep**

This hardy, bulbous plant comes from a wide area spreading from the Canary Islands, through the Mediterranean, North India to China and Japan and is characterized by the bunch of blooms on the flower stem of a single flower. The leaves are strap-like, and the plant will grow to a height of 30-45cm (12-18in). The blooms have white petals 3.8cm (1.5in) wide, with a shallow yellow cup. They have a strong perfume, and will flower in winter - among the earliest to bloom. Some of the varieties are half-hardy.

The bulbs should be planted 7.5-10cm (3-4in) deep in a well-drained moist soil where there is either full sun or partial shade. Gently cast the bulbs over the ground and plant them where they fall, to give a natural random spacing. Every few years the clumps of plants should be lifted, divided and replanted with more space around them to grow.

Narcissus – Trumpet Types

- **Light shade**
- **Moist well-drained soil**
- **Plant 7.5-10cm (3-4in) deep**

In this group the plants all have only one flower to a stem, and the trumpet is longer than the petals. It has been further sub-divided into sections with trumpet and petals yellow, trumpet yellow and petals white, trumpet and petals white, and any other combination. These are all of garden origin, and will grow to about 45cm (18in) tall. In this group are most of the popular daffodils, such as 'King Alfred' and 'Golden Harvest', with large blooms and fluted trumpets 7.5cm (3in) wide in spring.

These do equally well in the garden or forced in pots for earlier flowering. They should be planted in a good moist soil in late summer. Where they are grown in grass, do not use a mower until the leaves have turned yellow and the soil nutrients have been taken up by the bulbs. Lift and divide every few years to encourage large blooms and extra stock.

Nemesia strumosa

- **Sow in early spring**
- **Most soils, but well cultivated**
- **Sunny and slightly moist location**

In the wild, this half-hardy annual is rather untidy, but continued selection and breeding has led to today's more manageable plants. Many self colours are available but mixtures give a wide range of colours: usually included are shades of yellow, cream, pink, crimson, blue and purple. Individual blooms are 2.5cm (1in) across and funnel-shaped; these are carried on erect branching stems of up to 45cm (18in) long. The leaves are pale green and coarsely toothed; some change from green to a pinkish red.

This species is very useful as a bedding plant or in window boxes or other containers. Sow seeds under glass in early spring at a temperature of 16°C (60°F). Only just cover the seed, in boxes or pots of a good loam-based growing medium. Harden off slowly and plant out in flowering positions in early summer, at 15cm (6in) apart. Make a second sowing one month after the first, for succession.

| Narcissus pseudonarcissus | Narcissus tazetta | Narcissus – trumpet type | Nemesia strumosa |

Nemophila menziesii
(Nemophila insignis)
(Baby blue eyes)
- **Sow in spring**
- **Ordinary but moist soil**
- **Sun or partial shade**

Also known as *Nemophila insignis*, this is one of the more notable hardy annuals from California. Plants grow to a height of 23cm (9in), and have spreading slender stems on which deeply cut, feathery, light green leaves are carried. Appearing from early summer, the flowers are buttercup-shaped and of a beautiful sky blue with a white centre. Each bloom measures 4cm

(1.6in) in diameter. This species will tolerate partial shade.

Before sowing, fork in organic material if your soil is on the light side. This will ensure that moisture is retained in hot dry spells so that plants can survive. Sow seeds directly where they are to flower, in early spring. Take out shallow drills and only lightly cover the seed. Thin out seedlings to 15cm (6in) apart. In mild districts autumn sowings carried out in the same way will provide plants for flowering in late spring of the following year.

Below: Nepeta × faassenii, ideal for dry and light soils, has soft lavender-blue flowers.

Nepeta × faassenii
(Nepeta mussinii)
(Catmint)
- **Sunny location**
- **Well-drained soil**
- **Early and late summer flowering**

Cats love nestling in a clump of this hardy, herbaceous perennial. To prevent them sitting on your plants, insert a few prickly twigs; any cat will then soon realize that it is no place for a nap. This plant was for many years called *Nepeta mussinii*. The soft lavender-blue flowers have a long season of bloom from early summer to late summer, and often into early

autumn. The thin grey stems are 45cm (18in) tall.

It is not a particularly long-lived plant, especially on cold clay soils; it needs a light, well-drained soil. On heavy soil, work in sand or gritty material around the plants. Cut the plants back after the first flush of flowers; this encourages more flowers, and provides material to use as cuttings. Plant in spring, where an individual clump is required, putting four plants to a square metre (square yard). Propagate by softwood cuttings in early summer to midsummer.

Below: Nerine bowdenii brightens autumn, with rose or deep pink flowers clustered on tall stems.

Nemophila menziesii

Nepeta x faassenii

Nerine bowdenii

Nicotiana x sanderae 'Nicki Hybrids' F1

Nerine bowdenii
- **Sunny position**
- **Ordinary well-drained soil**
- **Plant just under the surface**

Nerine bowdenii, which comes from South Africa, is a sufficiently hardy bulbous plant to withstand most winters in the temperate zone. It will grow to a height of 60cm (24in). The blooms open in autumn, with up to eight flowers in each cluster. The clusters are 15cm (6in) across, usually rose or deep pink, but there is also a white form. The mid-green leaves are narrow and strap-like.

The bulbs should be planted in either late summer or early spring,

Below: Nicotiana × sanderae 'Nicki Hybrids' have richly scented flowers in many colours.

in an ordinary well-drained soil and in a sunny position. The bulbs are placed just under the surface or, if the soil is light, they can be set deeper – as much as 10cm (4in). Where there are bulbs near the surface they should be covered with a thick layer of compost to protect them. Keep them moist when growing. They can be lifted in spring, divided and replanted to encourage larger blooms.

Nicotiana × sanderae 'Nicki Hybrids' F1
(Flowering tobacco, Jasmine tobacco, Sweet-scented tobacco plant, Tobacco plant)
- **Sow in early spring**
- **Rich, well-drained soil**
- **Sun or partial shade**

The Nicki F1 Hybrids of this half-hardy annual are a lovely mixture of colours including red, pink, rose, lime green and white. Individual blooms are up to 6cm (2.4in) long, formed into loose clusters. Stems bearing the flowers carry large oblong leaves of a light green. This strain is dwarf and reaches only about 25cm (10in) in height. The blooms of this free-flowering cultivar are sweetly fragrant. Use as a bedding plant for formal beds or borders, beneath a window, or on a patio or yard where the scent can be appreciated, especially in the evening.

Sow seeds under glass in early spring, in a temperature of 18°C

(65°F). Seeds should be scattered thinly on top of prepared pots or boxes of a peat-based growing medium. Prick out in the usual way. Harden off and plant out in early summer, 23cm (9in) apart.

Nigella damascena
(Love-in-a-mist, Wild fennel)
- **Sow in early spring**
- **Well-cultivated ordinary soil**
- **Sunny position**

An old favourite, this hardy annual is particularly good for the annual border when planted towards the centre. Growing up to 60cm (24in), the stiff stems carry cornflower-like blooms of blue, mauve, purple, rose-pink or white. Bright green feathery foliage gives a light feeling to the plant. The semi-double blooms are followed by the seedpods, much prized for floral arrangements.

Being hardy annuals, these plants are easy to raise, simply by sowing where they are to flower. Rake down to a fine tilth the area to sow, take out shallow drills in early spring, sow the seeds and lightly cover over. When large enough to handle, thin out the seedlings to 23cm (9in) apart. In mild districts autumn sowings made in the same way will produce

earlier flowering plants the following year. Cut stems for drying when seedpods are a light brown.

Oenothera missouriensis
(Evening primrose)
- **Sunny location**
- **Well-drained soil**
- **Summer and autumn flowering**

This lovely herbaceous perennial ground-hugging plant, which belongs to the evening primrose family, is a native of the southern United States of America. The dark green narrow leaves lie prostrate on the ground, and above them are produced canary-yellow flowers about 7.5cm (3in) across, on 23cm (9in) reddish stems, in succession for many weeks during the summer. The flowers, which open in the evening and last for several days, are followed by equally large seedpods. Often the buds are spotted with red.

This is a superb plant for the front of a border, but to succeed it must have a well-drained soil. It is ideal for the rock garden but allow it sufficient space, because it can spread up to 60cm (24in). Propagate this species by seed in spring.

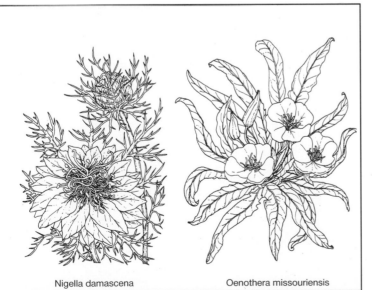

Nigella damascena

Oenothera missouriensis

Above: *Oenothera missouriensis has large, canary-yellow flowers on* reddish stems during summer. Plant in a large rock garden.

Olearia × haastii

(Daisy bush, Tree aster)
- **Sunny position**
- **Any soil, including chalk**
- **Summer flowering**

This bushy evergreen shrub is the hardiest of the olearias. It has a rounded habit, and reaches 1.2-2.7m (4-9ft) tall and 2-2.5m (6.5-8ft) wide. The alternate oval leaves are crowded on its branches; each leaf is 1.2-2.5cm (0.5-1in) long and nearly half as wide, dark shining green above and white felted beneath. The daisy-like white flowers are carried above the foliage, forming flattish clusters 5-7.5cm (2-3in) across. Each flower is made up of white ray florets and yellow disc florets.

For newly planted bushes, only light pruning is necessary in the first few years. If bushes become tall and stems bare, then during spring cut such stems well back into the old wood.

Propagate by taking half-ripe cuttings in late summer.

Onopordon acanthium

(Argentine thistle, Cotton thistle, Scotch thistle)
- **Sunny location**
- **Ordinary soil**
- **Summer flowering**

This hardy biennial is usually found growing in a hardy flower border. It is a handsome tall grey-leaved and grey-stemmed architectural plant. Both leaves and stems are covered with woolly cobweb-like hairs, and on top of its 1.5-2.1m (5-7ft) high stems are carried purplish mauve to pale lilac thistle-like flowers.

These plants seed themselves freely, and once a plant is established the owner will never be without a plant or two in the border. Nevertheless, it is easy to eradicate any unwanted seedlings, or to give them away to friends. Position these plants at the back of the border and allow at least 90cm (3ft) for them to spread. Stake plants, if necessary, in windswept borders. Propagate by seeds sown out of doors in well-drained soil in spring.

Ornithogalum thyrsoides

(African wonder flower, Chincherinchee, Wonder flower)
- **Partial shade**
- **Good soil or potting mixture**
- **Plant 10cm (4in) deep**

This slightly tender bulbous plant from South Africa has up to 30 white, cream or yellow star-like flowers grouped in a tight cluster at the top of the 45cm (18in) stem

Below: Olearia × haastii is a rounded, evergreen shrub with masses of white, daisy-like flowers during summer.

in summer. The mid-green leaves spring from the base of the plant and grow 30cm (12in) long. It is not hardy in the temperate zones where frosts occur, and should be grown in a pot.

Plant the bulbs in a 20cm (8in) pot of rich potting mixture in autumn and keep in a cool greenhouse for early spring flowering. In mild areas the bulbs can be planted out of doors in spring, with 10cm (4in) of soil over them. They should be well covered during the winter months with a thick mulch of bracken, leaf-mould or peat. Seeds can be sown but they will take up to four years to reach flowering size. Generally these are pest-free, but if sooty spots appear on the leaves, treat them with a fungicide, and if this has no effect, destroy the plant to stop the fungus spreading to other plants.

Below: Ornithogalum umbellatum is hardy and bulbous, with star-like white flowers in spring. Plant in grass and shrubberies.

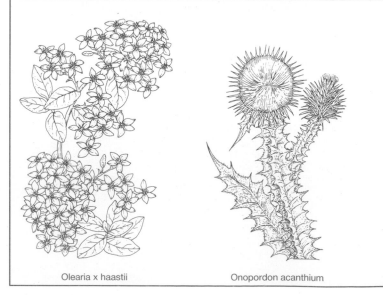

Olearia x haastii   Onoporbon acanthium

Left: Osmanthus delavayi, an evergreen shrub, has tiny, sweetly scented, jasmine-like white flowers in spring. Select a sheltered position for it.

need no atttention and will continue to produce masses of blossom. To increase stock, lift the clumps of bulbs in late summer after the leaves have died down, divide them, and replant with more space. Seeds can be sown, but take up to four years to reach flowering size.

Osmanthus × burkwoodii
- **Sun or light shade**
- **Any good loamy or chalk soil**
- **Spring flowering**

This hardy evergreen shrub was originally known as a bigeneric hybrid between *Osmanthus delavayi* and *Phillyrea decora*; but since the second parent is now called *Osmanthus decorus*, botanists now classify this shrub as a hybrid of *O. delavayi* and *O. decorus*. Whichever name it is sold under, buy it, for it is a real beauty. It has glossy, oval, dark olive-green toothed leaves, 2.5-5cm (1-2in) long. The terminal and axillary clusters of six or seven fragrant white flowers are produced in spring; they are not so sweetly scented as *O. delavayi*, but hardier. It is rather slow in growth, but eventually makes a

dense bushy shrub, 2.7-3.6m (9-12ft) in height and equally wide. Give it plenty of room to expand. It is a very desirable and useful evergreen.

Any pruning needed should be done once flowering has finished. Propagate by half-ripe cuttings, in late spring or early summer.

Osmanthus delavayi
- **Sun or light shade**
- **Any good loamy or chalk soil**
- **Spring flowering**

This hardy evergreen shrub has sweetly scented flowers. It is hardy except in the very coldest and frostiest areas, where it should be grown against a wall or fence. It has small dark green leathery leaves, with tiny dark spots beneath. The leaves are oval in shape and tapered at each end. In spring it has pure white, fragrant, jasmine-like flowers, which are produced in terminal and axillary clusters. In favoured localities it will reach a height of 3m (10ft), and sometimes more in overall width.

Plant this shrub where it will have protection from the overhanging branches of a nearby tree, or in a position where the sun will not reach the bush before the frost is off, so that damage to the flowers will be less. Any pruning needed should be done after flowering.

Propagate by half-ripe cuttings in late summer.

Ornithogalum umbellatum
(Dove's dung, Nap-at-noon, Star of Bethlehem, Summer snowflake)
- **Partial shade**
- **Ordinary well-drained soil**
- **Plant 7.5cm (3in) deep**

This hardy bulbous plant grows to a height of 30cm (12in), with a spread of up to 20cm (8in). In spring, the flower stem carries a profusion of white star-like blooms with green stripes on the outside. The plant is hardy, and ideal for edgings and mass effects, even naturalizing in short grass or in shrubberies.

Plant the bulbs in autumn, in ordinary well-drained soil with 7.5cm (3in) of soil over them in an area where there is some shade. If possible, dig in a good quantity of peat, compost or leaf-mould beforehand. Once planted they

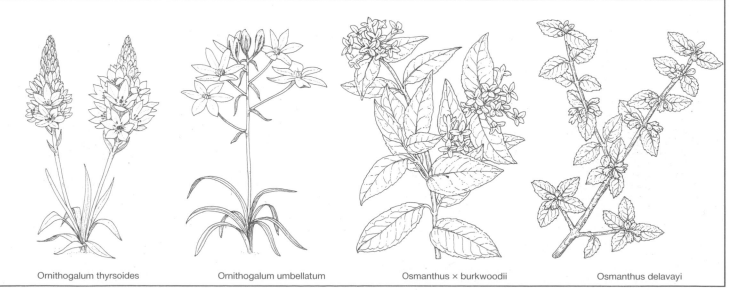

Ornithogalum thyrsoides   Ornithogalum umbellatum   Osmanthus × burkwoodii   Osmanthus delavayi

Osmunda regalis

(Flowering fern, Royal fern)
- **Partial shade**
- **Moist peaty soil**
- **Early spring flowering**

This deciduous hardy perennial needs a moist peaty soil, and is best grown in half shady places, though it can be grown in full sunshine if its roots are constantly in moist soil and the plant is sheltered from cold winds. The sterile, delicate, pale green fronds are 1.2-1.5m (4-5ft) long, whereas the fertile portion may be as much as 1.5-1.8m (5-6ft). As the elegant fronds emerge in spring, they look like shepherds' crooks, and in autumn they take on bright yellow and russet hues. Flower arrangers gather them because they press and dry well.

This fern can be propagated by sowing the spores during summer, but for the amateur, propagation by division in spring is more satisfactory. The mass of black roots needs to be sliced through with a sharp spade.

Oxalis adenophylla

- **Full sun**
- **Sandy peaty soil**
- **Plant 5cm (2in) deep**

These 7.5cm (3in) tall bulbous plants are ideal for the rock garden and edges of borders. They have delicate cup-shaped lilac-pink

flowers 2.5cm (1in) wide in midsummer, and small clusters of leaves that die down in winter.

The bulb-like rhizome should be planted in spring or autumn in a soil that is sandy but enriched with peat, leaf-mould or compost. Plant it 5cm (2in) deep in a sunny place, although it will stand partial shade. Keep the plant moist during

Below: Osmunda regalis, a hardy fern, is ideal for planting by the edge of a stream.

drought. When the bulbs have finished flowering in summer, they can be lifted, divided and replanted with more space around them. This can also be grown as a decorative pot plant, using a 20-25cm (8-10in) pot and ordinary potting mixture. Keep it in the cool until ready to flower, and then bring it indoors. Every alternate year move it to a larger pot with fresh soil, or divide it and keep in the same size pot with new potting mixture.

Above: Oxalis adenophylla reveals its cup-shaped, lilac-pink flowers, with a satin sheen. in clusters in summer.

Paeonia officinalis 'Rubra Plena'

(Old double crimson, Peony)
- **Full sun or partial shade**
- **Rich well-drained soil**
- **Late spring flowering**

Paeonia officinalis is a hardy herbaceous perennial. The variety 'Rubra Plena' is a beautiful old peony, introduced in the sixteenth century. The large heads of double blooms are held above deeply cut foliage on stems 45-60cm (18-24in) high. Apart from 'Rubra Plena' there is the white 'Alba Plena' and the larger flowered light pink 'Rosea Superba Plena'.

Peonies will grow in full sun or partial shade. Choose a site where the plants will not catch the early morning sun, as frosts can injure

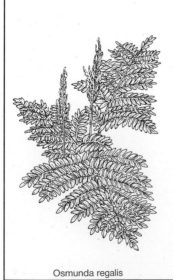

Osmunda regalis

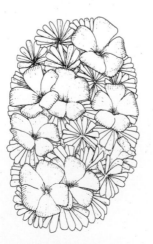

Oxalis adenophylla

Paeonia officinalis 'Rubra Plena'

Paeonia suffruticosa

flower buds. When preparing the site incorporate well-rotted farmyard manure, garden compost or leaf-mould. An application of liquid manure as the buds start to swell will be beneficial. A feed of bonemeal and a mulch of humus should be worked into the soil every autumn. See that these peonies have enough moisture in dry weather.

Propagate them by division in early autumn, or in early spring before new growth starts.

Below: Paeonia suffruticosa 'Rock's Variety' has dominant flowers, white petals blotched dark purple at their bases.

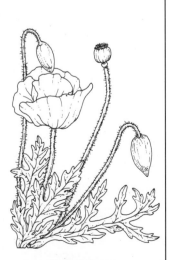

Paeonia suffruticosa
(Paeonia moutan)

(Moutan peony, Peony, Tree peony)
- **Some shade is preferable**
- **Any good garden soil**
- **Spring flowering**

This hardy deciduous flowering shrub is a slow grower, eventually reaching a height of 1.2-1.5m (4-5ft), sometimes 2m (6.5ft) and equally wide. It has gnarled twisted branches with elegant foliage. The doubly pinnate or double ternate leaves are 23-45cm (9-18in) long, dark to mid-green above and bluish grey beneath. The 15cm

(6in) wide flowers are white with a maroon-purple blotch at the base of each petal. *P.s.* 'Rock's Variety' is similar in colour.

Tree peonies need a protected position so that the early morning sun does not harm the blooms before any frost on them has thawed. Peonies need rich well-cultivated soil with liberal mulchings of leaf-mould. The only pruning necessary is to remove any dead wood after flowering. Propagate by grafting on to rootstocks of *P. officinalis* in spring.

Papaver orientale

(Oriental poppy, Poppy)
- **Full sun**
- **Well-drained soil**
- **Early summer flowering**

This hardy herbaceous perennial has flamboyant flowers, on plants that vary in height from 30cm-1m (1-3.3ft). The first colour break came in 1906 with the salmon-pink 'Mrs Perry', 90cm (3ft) tall. To name only a few other varieties: 'Fireball', with double orange-scarlet flowers, 30cm (12in) tall; 'Marcus Perry', orange-scarlet, 75cm (30in); 'Perry's White', 90cm (3ft); 'Curlilocks', ruffled vermilion petals, 75cm (30in); 'Black and White', white flowers with a black centre zone, 1m (3.3ft); and 'Cedric's Pink', with large greyish pink curled petals with a purple-black blotch at the base.

These poppies will thrive in full sunshine in a well-drained soil. Be careful not to let these poppies swamp less vigorous plants. Propagate by root cuttings in autumn or winter.

Papaver rhoeas

(Corn poppy, Field poppy, Flanders poppy, Poppy)
- **Sow in autumn or spring**
- **Light well-drained soil**
- **Sunny location**

From the common wild scarlet field poppy the Rev. W. Wilks made his famous selections from which, in the 1880s, the world-renowned Shirley poppy strain was introduced. This poppy is such an example and is a hardy annual. It is mainly in a range of pink, red and white, but also has bicoloured and picotee forms. Double strains now exist, but the single type are more allied to the original introductions. It can be grown in borders and in the odd pocket towards the back of a rock garden, as long as the position is sunny.

Up to 60cm (24in) in height, the stems carry lovely deeply lobed leaves above which the flowers are borne, about 7.5cm (3in) across.

Sow seeds in spring or autumn. Take out shallow drills where the plants are to flower. Sow seeds and lightly cover with soil. Thin out seedlings to 30cm (12in) apart. Spray against aphids. Flowers appear in early summer.

Papaver orientale

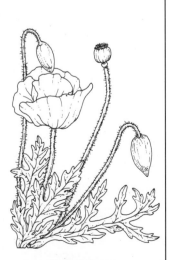

Papaver rhoeas

Above: Papaver rhoeas 'Lady Bird', a hardy annual, creates masses of scarlet poppies with dark centres throughout summer.

Papaver somniferum 'Paeony-flowered Mixed'

(Opium poppy, Poppy)
- **Sow in spring or autumn**
- **Ordinary soil**
- **Sunny position**

The large peony-flowered types of this hardy annual are superb garden plants. Individual double flowers measure up to 10cm (4in) across. Blue-green deeply lobed leaves are carried on smooth stems 75cm (30in) tall. Pink, white, red or purple blooms will appear in early summer and although relatively short-lived they are worth a place in the annual border. The flowers are followed by large bulbous seedpods much prized by flower arrangers.

These poppies are easily grown from seeds sown in the autumn in mild districts, or in the spring elsewhere. Take out drills large enough for the seeds, about 30cm (12in) apart. Cover the seeds lightly with soil. Thin out the seedlings to 30cm (12in) apart. Although fairly tall, these plants should not require staking. Spray them against mildew disease.

Above: Parahebe catarractae is a low-growing shrub with small and delicate purple flowers with darker purple centres.

Parahebe catarractae
- **Well-drained site in scree**
- **Neutral soil**
- **Evergreen**

Related to the veronicas and hebes, where it may sometimes be found listed, this deciduous, low-growing, sub-shrub is well worth growing. Care should be taken to obtain the correct plant; one listed as *Hebe catarractae* is totally different in height and colour.

Parahebe catarractae, its name giving an idea of its behaviour, requires a neutral soil and a little sun. It looks its best when it can tumble down between rocks. It bears ovate mid-green leaves and produces in summer a mass of terminal sprays of loosely borne white flowers, with a purple centre.

Propagation is by soft cuttings taken from midsummer to late summer and inserted in a sandy frame. Make sure to stop them to produce neat plants, which will be ready by the next spring.

Penstemon newberryi
- **Warm, well-drained site**
- **Any soil**
- **Semi-evergreen**

This plant is sometimes confused with *Penstemon menziesii*, which it resembles. This is another genus where there is considerable confusion of names. There are a number of attractive species, whatever their correct names may be, mostly originating in North America. Though technically hardy, they do suffer in severe winters, so a stock of young plants should be kept in reserve. They do well in any open, well-drained soil, but an excess of moisture may kill them.

P. newberryi will form a bushy sub-shrub some 20cm (8in) tall and will spread to 30-40cm (12-16in). Racemes of snapdragon-like pink to rose-purple flowers, about 3-4cm (1.25-1.6in) long, appear in midsummer.

Propagation is by 5-7.5cm (2-3in) long cuttings, taken in late summer or early autumn, which will be ready by the next spring. Seed, sown in winter, is variable.

Pernettya mucronata
- **Full sun or partial shade**
- **Moist loamy lime-free soil**
- **Spring and summer flowers; autumn and winter berries**

This is one of the most decorative hardy evergreen shrubs. It has

nodding cylindrical white flowers produced singly in the leaf axils in spring and summer, followed by 1cm (0.4in) berries in autumn and winter in varying colours of pure white to lilac-pink, purple, crimson and red. The branches are densely covered with alternate, shining, dark green, toothed leaves ending in a sharp point.

It tolerates sun but is equally happy in partial shade. Its chief needs are a moist gritty sand-peat soil.

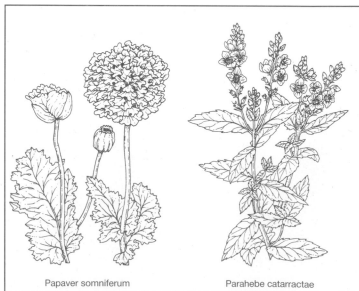

Papaver somniferum

Parahebe catarractae

One male should be planted for up to four or five female bushes in order to have berries, as the sexes are on different plants. There are, however, hermaphrodite forms such as 'Bell's Seedling' and Davis's Hybrids. No regular pruning is needed.

Propagate by seeds, by suckers, or by cuttings in late summer.

Below: Penstemon newberryi prettily scrambles and trails over dry stone walls.

Above: This petunia has deep pink flowers amidst mid-green leaves during the summer.

Perovskia atriplicifolia

(Russian sage)
- **Sunny location**
- **Well-drained soil**
- **Late summer flowering**

This is a sub-shrubby, deciduous, hardy perennial, though more often than not it is grown in herbaceous borders rather than among shrubs. The whole plant has a sage-like odour, especially when it is brushed against. It has coarsely toothed, grey-green foliage, and a profusion of soft lavender-blue flowers during late summer. A variety worth growing is 'Blue Spire', with deeply cut leaves and larger lavender-blue flowers.

This species needs to be grown in full sun, in well-drained loamy soil. An annual pruning should be given just as buds start to break in spring; cut all shoots hard back to the base, leaving perhaps two buds to develop on each. The plant will then send up new shoots 90-150cm (3-5ft) high. Propagate by cuttings of half-ripe shoots in midsummer, inserted in sandy cuttings mixture in a propagating frame.

Petunia Hybrids
- **Sow in early spring**
- **Ordinary well-cultivated soil**
- **Sunny location**

This half-hardy perennial is usually grown as a half-hardy annual. In a good sunny summer, it is second to none for its profusion of colour and versatility of use. Flowers are trumpet-shaped, up to 10cm (4in) across. Leaves and stems will be a mid- to dark green; leaves vary in size but are usually ovate. The whole plant feels sticky to the touch. Use these petunias for a wide range of purposes including formal bedding, borders, containers, window boxes and hanging baskets.

All petunias love a sunny position and benefit from being grown in a well-cultivated soil. Avoid having the soil over-rich, as this can lead to a lot of growth and few flowers. Seeds will need to be sown under glass in early spring. Sow thinly on top of a peat-based growing medium in pots or boxes. Prick off the seedlings into boxes, harden off and plant out in early summer.

Penstemon newberryi

Pernettya mucronata

Perovskia altriplicifolia

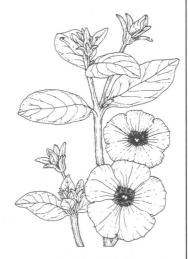

Petunia hybrid

Phacelia campanularia

- **Sow in early spring**
- **Light, sandy, well-drained soil**
- **Sunny site**

This is one of the most striking hardy annuals. The gentian-blue clusters of upturned bell-shaped flowers are worth a place in any annual border. Blooms appear from early summer. Each individual flower has lovely contrasting pale yellow stamens; overall, blooms are about 2.5cm (1in) across. Plants are dwarf and branching in character, about 23cm (9in) high. Stems carry ovate leaves that are cut or toothed along the edge, and dark greyish green in colour. Loved by bees, these plants are ideally suited to the edge of a border or pathway.

In early spring rake down the soil to a fine tilth, sow the seeds thinly in shallow drills where they are to flower and cover lightly. Thin out the subsequent seedlings to 15cm (6in) apart. If your garden is in a relatively mild area, then seeds can be sown in autumn. Plants grown through the winter will flower somewhat earlier. Take care to watch out for slugs.

Below: Philadelphus coronarius 'Aureus' in spring is clothed with bright-golden leaves, which dull as the season progresses.

Philadelphus coronarius 'Aureus'

(Golden-leaved mock orange)
- **Full sun**
- **Any good garden soil**
- **Summer flowering**

This hardy deciduous shrub is one of the sweetest scented shrubs. 'Aureus' is the golden-leaved cultivar; in spring the foliage is a bright golden-yellow, but it becomes duller after midsummer. The oval lance-shaped leaves are 4-8cm (1.6-3.2in) long, and slightly toothed. The creamy white sweetly scented flowers in summer make this golden beauty an ideal fragrant shrub.

It rarely grows to more than 2.7m (9ft), so it is ideal for the small or medium-sized garden. Do not provide too rich a soil, and it will tolerate chalk soils; it is a good shrub for growing in coastal areas. As the flowers are produced on the previous year's shoots, pruning should be carried out as soon as the flowers are over; cut back old flowering wood to strong new growths to encourage healthy flowers the following season.

Propagate by hardwood cuttings in autumn, and insert out of doors.

Below: Phlomis fruticosa bears yellow flowers in whorls amid attractive grey-green leaves on upright stems.

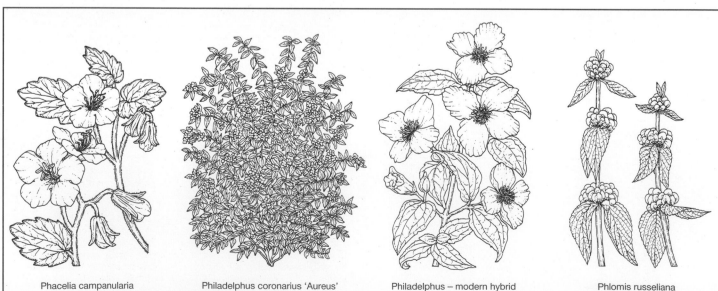

Phacelia campanularia

Philadelphus coronarius 'Aureus'

Philadelphus – modern hybrid

Phlomis russeliana

Philadelphus – Modern Hybrids

(Mock orange)
- **Full sun**
- **Any good garden soil**
- **Summer flowering**

Over the years many beautiful hybrid varieties of this hardy deciduous shrub have been raised and introduced. The following are worthy of space in a small or medium-sized garden. 'Belle Etoile' has fragrant white flowers with a reddish blotch in the centre of each flower. Its height is 1.5-2m (5-6.5ft). The variety 'Sybille' has large, saucer-shaped, fragrant flowers up to 5cm (2in) wide, borne

Above: *Phlox drummondii 'Carnival', a half-hardy annual, becomes smothered with brightly coloured flowers.*

singly or in twos or threes; the blooms are purplish white at the base of each petal, with sea-green foliage, and the shrub is 1.2-2m (4-6.5ft) tall. A third beauty is the double or semi-double white, cup-shaped, fragrant 'Virginal', which reaches 2-2.5m (6.5-8ft) tall. The compact 'Manteau d'Hermine', with creamy white fragrant flowers borne usually in threes, is about 1m (3.3ft) tall.

The general care and cultivation, pruning and propagation of all these varieties are exactly the same as for *P. coronarius* 'Aureus'.

Phlomis russeliana

- **Sunny location**
- **Well-drained ordinary soil**
- **Summer flowering**

This hardy herbaceous perennial is a handsome weed-smothering plant or ground coverer which has large, rough, puckered, heart-shaped, sage-like, grey-green leaves. Among the foliage, stout flower spikes, 75-90cm (30-36in) high, carry whorls of soft, rich, yellow, hooded flowers in early summer to midsummer. Phlomis will grow in ordinary garden soil in an open, sunny location.

Phlomis fruticosa, another member of this genus, is a shrubby evergreen species and is well-known as the Jerusalem sage.

Propagate *P. russeliana* by seed, cuttings or division, in spring or autumn.

Above: *Phlox paniculata 'Windsor', an herbaceous phlox, has beautiful carmine-rose flowers with magenta eyes.*

Phlox drummondii 'Carnival'

- **Sow in spring**
- **Ordinary well-drained soil**
- **Open, sunny site**

This half-hardy annual will give a succession of colour throughout the summer. For a really bright display try the cultivar 'Carnival'. This mixture has pink, rose, salmon, scarlet, blue and violet flowers. These are borne on stems 30cm (12in) high, carrying light green lanceolate leaves. Blooms are produced in early summer as dense heads up to 10cm (4in) in diameter; each individual flower is rounded. These plants are ideally suited for low-growing areas of the garden, especially the rock garden, where pockets can be filled to give constant colour.

In spring, sow seeds under glass in a temperature of 16°C (60°F). Use any good growing medium for sowing. Sow the seeds thinly and cover them lightly. Prick off the young seedlings, when large enough to handle, into boxes or trays. Harden off and plant out in flowering positions in early summer at 23cm (9in) intervals. Dead-head to prolong flowering.

Phlox paniculata

(Phlox decussata)
(Border phlox, Perennial phlox, Summer perennial phlox)
- **Sun or light shade**
- **Light fertile soil**
- **Summer to late summer flowering**

This hardy herbaceous perennial is a well-known garden plant, also called *Phlox decussata*. It develops 15cm (6in) long, terminal, tapering heads of flowers each up to 2.5cm (1in) wide from midsummer to late summer.

There is a wide range of colourful varieties: 'Balmoral' has clear pink flowers and is 1m (3.3ft) tall; 'Blue Ice' has pink buds opening to reveal white flowers with deep pink eyes and is 90cm (3ft) tall; 'Chintz', 75cm (30in) tall, has warm pink flowers with red eyes; 'Fujiyama', 75cm (30in) tall, has pure white flowers. There are also 'July Glow', 75cm (30in) tall, with carmine-crimson flowers; 'Prospero', 90cm (3ft) tall, with pale lilac flowers; 'Vintage Wine', 75cm (30in), with purple-red flowers; and 'Windsor', 75cm (30in), carmine-rose flowers.

Plant in light, fertile and compost-rich soil. Eelworms infest these phlox. To avoid them, increase plants from root-cuttings in autumn or winter. Do not let plants dry out.

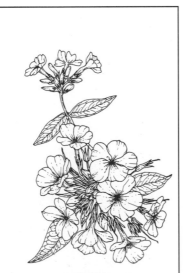

Phlox drummondii 'Carnival'

Phlox paniculata

Phlox subulata 'Daniel's Cushion'

(Moss phlox, Moss pink)
● **Open sunny situation**
● **Neutral soil**
● **Evergreen**

The true species of this technically sub-shrubby plant is never seen in cultivation, having been supplanted by several named varieties, lists of which can be found in specialist catalogues. 'Apple Blossom' is pale pink; 'G.F. Wilson', clear lilac; and 'Temiscaming', a brilliant magenta-red. These form spreading mats up to 45cm (18in) across and no more than 10cm (4in) tall when in flower. They look particularly well cascading over rocks and dry walls, producing their 1.5-2cm (0.6-0.8in) wide flowers *en masse* in late spring.

'Daniel's Cushion', however, has a less spreading tendency, possibly a maximum of 25-30cm (10-12in), and so is suitable for the scree or where it cannot be over-shadowed by taller plants.

Propagation is by soft cuttings taken in midsummer to late summer and inserted in a sand frame.

Above: Phlox subulata 'Daniel's Cushion' is a superb rock garden phlox, or for a scree bed.

Phuopsis stylosa

(Crucinella stylosa)
(Crosswort)
● **Full sun**
● **Sandy or chalky soils**
● **Summer flowering**

This little, mat-forming, hardy, herbaceous perennial from Persia and the Caucasus was for many years known as *Crucinella stylosa*, but now its genus is *Phuopsis*. The 25-30cm (10-12in) stems are clothed in small slender foliage. On these stems are borne pretty little tubular flowers that form a crosswise design, hence its common name, crosswort. The bright rosy-pink flower clusters make an attractive display throughout the summer. It is a first-rate plant for the front of the border or as an edging plant to a path. There are other coloured forms with scarlet and purple flowers. This plant likes sun.

Propagate crosswort by sowing seeds in the open ground in spring, or by division of the roots in early autumn.

Physostegia virginiana

(Obedience, Obedient plant)
● **Sun or partial shade**
● **Any good fertile soil**
● **Late summer flowering**

This hardy herbaceous perennial is well named the obedient plant, because its flowers have hinged stalks and can be moved from side to side and remain as altered on their square stems. The long, narrow, dark green, glossy leaves are toothed and grow in four columns. The dull rose-pink flowers terminate the square tapering spikes, 45-105cm (18-42in) tall. They bloom from summer to autumn, until the frosts spoil their beauty. Physostegia has vigorous stoloniferous rootstocks that spread underground. Give this plant sufficient moisture during dry summer weather.

There are several good varieties: 'Rose Bouquet' has pinkish mauve trumpet flowers; 'Summer Snow', pure white, is about 75cm (30in) high; and 'Vivid' bears rose-crimson flowers on stalks 30-45cm (12-18in) tall.

Propagate by division in spring, or by root cuttings in winter.

Below: Physostegia virginiana 'Rose Bouquet' bears pinkish-mauve trumpet-shaped flowers on spikes in late summer.

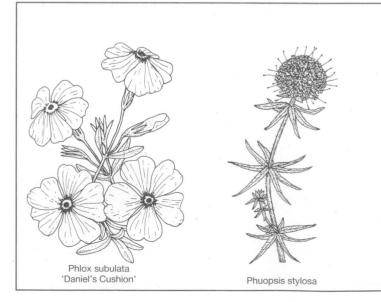

Phlox subulata 'Daniel's Cushion'

Phuopsis stylosa

Picea abies 'Little Gem'
- **Sun or light shade**
- **Deep moist soil**
- **Slow-growing dwarf bush**

This small, evergreen conifer mades a round, bun-shaped bush that is very slow-growing, reaching only about 30cm (12in) tall and wide in ten years, with a possible ultimate size of 60cm (24in) tall and a spread of 1m (3.3ft). The leaves are small and densely packed on to the shrub. It makes an ideal subject for a rockery, or a sink or scree garden.

Seeds can be sown, but careful selection must be made to keep the form and colour of the parent. Cuttings are best taken under nursery conditions; they need to be kept in protected nursery beds for at least two years before being planted out into their final positions. Grow in an open sunny or lightly shaded site that is not exposed to cold winds.

Picea glauca albertiana 'Conica'
- **Full sun or light shade**
- **Moist deep soil**
- **Slow-growing dwarf bush**

This small, evergreen conifer makes a perfect cone shape of soft dense grass-green foliage. It will make a bush with a height of 80cm (32in) and a width of 30cm (12in) at the base in ten years; it reaches 1.2m (4ft) tall and 75cm (30in) wide in 20 years, with an ultimate height of about 3m (10ft). The plant can be trimmed to fit the available space. The cones are brown when ripe, about 2.5cm (1in) long.

The seeds should be sown in pots in spring, and put out the following year into nursery beds for two years. Choose the best forms and colours to plant out into their final positions. Select an open site in full sun or light shade, with a deep moist soil on the acid side. Water young plants in droughts. The young tree has a peak growth rate in spring and summer.

Picea mariana
(Black spruce)
- **Open sun or light shade**
- **Deep moist soil**
- **Medium tree of medium growth**

This medium-sized evergreen conifer normally makes a height of 9m (29.5ft) in cultivation, but often reaches 30m (98ft) in the wild. As a cultivated plant it may be short-lived unless conditions are right, and it keeps a conical shape instead of the tall columnar form of its natural state. In ten years it should grow to 2.4m (8ft) high with a width of 1.5m (5ft); in 20 years it makes a tree 4.5m (15ft) tall with a spread of 3m (10ft). The stems are densely packed on the upper surfaces with dark blue-green needles, which when crushed smell of menthol. Cones are borne in large numbers; they are 3.7cm (1.5in) long, and dark purple, turning brown.

The dwarf form 'Nana' makes a very slow-growing bun shape, 30cm (12in) tall with a spread of 60cm (24in), ideal for the rockery.

Seeds can be sown in pots and grown on for three years before planting out into a deep moist soil, in sun or light shade.

Below: Picea glauca albertina 'Conica' forms an eye-catching cone of grass-green needles.

Physostegia virginiana

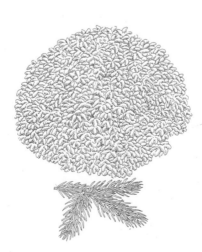

Picea abies 'Little Gem'

Picea glauca albertiana 'Conica'

Picea mariana

Picea pungens 'Koster'
- **Open sun**
- **Deep moist soil**
- **Small to medium tree**

This evergreen conifer is the most popular of the blue spruces, because of its intensely blue foliage, its neat habit of growth and its ability to fit into formal and informal gardens. It grows with an upright pyramidal shape to 2m (6.5ft) tall and 1m (3.3ft) wide in ten years, with an eventual height of some 9m (29.5ft) with a spread of 3m (10ft) in good conditions. Tassels of blue leaves are enriched

with pale blue tufts when new growth breaks in spring. Cones are about 10cm (4in) long, with pointed scales, and ripen to a pale brown colour.

Propagation is preferably by grafting good leader material on to a *P. pungens* stock to encourage a good upright form; this makes the plant scarce and expensive. Growing from seed gives a wide variation in both colour and form. Plant in a good deep moist soil in open sun. Keep young plants moist.

Below: *Pimelea coarctata is a small, prostrate, evergreen shrub, ideal for a rock garden.*

Pieris 'Forest Flame'
- **Sun with overhead shade**
- **Peaty soil or lime-free loam**
- **Spring flowers and foliage**

An evergreen hardy shrub, reaching at least 2m (6.5ft) in height, with attractive flowers and coloured foliage in spring. The oblong lance-like leaves, with a narrowly tapered base, are up to 13cm (5in) long by 3cm (1.2in) wide. 'Forest Flame' comes into growth earlier than the cultivar 'Wakehurst', but the elegant foliage is less vivid. Even so, the young growths are at first brilliant red, later changing through pink to creamy white, and finally to green. The white pitcher-shaped flowers are produced in a cluster of panicles and borne at the end of the previous year's shoots.

'Forest Flame' needs a light lime-free peaty soil, with light overhead shade and a protected position.

Propagate by seed, by half-ripe heel cuttings in summer, or by layering in autumn.

Pimelea coarctata
(Pimelea prostrata)
- **Sunny sheltered position**
- **Lime-free soil**
- **Evergreen shrub**

This is a small-leaved, prostrate, evergreen shrub that has name problems. It may also be listed as

Pimelea prostrata, of which it is said to be a congested form. The plant under description forms flat mats of leafy twigs. The leaves are grey-green and tiny, occasionally rimmed red. The flower heads are borne at the tips of the many twigs. Although the individual waxy white flowers are minute, there are so many that they form a mass. The plant rises only a few centimetres off the ground, but a happy plant will spread to 60cm (24in). After it flowers in early summer, fleshy white berries appear.

It likes a moist but well-drained soil, and where it is happy the stems will root as they spread. This gives a direct clue to propagation, as these rooted twigs can be removed and potted up in autumn. Take care to protect this plant from extreme cold.

Piptanthus laburnifolius
(Evergreen laburnum)
- **Sunny sheltered position**
- **Well-drained or chalky soils**
- **Late spring flowering**

This almost evergreen shrub, deciduous in severe winters, is best planted with the protection of a wall or fence. It will reach a height of 2-2.5m (6.5-8ft). The alternate foliage consists of trifoliate lance-like stalkless leaflets, 8-15cm (3.2-6in) long and about 3-5cm (1.2-2in) wide, dark

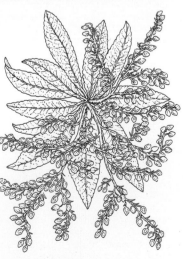
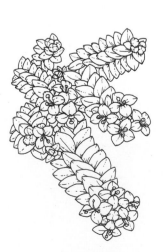

Picea pungens 'Koster'   Pieris 'Forest Flame'   Pimelea coarctata   Piptanthus laburnifolius

green above and bluish grey beneath. In late spring bright yellow laburnum-like flowers are produced and borne on erect stiff racemes 5-8cm (2-3.2in) long.

Although this is a vigorous shrub, it is not long-lived, but can be easily renewed from seeds, which are freely produced. It dislikes root disturbance, so always use pot-grown plants. In mild areas it will remain evergreen, but in colder areas it is often deciduous. Bushes should be allowed to grow freely; if they are

badly frosted, prune hard back in spring, tipping back uninjured healthy branches. Give it some protection. Propagate from seed sown in spring, or from half-ripe cuttings in summer.

Right: Polygala chamaebuxus 'Rhodoptera' is a dwarf shrub with spectacular flowers.

Below: Polemonium foliosissimum has beautifully dissected leaves as well as lavender-blue flowers from early to late summer.

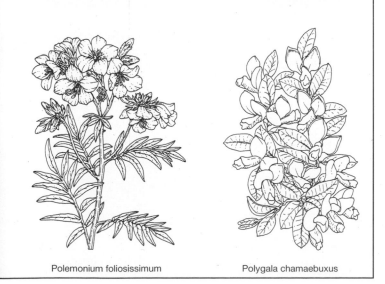

Polemonium foliosissimum

Polygala chamaebuxus

Polemonium foliosissimum

(Charity, Greek valerian, Jacob's ladder)
● **Sunny location**
● **Deep rich fertile soil**
● **Early to late summer flowering**

This hardy herbaceous perennial has been known since Roman times, and its generic name is after King Polemon of Pontus. Most gardeners know *P. caeruleum*, which seeds so freely. *P. foliosissimum* is the longest-lived of these hardy perennials. It has pinnate foliage bearing clusters of pretty five-petalled lavender-blue flowers, enriched by orange-yellow stamens, and massed together on upright 75cm (30in) stems from early to late summer. There is also an earlier flowering variety called 'Sapphire', which has light blue flowers on 45cm (18in) stems and is equally long lived.

Grow polemoniums in a rich fertile soil for a fine display of flowers. Buy plants, as it hardly ever produces seed. Propagate these polemoniums by division in early autumn, after flowering has finished, or in spring.

Polygala chamaebuxus

(Ground box, Milkwort)
● **Light shade**
● **Peaty, leafy soil**
● **Evergreen sub-shrub**

This spreading, ground-hugging evergreen shrub from the Alps does well in gardens. It forms small bushes 10-15cm (4-6in) tall with box-like leaves and a spread of about 20-30cm (8-12in). Cream and yellow flowers tipped with purple appear from late spring to midsummer, up to six flowers on each stem. In the form illustrated, the flowers are carmine and yellow, and thus slightly more spectacular. This may be seen catalogued as 'Purpurea', 'Rhodoptera' or 'Grandiflora'.

Growing as it does on the edge of woodland, this species appreciates a leafy soil and some light shade.

Propagation is by soft cuttings taken in midsummer to late summer and inserted in the shaded peat frame. Pot on, making sure to pinch out the tips to obtain a bushy plant. The plants can be divided in spring.

Polygonatum × hybridum
(Solomon's seal)
- **Sun or shade**
- **Fertile retentive soil**
- **Late spring flowering**

This is a most graceful hardy herbaceous perennial, with fat rhizomatous roots that need to be grown in groups. The 90cm (3ft) stems, which have a pretty arching habit, are clothed with stalkless, alternate, broad, ribbed, lance-like foliage. On the opposite side to each leaf, pretty little greenish white fragrant bells hang down from horizontal arching stems. Gather when in bud and take them indoors for their scent.

The rhizomes should be just below soil level. Solomon's seal is happiest in a retentive soil well endowed with leaf-mould or well-rotted garden compost. Propagate it by division in autumn or spring.

Foliage can be skeletonized by the Solomon's seal sawfly. At the first sign of a holed leaf, spray with an insecticide.

Polygonum affine 'Darjeeling Red'
(Fleece flower, Knotweed)
- **Any situation**
- **Any soil**
- **Ground cover**

This is a hardy herbaceous perennial. It is vigorous, and covers an area up to 45cm (18in) across and it is invaluable for its upright spikes of clear pink flowers in late summer and early autumn. 'Darjeeling Red' is as vigorous, but the 15cm (6in) flower spikes are deep pink. The narrow dark green leaves turn bronzy red in winter, finishing up as an acceptable russet-brown in midwinter.

Any soil or situation will suit this species, but perhaps full shade and damp would not encourage it to produce so many flowers. This is an accommodating and completely hardy plant. It may swamp less vigorous plants.

Propagation is by division in early spring as growth begins; plant out direct or pot up in a normal compost.

Above: Polygonum vacciniifolium is low-growing and spreading, ideal for clambering over large rocks and dry stone walls.

Polygonum vacciniifolium
(Fleece flower, Knotweed)
- **Sunny situation**
- **Any soil**
- **Ground cover**

The spikes of this vigorous, mat-forming, evergreen perennial extend the flowering season well into the autumn and it is sometimes possible to pick a small bunch of its pink spikes in midwinter. Although it will cover the ground, it looks best cascading down a dry wall or over a rock face. The small pointed oval leaves take on autumn tints, and the slender rose-pink flower spikes rise 5-10cm (2-4in) from the flat mat.

P. vacciniifolium will give of its best in a light well-drained soil and sunny position, although it is quite hardy. Do not give too rich a diet, or it may produce soft leafy growth instead of flowers. Despite its vigorous habits it is by no means invasive, and can easily be kept under control.

Propagation is by division in spring or autumn, or by cuttings taken from midsummer onwards and inserted in the sand frame.

Above: Polygonum affine 'Darjeeling Red' forms a dense mat, with spikes of deep pink flowers in late summer.

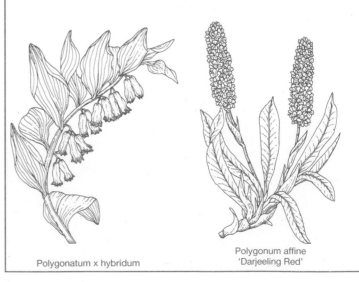

Polygonatum x hybridum

Polygonum affine 'Darjeeling Red'

Right: Potentilla crantzii, low-growing and tufted, has broad-petalled yellow flowers.

Portulaca grandiflora
(Eleven o'clock, Rose moss,
Sun plant)
- **Sow in spring**
- **Ordinary well-drained soil**
- **Full sun**

Originating from Brazil, this half-hardy annual has now come into its own as a worthwhile plant for the annual border or (more especially) for pockets in the rock garden. In some areas they can be temperamental but given a good sunny site they should thrive well on most soils. The flowers of *P. grandiflora* are produced on semi-prostrate stems of a reddish colour, usually up to 23cm (9in) in height. Red, purple, rose, orange-scarlet, yellow and white, the blooms can be over 2.5cm (1in) across. Each centre has pronounced yellow stamens. Leaves are narrow, round and fleshy.

Sow seed in early spring under glass, in a temperature of 18°C (65°F). Use any good growing medium for this purpose and for the subsequent pricking-off of seedlings. Harden off in a cold frame and plant out in early summer, 15cm (6in) apart. Alternatively, sow where they are to flower, in mid-spring. Water established plants only in extreme temperatures.

Potentilla atrosanguinea
(Cinquefoil)
- **Full sun**
- **Fertile well-drained soil**
- **Early and late summer flowering**

The best-known variety of this hardy herbaceous perennial is 'Gibson's Scarlet', which has brilliant single red flowers on 30cm (12in) stems from midsummer to late summer. Larger-flowered varieties include the double orange-flame 'William Rollison', also the double mahogany-coloured 'Monsieur Rouillard'; and the grey-foliaged 'Gloire de Nancy', which has semi-double orange-crimson flowers almost 5cm (2in) across, on 45cm (18in) branching stems.

The potentillas, with strawberry-like foliage, are best in full sun, but can tolerate partial shade. They enjoy good well-drained soil, but if the soil is too rich it results in extra lush foliage at the expense of the flowers. These potentillas sprawl, so give ample space; plant in groups.

Propagate by division in spring or autumn.

Potentilla crantzii
(Cinquefoil)
- **Sunny exposure**
- **Any soil**
- **Herbaceous**

This hardy herbaceous perennial is an inhabitant of grassy meadows in the Alps, North America and Asia. It forms a tuft of 5-15cm (2-6in) stalks, with small palmate leaves and broad-petalled yellow flowers blotched orange at the base of each petal.

The flowering period in gardens is midsummer to late summer, and the length of the flowering stem depends on the plant's environment and whether it is drawn up by its neighbours. It does well on a light open soil and in full sun, where it will flower well. In its native habitat it lives in a limy soil, but in cultivation it is quite accommodating in this respect.

There are two ways of propagating this plant: by seed, in late winter or early spring, though this may not result in the right plant; and by division in the autumn, which is preferable.

Polygonum vacciniifolium

Portulaca grandiflora

Potentilla atrosanguinea

Potentilla crantzii

Potentilla 'Elizabeth'
(Cinquefoil)
- **Sun or partial shade**
- **Any good soil**
- **Flowers from late spring to early autumn**

The hardy, deciduous shrubby potentillas are robust and free-flowering; there are many varieties and hybrids. 'Elizabeth' is probably a hybrid between *P. arbuscula* and *P. dahurica* var. *veitchii*; and originally it was grown under the species *P. arbuscula*. This deciduous dome-shaped bush is about 1m (3.3ft) high, and as much in width. From late spring to early autumn it is adorned with large, rich, primrose-yellow strawberry-like flowers up to 4cm (1.6in) in diameter. Today there are many potentillas to choose from: 'Katherine Dykes' has primrose-yellow flowers, and 'Red Ace' has vermilion-flame backed by pale yellow flowers.

To keep potentillas vigorous, occasionally remove old worn-out stems down to ground level. They thrive in any good garden soil, and do well in full sun, but also tolerate partial shade. Propagate by seeds in late winter, or by half-ripe cuttings in late summer.

Below: Potentilla 'Elizabeth' is a hardy hybrid with bright-faced yellow flowers throughout summer.

Primula denticulata
(Drumstick primula)
- **Any situation**
- **Any soil**
- **Herbaceous**

This hardy perennial is usually grown as an annual or biennial, and is one of the easiest, most reliable and most accommodating plants for the rock garden. Its globose drumstick heads of flowers vary from pure white to deep rose-red. There are several named forms, but self-sown seedlings provide sufficient variation if you begin with a good colour form. The foliage is tough and strong – almost coarse – with the flower heads rising from the centre of a tuft in early spring.

They thrive best in moist loam, but would do well planted at the base of a rock in the cool. This is a striking plant.

Propagation is best done by seed in midsummer. Sow in normal soil, and the young plants will be ready by the next spring. Any good colour forms should be increased by root cuttings taken in late summer.

Primula juliae
- **Cool situation**
- **Leafy soil**
- **Evergreen**

This hardy perennial forms mats of heart-shaped leaves on a tangle of underground stems or rhizomes. These in turn produce clusters of short-stemmed magenta flowers, about 10cm (4in) tall, which nestle in the tufts of leaves.

It is a very easy plant on most soils, given a cool site, but its preference is for a leafy humus. It has hybridized with other species to form some well-known hybrids: *Primula* × 'Garryarde' with bronze flushed leaves, or the well-known 'Wanda', with claret-coloured

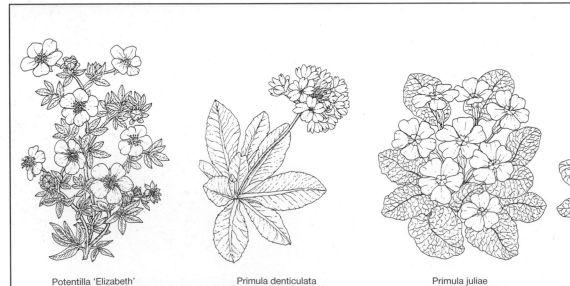

| Potentilla 'Elizabeth' | Primula denticulata | Primula juliae | Primula viallii |

flowers sometimes appearing in midwinter.

Propagation is by division in late summer, planting direct into the garden or potting up for distribution. The roots may well be entangled and will need firm pulling apart, particularly in older specimens.

Below: Prunus 'Cheal's Weeping' becomes smothered in double, deep pink flowers in spring.

Primula viallii
- **Light shade**
- **Light rich soil**
- **Herbaceous**

The comparison of this hardy perennial to an 'elegant red hot poker' (*Kniphofia*) is apt, for the distinctive upright flower spikes have just that appearance. The scarlet buds open to reveal small lavender flowers. The 7-12cm (2.75-4.75in) long dense spikes are on a flower stalk of a total height of 30cm (12in) and appear in midsummer. The narrow lanceolate leaves form a tuft and the flowers are slightly scented.

Although this plant needs a moist soil, it also requires the ground to be well-drained – not always an easy combination to achieve.

Propagation is by division of congested clumps in early spring or by sowing fresh seed immediately after it has been gathered.

Prunus – Japanese Cherries
(Japanese cherry)
- **Full sun**
- **Any well-drained soil**
- **Spring flowering**

The following two deciduous trees are especially suitable for small and medium-sized gardens. The erect *Prunus* 'Amanogawa' is a columnar tree which can eventually become 5m (16.4ft) tall. At first the young foliage is yellowish, before turning green. In early to mid-spring this tree is bedecked with fragrant semi-double soft pink flowers, and in autumn it has coloured foliage.

Where an attractive pendulous tree is wanted, grow 'Cheal's Weeping'. This small tree has attractive arching branches covered with deep pink double flowers. The young leaves are bronze-green, changing later to a glossy green; it is also colourful in autumn. Mature specimens can be 4.5m (15ft) or taller. To encourage this cherry to flower freely, pinch out the tips of all lateral shoots when they are 1-1.2m (3.3-4ft) long. Propagate both these cherries by budding in the summer, or by grafting in early spring on to appropriate stocks.

Below: Prunus laurocerasus 'Otto Luyken' develops candle-like white flowers in spring.

Prunus laurocerasus 'Otto Luyken'
- **Sun or dappled shade**
- **Good fertile soil; not chalk soils**
- **Spring flowering**

A low-growing, hardy, evergreen shrub 1-1.2m (3.3-4ft) tall with a spread of (eventually) 2.1-2.7m (7-9ft). It has glossy, deep green, leathery foliage; the leaves almost 2.5cm (1in) wide, and pointed at either end. The leaves are thickly set on ascending branches, which grow at a semi-erect angle from the ground. This free-flowering variety produces vertical terminal racemes of white flowers. It is outstanding for small or medium-sized gardens.

Normally pruning will not be necessary, but if it has to be done, choose spring or early summer.

Propagate during the summer by hardwood cuttings inserted out of doors in a border facing away from the sun.

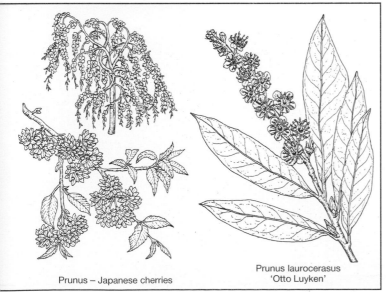

Prunus – Japanese cherries

Prunus laurocerasus 'Otto Luyken'

145

Prunus sargentii
(Sargent cherry)
- **Sunny position**
- **Any fertile loamy neutral soil**
- **Spring flowering**

This splendid deciduous ornamental tree reaches 7.6-10.7m (25-35ft) with a spread of 5.5-7.6m (18-25ft); these measurements are for mature trees. The oval, sharply toothed slender pointed leaves are 5-10cm (2-4in) long and half as wide. The young foliage is coppery red, changing to orange-scarlet in early autumn. The tree flowers early in spring. Its large, deep, blush-pink single flowers, 3.5-4cm (1.4-1.6in) across, are borne in clusters of two to six on long stalks. The bark is a pleasing dark chestnut-brown.

Plant *Prunus sargentii* in an open sunny position. Any pruning necessary should be done either just before or just after flowering. Take care to remove suckers from the stock.

Propagate by budding in summer, or by grafting in spring.

Prunus subhirtella 'Pendula'
(Weeping spring cherry)
- **Full sun**
- **Any fertile loamy neutral soil**
- **Spring flowering**

Prunus subhirtella 'Pendula' is an excellent pendulous, deciduous

tree for a small garden, as it reaches only 3.6-5.5m (12-18ft) in height with a spread of about 6m (20ft). The tiny pale pink blossoms are freely produced in spring on the base branches of this deciduous weeping tree.

Another form of *P. subhirtella* is the cultivar 'Autumnalis', which grows to 5-6m (16.4-20ft) tall, producing almond-scented semi-

Below: Prunus sargentii creates a mass of deep blush-pink single flowers in spring. The leaves turn orange-scarlet in autumn.

double white flowers from late autumn throughout the winter until early spring. It makes a wide-branched small tree with a dense twiggy crown. The autumn apricot tints are very attractive.

No regular pruning is necessary. Propagate by budding in summer, or by grafting on to suitable stocks in spring. Remove any suckers which arise from the stocks.

Above: Pseudotsuga menziesii 'Fletcheri' forms a wide-spreading, dwarf conifer.

Pseudotsuga menziesii 'Fletcheri'
(Pseudotsuga glauca 'Fletcheri')
- **Open position**
- **Deep moist well-drained soil**
- **Slow-growing dwarf shrub**

This evergreen conifer is also called *P. glauca* 'Fletcheri'. It forms an irregular round bush with a flat top and may eventually reach 2m (6.5ft) high and wide. In ten years a plant 35cm (14in) tall and with a similar spread can be expected; it will reach 60cm (24in) in both

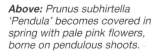

Above: Prunus subhirtella 'Pendula' becomes covered in spring with pale pink flowers, borne on pendulous shoots.

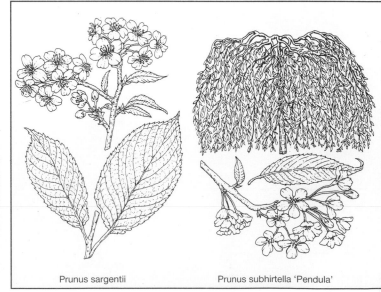

Prunus sargentii

Prunus subhirtella 'Pendula'

Above: Ptilotrichum spinosum, a diminutive shrublet, has white flowers and greyish leaves.

height and width in 20 years. This size makes it ideal for a rockery or border, where it can grow undisturbed for years. The dense foliage is arranged on each side of the branch, with short blue-green needles; in spring the plant has a spotted effect because of the pale buds opening on the branch ends. It can be pruned to shape.

This tree rarely produces cones. Propagate by either cuttings or grafting. The young plant should be kept under nursery conditions for several years to ensure that the graft is satisfactory or the cutting healthy. Also keep young plants watered. Plant in an open position with a moist well-drained soil, preferably acid or neutral.

Ptilotrichum spinosum

(Alyssum spinosum)
● **Full sun**
● **Any good well-drained soil**
● **Evergreen shrublet**

This small, evergreen shrublet comes from the rocks and screes of southern France and central and southern Spain. It has a wildly confused nomenclature, and may be listed as *Alyssum spinosum*. It forms a much-branched little shrub with small grey leaves, which can spread up to 40cm (16in). The small flowers are white or pink, and you should see it in flower before purchasing.

This species is easy to cultivate; it is not particular about its requirements, apart from needing some sunshine and soil with good drainage.

Seed is the best method of propagation, but germination is not easy, so keep a look-out for self-sown seedlings, which can be dug up and potted in early autumn. Take care not to damage the root system too much.

Pulsatilla vulgaris

(Pasque flower)
● **Open situation**
● **Likes some lime**
● **Herbaceous**

This hardy herbaceous perennial is one of the glories of alpine pastures and chalk downs, from England to the Ukraine. In cultivation this plant makes bushy clumps, and when mature these produce up to two dozen dark to pale purple cup-shaped flowers on 25-30cm (10-12in) stems; the flowers can be as wide as 8.5cm (3.3in). The foliage is hairy and deeply cut, resembling a fern or carrot leaf, and after flowering there appear most attractive fluffy seed heads.

This plant is very easy to cultivate, given a sunny spot and a good soil, but it appreciates some lime, which could be given as limestone chippings.

Propagation is easy by seed, which germinates quite quickly after midsummer sowing. Water well until the foliage dies down, and plant out the following spring. Good forms of pulsatilla can be increased by root cuttings. Do not move this plant, once it is established.

Puschkinia scilloides

(Lebanon squill, Striped squill)
● **Sun or partial shade**
● **Good sandy garden soil**
● **Plant 5cm (2in) deep**

This spring-flowering hardy bulbous plant from Asia Minor is highly suitable for growing in low grass, in rockeries, or as a pot plant in a cool greenhouse. It grows to a height of 20cm (8in), with mid-green strap-like leaves and six-petalled bell-shaped flowers of silvery-blue, 1.25cm (0.5in) long, with a greenish blue stripe in the centre of each petal. There are up to six blooms on each stem.

In autumn, plant the bulbs 5cm (2in) deep in a good sandy garden soil, in either sun or partial shade, and leave them untouched unless you need to increase your stock. This can be done when the leaves have died down; lift the plants and remove offsets, dry them and then replant. This is far quicker than growing by seed, which can take up to four years to mature. Where possible leave the plants to form mats or carpets of flowers in drifts under mature trees or shrubs.

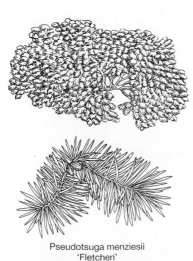

Pseudotsuga menziesii 'Fletcheri'

Ptilotrichum spinosum

Pulsatilla vulgaris

Puschkinia scilloides

Pyracantha 'Watereri'
(Firethorn)
- **Prefers sun**
- **All good garden soil, or chalk**
- **Summer flowers; autumn fruits**

Pyracantha 'Watereri' is probably a hybrid between *P. atalantioides* and *P. rogersiana*, the first parent a tall and not so spiny evergreen, the other parent shorter and very spiny; both have an erect habit. 'Watereri' is dense and twiggy, making a vigorous bushy, evergreen shrub growing to 2.5-3m (8-10ft) in height and at least as wide, sometimes wider. In early summer, bushes are smothered in foamy clusters of white flowers, followed in autumn by masses of bright red berries. Pyracantha makes a handsome free-growing bush.

The only pruning needed is to keep bushes within bounds.

Propagate by cuttings of the current year's growth with a heel in late summer, or by hardwood cuttings in autumn.

Pyrus salicifolia 'Pendula'
(Willow-leaved pear)
- **Full sun**
- **All types of fertile soil; excellent in lime soils**
- **Flowers in late spring**

Pyrus salicifolia 'Pendula' is a superb deciduous tree for a small or medium-sized garden, and looks good even when not in flower. Well-grown standard trees can be anything from 4.5-7.6m (15-25ft) tall, with a spread of 7.6m (25ft) for a mature tree, but it is easy enough to keep them within bounds. Until early summer the foliage is covered with silky white down, later changing to silvery grey, which it keeps until autumn. In spring pure white flowers are produced in small closely packed clusters.

Newly planted specimens will need to be securely staked, especially if the tree has been budded or grafted near the base, but even top-worked trees – those that were budded or grafted to a standard tree stock – will need similar support at first. No pruning is usually necessary. Plant only dwarf shrubs beneath this weeping tree.

Propagate by budding in the summer or by grafting in spring, on to suitable stocks.

Ramonda myconi
- **Semi-shade**
- **Acid soil**
- **Evergreen**

This hardy, rosette-forming evergreen plant is found growing on rocks in the Pyrenees, where it makes flat rosettes of slightly woolly dark green crinkled leaves. The flat-faced 2.5-4cm (1-1.6in) wide flowers appear on 10-15cm (4-6in) stems in late spring. They are lilac-blue with prominent golden stamens.

This is one of the plants that benefits from being planted on its side to prevent winter wetness from nestling in the hairy rosettes. It is ideal for a north-facing aspect, planted in a rock crevice or between peat blocks. Though it likes a leafy soil, it must have good drainage. It is not a plant for a hot sunny alkaline soil.

If you want this plant in quantity, seed is the best method of propagation; you may then get some of the pink- or white-flowered forms germinating.

Below: Pyrus salicifolia 'Pendula' has silvery-grey leaves and white flowers in spring.

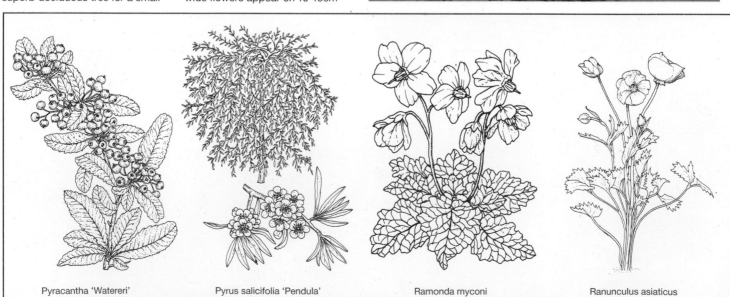

| Pyracantha 'Watereri' | Pyrus salicifolia 'Pendula' | Ramonda myconi | Ranunculus asiaticus |

Above: Ramonda myconi forms a rosette of leaves and lilac-blue flowers with golden stamens.

Ranunculus asiaticus

(Persian buttercup)
- Sunny position
- Ordinary garden soil
- Plant 5cm (2in) deep

These tuberous plants are hardy in milder areas, but in colder parts they should be kept in a frost-free place during winter. Most of these plants have deeply cut leaves of mid-green, and semi-double blooms up to 7.5cm (3in) wide that are fine as cut flowers because they last well.

At first sight they look a little like anemones, with flowers of crimson, pink, orange, gold or white.

They bloom in early summer, and should be placed in the sun in a good soil that has been well dug over with plenty of compost, peat or well-rotted manure added. The tubers should be planted at any time from midwinter to spring, 5cm (2in) deep, with the claw-like roots pointing downwards. In less mild areas the plant should be lifted when its leaves turn yellow; dry off the root system in the sun, and store in a frost-free place until replanting in spring. At this time the tubers can be divided to increase your stock.

Ranunculus ficaria 'Flore Plena'

(Double lesser celandine)
- Open or semi-shaded site
- Damp leafy soil
- Herbaceous

The perennial, fibrous-rooted British plant, lesser celandine, is far too invasive to be considered for planting in a garden, but it has some attractive colour forms – white, creamy yellow and copper. It also has a double form, 'Flore Plena', which is a rich double yellow, and less badly behaved than the type species. The flat glossy heart-shaped leaves are attractive, with silver and mahogany mottling.

This species should be planted in the dampest corner in a leafy soil; it does not mind some sun or mild shade.

Propagation is by division at almost any time of the year, provided the plants can be kept moist.

Below: Ranunculus gramineus develops yellow, buttercup-like flowers on tall stems.

Ranunculus gramineus

- Sow in early spring
- Ordinary soil
- Sun or partial shade

This herbaceous perennial is a member of the buttercup family and an extremely valuable plant to have in the garden. Buttercup flowers are produced in sprays on 30cm (12in) stems. The leaves are grey-green and grass-like. Appearing from late spring to midsummer, the yellow blooms are 2cm (0.8in) in diameter, shiny in texture and very free flowering. Mainly used in drifts in slightly moist areas, these plants will also give a good account of themselves in most borders.

Raise plants each year from seed by sowing in a frame or under cloches. Sow directly into the ground during early spring in shallow drills. Thin out the seedlings and remove the frame top or cloche in mid-spring. Grow on until autumn, then plant in final flowering positions. Keep young plants cool through the summer months.

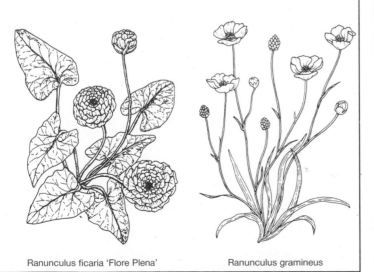

Ranunculus ficaria 'Flore Plena'　　　Ranunculus gramineus

Above: Reseda odorata is a hardy annual that for centuries has been grown for its sweetly scented summer flowers.

Reseda odorata

(Common mignonette, Mignonette)
- **Sow in early spring or autumn**
- **Most soils except very acid ones**
- **Sunny location**

Having a very distinctive sweet scent, this hardy annual has long been a favourite. Flowers are carried on branching upright stems 75cm (30in) in height. Individual flowers are made up of very small petals in the centre of which is a mass of orange tufted stamens; clusters of these blooms are formed into a loose head. Leaves are a light green and spathe-shaped, smooth and terminating just below the blooms.

Sow seeds where they are to flower, in early spring or autumn. Take out drills and lightly cover the seed. To assist germination and better-shaped plants, firm the soil well after sowing, either with the back of the rake or by treading lightly with your feet. Thin out subsequent seedlings to 15-23cm (6-9in) apart. Do not overwater mature plants. Flowers will appear from early summer onwards.

Rhododendron – Deciduous Hybrid Azaleas
- **Light shade**
- **Lime-free soil**
- **Late spring and early summer flowering**

These deciduous, ericaceous shrubs need lime-free soil, peaty, medium or light loams; clay or heavy soils must be lightened. Botanically, azaleas are rhododendrons. Ghent 'Nancy Waterer' is large, and a brilliant golden-yellow; Ghent 'Daviesii' is white with a pale yellow eye, and very fragrant; Knap Hill 'Annabella' is bright orange, opening to golden-yellow; and Occidentale 'Irene Koster' is rose pink and fragrant; all four reach 2m (6.5ft). Mollis 'M. Oosthoek' is a deep-orange red; Ghent 'Narcissiflora' is pale yellow and double; both are 1.5m (5ft). Rustica 'Norma' is rose-red with a salmon glow, double, 1.2m (4ft) tall.

On heavy or poor soils work in well-rotted farmyard manure or use leaf-mould or well-moistened peat. No regular pruning is needed. Take care to remove the seedpods.

Propagate by half-ripe cuttings in summer, or by layering in late spring or early summer.

Rhododendron – Evergreen Azaleas
- **Dappled shade**
- **Lime-free soil**
- **Late spring flowering**

The evergreen azaleas at one time were all called Japanese azaleas, but over the years they have been so freely hybridized that it is, in our case, sufficient to class them as evergreen azaleas. All are late spring flowering, about 1m (3.3ft) tall and good ground cover plants. The obtusum azaleas have horizontal, dense branches and create wide-spreading shrubs. 'Mikado' is salmon-orange; 'Apple Blossom' has hose in hose flowers, white tinged with pink; 'Hatsugiri' is magenta-purple; 'Hinomayo' is a clear pink; 'Hinodegiri' is bright crimson; 'Shin-seikai', also hose in hose, is white; and 'Amoenum' is very hardy and wide-spreading, rose-purple or brilliant magenta.

They prefer some shade as in full sun their flowers are apt to be scorched. During very dry weather and certainly in times of drought, keep their roots moist. Other particulars as for the deciduous azaleas.

Below: Rhododendron 'Blue Diamond' is an evergreen hybrid with rich lavender-blue flowers during spring.

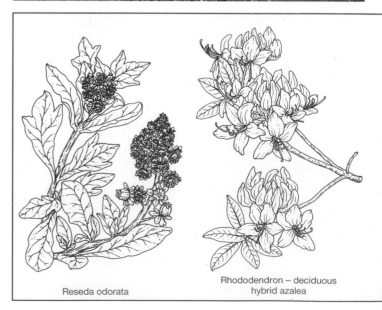

Reseda odorata

Rhododendron – deciduous hybrid azalea

Right: Rhus typhina is a deciduous shrub famed for its deeply dissected leaves that turn rich colours in autumn.

Rhododendron – Hardy Hybrids
- Full sun or dappled shade
- Well-drained lime-free soil
- Spring and early summer flowering

These hardy hybrids are evergreen, and include many varieties. 'Pink Pearl' has large trusses of frilly-edged flesh-pink flowers, paling later; 'Goldsworth Orange' is apricot or orange; and 'Unique' is a pale ochre-yellow flushed with pink. These three are all 2m (6.5ft). 'Britannia', with gloxinia-shaped flowers of cerise scarlet and light green foliage, is 2.5m (8ft). 'Sappho', mauve in bud, later becoming white with dark blotches, is 1.8m (6ft) tall. 'Doncaster' (very hardy) is red with dark spots.

The hardy hybrid rhododendrons are lime-haters, and happiest in moist sandy loam enriched with leaf-mould, moistened peat or well-rotted farmyard manure. Rhododendrons are surface-rooted, so do not plant too deeply. Planting can be done between early autumn and early spring. If they become straggly or too large, prune them back in very late winter or early spring. Remove faded flower heads. Propagation is as for deciduous azaleas.

Rhodohypoxis baurii
- Sunny position
- Well-drained peaty soil
- Bulbous

It was long thought that this dwarf bulb from South Africa was not too hardy, but it has now been in cultivation long enough to prove otherwise. Tufts of pale green hairy linear leaves appear in late spring, followed by the distinctive flat pink flower heads with overlapping petals, which are just above the leaves and about 8cm (3.2in) tall.

This plant thrives in sunshine and a warm pocket at the base of some rocks, but it is surprising how well it will tolerate extreme winter conditions. However, it does not like wet conditions. There are some good colour forms in circulation, from pale to deep rose, and there is a particularly good clear white.

Propagation is simply by division: lift the clumps of bulbs after flowering in late summer, separate and replant the larger ones, potting up the smaller bulbs for later planting. Seed can be sown in early spring.

Rhus typhina
(Staghorn sumach, Velvet sumach, Virginian sumach)
- Best in full sun
- Any soil, including chalk or lime
- Summer flowers, autumn foliage

This hardy deciduous shrub or small tree has large pinnate foliage, 30-60cm (1-2ft) long, with 13 or more lance-shaped leaflets. The downy green summer leaves change to yellow, rich orange, red or purple in autumn. There are erect green clusters of male flowers, with smaller female clusters on separate plants. In late autumn the female flowers produce conical hairy fruits.

This shrub produces thickets of suckering shoots, which need to be reduced unless there is ample room for them to spread. Each spring cut surplus shoots down to within an eye or two of the old wood. Bushes can be at least 4.5m (15ft) high, and trees with a short stem reach 4.5-6m (15-20ft).

Propagate by root cuttings in spring, or by removal of suckers in autumn.

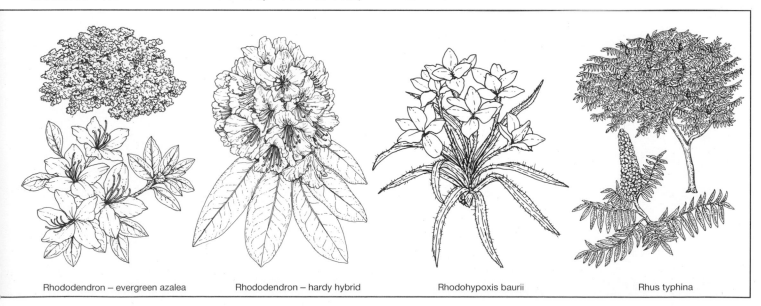

Rhododendron – evergreen azalea   Rhododendron – hardy hybrid   Rhodohypoxis baurii   Rhus typhina

Ribes sanguineum 'Pulborough Scarlet'
(Flowering currant)
- **Sunny position**
- **Any good garden soil**
- **Spring flowering**

This deciduous spring-flowering shrub has produced a number of cultivars. 'Pulborough Scarlet' has deep red flowers. These make a pleasing contrast to the rich moss-green foliage as it unfolds at the time of flowering. Sprays of 20 to 30 flowers are borne on long wand-like growths. This vigorous shrub reaches a height of 2-2.5m (6.5-8ft) or higher, and as much in width. Give ample room to expand. The palmately three- to five-lobed leaves have a heart-shaped base 5-10cm (2-4in) wide but less in length. This attractive shrub is disliked by some people because of the pungent smell of its flowers and foliage.

Prune by removing an occasional old branch or a few side shoots after flowering has finished.

Propagate by hardwood cuttings, in autumn or winter.

Below: Ribes sanguineum becomes aflame with sprays of deep red flowers in spring, amid attractive moss-green foliage.

Robinia pseudoacacia 'Frisia'
(Black locust, False acacia, Yellow locust)
- **Full sun**
- **Any well-drained soil**
- **Coloured foliage from spring to autumn**

This hardy, deciduous tree grows well in industrial areas. 'Frisia' has become very popular, partly because it makes a small to medium-sized tree and is therefore suited to a small or medium-sized garden. It has rich golden-yellow pinnate foliage that creates a superb splash of colour from spring through to autumn. Trees can be anything from 6-8m (20-26ft) high. The thorns on young growths are red, which with the young golden-yellow foliage makes a striking sight.

Any pruning that is necessary should be carried out during midsummer or late summer, as there is then less chance of the tree bleeding. Where large wounds are left, treat them with a suitable tree paint.

Propagate by grafting 'Frisia' on to stocks of *R. pseudoacacia* in spring out of doors.

Above: Robinia pseudoacacia 'Frisia' has yellow leaves.

Rosa canina
(Dog rose, Rose)
- **Full sun or light shade**
- **Well-drained and fertile soil**
- **Midsummer flowering**

The superb variety 'Abbotswood' of the well-known dog rose is a deciduous shrub. During midsummer it develops fragrant, fairly double, pink, cup-shaped flowers borne in graceful sprays of light green leaves. During autumn it also bears orange-red, oval hips (also known as heps). It forms a bush about 1.8m (6ft) high and 2.4m (8ft) wide.

Rose canina 'Andersonii' is another superb variety, with deep pink flowers on arching stems during midsummer. These are followed by bright orange-red, egg-shaped hips. The flowers have a superb raspberry-drop fragrance.

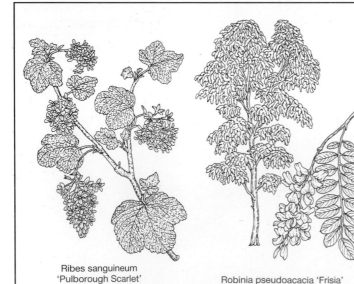

Ribes sanguineum 'Pulborough Scarlet'

Robinia pseudoacacia 'Frisia'

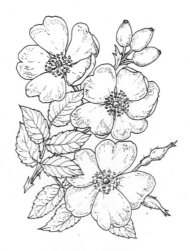

Rosa canina

Rosa – climber

Little pruning is needed, other than cutting out dead and congested shoots in late winter. Do not prune before the rosehips have fallen.

Rosa – Climbers and Ramblers

(Rose)
- **Full sun or partial shade**
- **Well-drained and fertile soil**
- **Midsummer flowering – and often again later in the year**

These are well-known deciduous shrubs. Climbers, in the main, bear most of their flowers on lateral or sub-lateral shoots from the main stems. These main stems are retained as long as they continue to grow vigorously. They are ideal for training against walls and fences. Ramblers, however, develop long, flexible stems along which flowers are borne on numerous lateral shoots. They are best grown over arches, pergolas and rustic fences.

Regular yearly pruning is needed, but this can vary between varieties and types. However, little major pruning is needed for climbers, other than cutting out overcrowded shoots and removing dead and twiggy wood. Also, cut old laterals back to two or three buds from the main stem. Ramblers need to be encouraged yearly to produce fresh shoots from ground level. Therefore, after flowering, cut out all canes that have flowered and tie in those which have yet to flower.

Rosa damascena

(Damask rose, Rose)
- **Full sun or light shade**
- **Well-drained and very fertile soil**
- **Midsummer flowering**

This is a well-known, hardy, deciduous shrub, bearing double flowers during midsummer. In bud they are pink, fading with age to near white. However, it is the attractive varieties which are mainly grown, which include the York and Lancaster rose (*Rosa damascena* 'Versicolor'). This bears semi-double, rather untidy flowers which can be pink or bluish-white, or even a mixture on different petals. However, they are never striped or splashed.

It grows about 1.8m (6ft) high and with a similar spread.

Little pruning is needed, other than shaping the plant when young to remove twiggy shoots. When established, all that is needed is to remove congested shoots and to cut long shoots back by one-third of their length in late winter. Each year cut out a few very old shoots at their bases to encourage fresh ones to develop.

Rosa – Floribunda

(Cluster-flowered Bush rose)
(Rose)
- **Full sun or partial shade**
- **Well-drained and fertile soil**
- **Midsummer flowers, then repeat flowering in late summer and autumn**

This group of roses is now known as Cluster-flowered Bush roses, but invariably they are still known by their earlier name.

They are hardy and deciduous shrubs, with flowers borne on variably prickly stems. Each flower is 6-8cm (2.4-3.2in) across and borne in terminal clusters during midsummer, and often again in late summer and into autumn.

Regular pruning is essential. In autumn cut off long tops from stems to reduce the area exposed to wind that may rock the bush. In early spring, cut out all dead and diseased shoots. Also, cut back – to outward-facing buds – shoots to about half the previous year's growth. There is a wide range of varieties and each year many more are introduced into cultivation.

Avoid planting them in exposed places where they become buffeted by wind, or positions under trees where water can drip upon them. If they are in exposed areas, refirm soil around roots in spring.

Below: Rosa 'Masquerade' is a floribunda with yellow and red flowers in midsummer.

Above: Rosa canina 'Abbotswood' is a beautiful form of the dog rose, with the bonus of oval, orange-red hips in autumn.

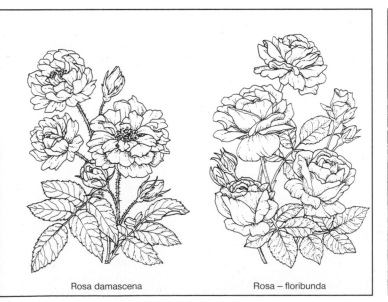

Rosa damascena   Rosa – floribunda

Above: *Rosa gallica 'Versicolor'* bears fragrant, crimson flowers splashed and striped with white.

Rosa gallica 'Versicolor'

(Rosa Mundi)
- **Full sun or light shade**
- **Well-drained and fertile soil**
- **Midsummer flowering**

This hardy, deciduous shrub is also known as 'Rosa Mundi' and is a very showy rose. During midsummer it bears crimson, richly fragrant, semi-double flowers striped with white. Each flower is 5-7.5cm (2-3in) wide.

It forms a neat and compact bush, about 1.2m (4ft) high and wide, and will also create a good low hedge. Plant it where it can be readily seen.

Little pruning is needed, other than shaping the plant when young to remove twiggy shoots and to allow more air to penetrate into it. When established, all that is needed is to remove congested shoots and to cut long shoots back by one-third of their length in late winter. Each year cut out a few very old shoots at their bases to encourage fresh ones to develop from the plant's base.

Rosa – Hybrid Tea

(Large-flowered Bush rose)
(Rose)
- **Full sun or partial shade**
- **Well-drained and fertile soil**
- **Midsummer to late summer flowering**

This group of roses is now known as Large-flowered Bush roses, but in most catalogues you will find them grouped under their old and established name.

They are hardy and deciduous shrubs, with flowers borne on stems which are sparsely or abundantly prickly. The bowl-shaped flowers are 10-15cm (4-6in) across, and appear from midsummer to late summer. Some of the varieties are richly scented. The range of varieties is very wide, and each year many more are introduced.

Avoid sites where the roses will be continually buffeted by strong winds, and keep them away from tall trees which will drip water on the flowers after a shower or rain, and spoil petals.

Each year the bushes need to be pruned. Prune as for Floribunda roses. Regular, yearly pruning is essential for a long-lived bush.

Rosa – Miniature

(Rose)
- **Full sun or partial shade**
- **Well-drained soil**
- **Midsummer flowering – and often again later in the year**

This group of roses can be grown in most gardens, in small raised beds, window-boxes and pots.

They are small – often 15-23cm (6-9in) high – hardy, deciduous shrubs. They have semi-double or double flowers which open flat and generally measure up to 4cm (1.5in) across. The range of varieties is wide and continually growing, with even miniature-flowered roses which climb up to about 2.4m (8ft) high.

When grown in containers, ensure that they are deep enough to accommodate the roots. If the area is too small, the compost will dry out rapidly in summer.

These roses need little pruning, other than trimming to shape in spring to prevent them becoming straggly. Also, cut out some of the thinnest shoots to prevent centres becoming overcrowded.

Above: *Rosa rugosa 'Frau Dagmar Hastrup'* is a rose bush for a small garden. It has fragrant, rose-pink flowers.

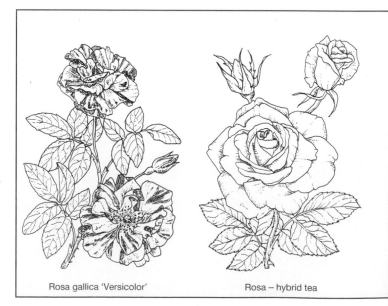

Rosa gallica 'Versicolor'

Rosa – hybrid tea

Rosa rugosa 'Frau Dagmar Hastrup'
(Rose)
- **Sun, but tolerates shade**
- **Most soils; avoid chalk or clay**
- **Perpetual flowering**

Rosa rugosa 'Frau Dagmar Hastrup' is a form of the Ramanas rose that is particularly suitable for the small garden. Like other rugosas it has thick dark green wrinkled foliage. The fairly large rose-pink flowers have a conspicuous centre of creamy yellow stamens; the buds are a rich deep pink. The beautiful blooms are moderately scented and continuously produced. The bush has a compact habit, reaching 1.5m (5ft) tall and 1.2m (4ft) wide. The foliage has splendid autumn colouring, and from summer into autumn there are rich crimson tomato-shaped hips.

Very little pruning is needed; but if bushes become overcrowded and ungainly, they can be severely cut back in early spring.

Propagate by cuttings 23cm (9in) long, with a heel or cut just below a bud, in autumn.

Roscoea cautleoides
- **Light shade**
- **Cool soil**
- **Herbaceous**

It has been said that roscoeas hardly qualify as alpine plants, but by common usage on rock gardens they merit inclusion in this book. Of all of these hardy herbaceous perennials, *R. cautleoides* is probably the most handsome. Its mid-green lanceolate leaves reach from 30-40cm (12-16in) and a profusion of soft luminous yellow orchid-like flowers appear just above this foliage in summer.

They prefer a cool situation, the peat garden being an appropriate spot where they can enjoy the moist peaty soil.

Propagation is by division of the dormant roots in spring. Self-sown seedlings can be potted up in late

Above: Roscoea cautleoides brightens rock gardens in summer, with soft yellow flowers borne above strap-like leaves.

summer, or seed sown in late winter, keeping the young plants shaded during the summer. Plant roscoeas deeply and they will survive hard winters. The fleshy roots do not like being confined in a small pot, so do not delay planting out.

Rosmarinus officinalis 'Sissinghurst Blue'
(Rosemary)
- **Full sun**
- **A light well-drained soil**
- **Late spring flowering**

This lovely evergreen shrub has leaves that are a glossy mid-green above, silvery white beneath, and pungently fragrant. From the opposite tufts of narrow 2cm (0.8in) long leaves, flower buds are formed which produce pretty light blue flowers in late spring. 'Sissinghurst Blue' growing at the foot of the rose 'Helen Knight', which has clear yellow flowers, makes an attractive display. Plants are usually about 1.2m (4ft) high and as wide, but may become taller and wider eventually. The fresh or dried leaves are used as a flavouring with meat, particularly lamb. Pruning is necessary only when bushes become overgrown; in that case cut them back into old wood during the spring.

Propagate by half-ripe cuttings in summer. Plant in a sunny sheltered position.

Rosa – miniature

Rosa rugosa 'Frau Dagmar Hastrup'

Roscoea cautleoides

Rosmarinus officinalis 'Sissinghurst Blue'

Rubus Tridel 'Benenden'

- **Sun or partial shade**
- **Ordinary well-drained loamy or chalk soil**
- **Late spring flowering**

This deciduous, hardy, flowering shrub is a hybrid between *Rubus trilobus* and *R. deliciosus* giving it a group name of Tridel, whereas the clone name is 'Benenden'. It has dark green leaves with three to five lobes. This vigorous shrub of the bramble family has spineless stems with peeling bark. The tall arching branches reach a height of 2.5-3m (8-10ft). In late spring the shrub produces many single pure white scented flowers, 6-8cm (2.3-3.2in) across, each flower with a central boss of golden-yellow stamens.

Pruning consists of cutting out the oldest wood after flowering, to encourage an annual supply of new growth from the base; this will produce flowers in the following year. Do not cut out too much old wood.

Propagate by layering in spring, even though they may take 12 months to root. Encourage young growths to develop from the base of the shrub.

Below: Rudbeckia fulgida bears dark-centred golden-yellow flowers in late summer.

Above: Rudbeckia hirta 'Marmalade' has rich yellow, purple-black centred, flowers.

Rudbeckia fulgida

(Rudbeckia newmanii, Rudbeckia speciosa)

(Black-eyed Susan, Coneflower)

- **Full sun**
- **Moist fertile soil**
- **Late summer and autumn flowering**

This hardy herbaceous perennial has also been known as *R.* speciosa and *R. newmanii*. Whatever one calls it, it is one of the most useful border and cut flowers in late summer and autumn. Erect 60cm (24in) stems rise from leafy clumps, displaying several large golden-yellow daisy-like flowers with short blackish-purple central discs or cones, hence the name black-eyed Susan. The narrow leaves are rather rough to handle. Other garden forms of *R. fulgida* are the free-flowering *R. deamii*, 90cm (3ft) tall, and 'Goldsturm', which above its bushy growth has stems 60cm

Rubus Tridel 'Benenden' Rudbeckia fulgida Rudbeckia hirta 'Marmalade' Ruta graveolens 'Jackman's Blue'

(24in) tall carrying chrome-yellow flowers with dark brown cones. Rudbeckias make good cut flowers and blend very well with *Aster amellus* 'King George'.

Propagate by dividing the plants, in autumn or spring.

Rudbeckia hirta 'Marmalade'

(Black-eyed Susan, Coneflower)
- **Sow in spring**
- **Any soil**
- **Sunny position**

The common names of this hardy annual allude to the centre of the flower, which has a very dark brown to purple colour and is cone-shaped. The outer petals are lovely shades of yellow, gold and brown, and the cultivar 'Marmalade' is a rich yellow with a central cone of purple-black – very striking. It flowers from early summer, and blooms will be carried in great profusion until late autumn on stems 45cm (18in) long. Individual flowers will be up to 10cm (4in) across.

To obtain flowering plants each year, sow seeds in boxes of any good growing medium in spring. They can be raised in a cold greenhouse or a frame. Prick out the young seedlings into boxes and place these in a cold frame to protect them from frosts. Harden off in late spring and plant out into flowering positions in very early summer, 23cm (9in) apart.

Ruta graveolens 'Jackman's Blue'

(Common rue, Herb of grace, Rue)
- **Sunny position**
- **Any well-drained or lime soil**
- **Summer flowering**

This evergreen shrub has been used both for cooking and for medicinal purposes, but today it makes a useful low-growing decorative shrub. The cultivar known as 'Jackman's Blue' has opalescent blue fern-like foliage,

and dull yellow flowers are produced above the foliage during the summer. This shrub is grown more for its foliage than for its flowers; in fact, some growers remove the flower spikes as they appear. Bushes reach a height of 75cm-1m (30-39in) with a spread of 90cm-1.2m (3-4ft).

To keep bushes neat and tidy, prune them each spring by cutting back fairly severely to sound wood. Remove weaker growths.

Propagate by half-ripe cuttings in summer; insert in a cold frame.

Above: *Ruta graveolens 'Jackman's Blue', with blue-green leaves, is ideal for path edges.*

Below: *Sagina procumbens 'Aurea' creates a mat of golden-green leaves and white flowers.*

Sagina procumbens 'Aurea'

(Golden procumbent pearlwort, Pearlwort)
- **Open situation**
- **Any well-drained soil**
- **Ground cover**

The ordinary pearlwort is a tufted perennial that is usually considered to be a weed. However, *S. procumbens* 'Aurea', with its attractive gold foliage, has a place on the rock garden, where it can be allowed to invade an area about 30cm (12in) in diameter. If you want to make an alpine lawn of low-growing plants, this is a candidate. The flowers are minute, off-white and totally insignificant.

It seems to tolerate a wide variety of soils, but you should incorporate some drainage in the form of grit or very sharp sand in the top layer of soil. It is very tolerant as a cover for the smaller early-flowering crocus or narcissus bulbs. Be careful not to plant in the shade, where it may be drawn up.

Propagation is by division at almost any time, but is best in early autumn; plant out direct or over-winter in a pot.

Salix arbuscula
- **Open situation but not too sunny in summer**
- **Not too dry a soil**
- **Deciduous shrub**

There are a number of dwarf willows suitable for the rock garden, mostly from the European Alps. Creeping woody stems throw up a number of other stems, which end up making a gnarled bush in time, with a maximum height of 40-45cm (16-18in) and a spread of 60cm (24in). The leaves are a deep green, and glaucous beneath; the slender grey catkins appear in mid-spring.

This deciduous shrub needs a moist soil of any composition, but not too rich, in an open situation. It does not like the direct hot sunshine of midsummer, and requires moisture all the year round.

Propagation is by cuttings with a heel, taken from midsummer to early autumn and inserted in a sandy frame. Make sure the tips are pinched out, to encourage bushy growth.

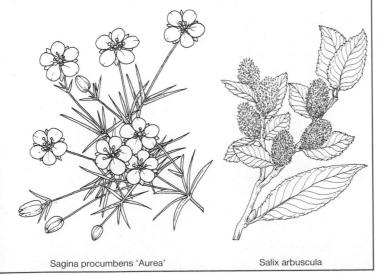

Sagina procumbens 'Aurea'   Salix arbuscula

Salpiglossis sinuata 'Grandiflora'

(Painted tongue)
- **Sow in very early spring**
- **Ordinary but well-cultivated soil**
- **Open and sunny position**

Although usually grown as a pot plant this half-hardy annual is a worthwhile plant to use outdoors in summer as a bedding plant.

'Grandiflora' and its hybrids will provide a wealth of colour in shades of crimson, scarlet, gold, rose, blue and yellow. Each flower has a velvet texture and the throat of the tubular flowers is often deeply veined with a contrasting colour. Size of individual blooms will vary between named cultivars of the species but they are on average about 5cm (2in) long and the same in diameter. Up to 60cm (24in) in height, the stems are slender and carry wavy-edged narrow leaves of a dark green.

Sow seed under glass in very early spring to produce plants for growing outdoors in summer. Use a peat-based growing medium for raising the seed, and keep in a temperature of 18°C (65°F). Prick out seedlings into boxes, harden off and plant out in early summer, 23cm (9in) apart. Keep well watered at all times.

Salvia horminum

- **Sow in early spring or autumn**
- **Ordinary well-drained soil**
- **Sunny position**

This hardy annual salvia provides a completely different range of colour from the *S. splendens* scarlet cultivars. Dark blue or purple bracts are produced around the insignificant true flowers. Mixtures are available, but the cultivar 'Blue Beard' is recommended for its very deep purple bracts on erect branching

square stems, 45cm (18in) high. These also carry the ovate mid-green leaves. Grow towards the front of a border, or as a formal bedding plant with a few silver spot plants.

These hardy annuals may be sown direct outdoors in spring or autumn. If earlier colour is required plants can be raised under glass by sowing in seed mixture in spring at a temperature of 18°C (65°F). Prick off into individual pots or seed trays. Grow on cooler and harden off to plant out at 23cm (9in) apart in early summer. Thin seedlings sown outdoors before they become crowded. Too high temperatures will produce soft elongated growth.

Above: Salvia sclarea is a hardy biennial – sometimes grown in herb gardens – with spires of bright flowers during summer.

Salvia sclarea

(Clary)
- **Sow in spring**
- **Light and fertile soil**
- **Full sun**

This handsome hardy biennial was grown in the past for use as a culinary herb but is now surpassed by the various species of sage. The oil, however, is still extracted commercially for use in the manufacture of perfumes. Reaching a height of 75cm (30in),

Above: Salvia horminum creates numerous branches and upright stiff stems clouded at their tops with dark purple bracts.

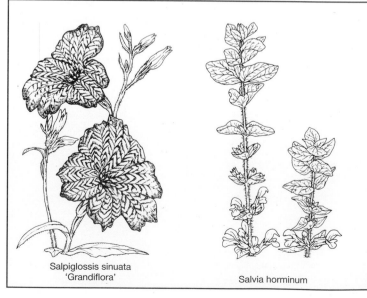

Salpiglossis sinuata 'Grandiflora'

Salvia horminum

the stems carry large, very hairy triangular leaves of mid-green. Flowers are tubular in shape, about 2.5cm (1in) long, and white-blue in colour. Below the true flowers, bracts of purple or yellow will accentuate the whole blooms, which show colour from midsummer onward. These are good border plants, which will enhance an otherwise flat area.

The seeds are sown in spring where they are to flower. Take out drills 38cm (15in) apart; thin out seedlings to 30cm (12in) apart when they are large enough to handle.

Salvia splendens 'Flarepath'

(Scarlet sage)
- **Sow in early spring**
- **Ordinary well-drained soil**
- **Sunny position**

Of all summer half-hardy annuals the scarlet flowers (actually, bracts) of *S. splendens* must be the most vivid. Planted in formal beds or borders with contrasting silver- or grey-leaved plants they provide a stunning spectacle. Of the many cultivars available, 'Flarepath' is well recommended. The flowers are produced on 30cm (12in) stems.

This tender plant requires a greenhouse for propagation. Sow seed in early spring in a peat-based growing compost. Keep the temperature about 18°C (65°F).

Prick out seedlings into individual small pots and grow on in a slightly lower temperature. Harden off and plant out in summer about 23cm (9in) apart after late frosts are over. Provide ample moisture when the plants are established.

Salvia × superba

(Salvia nemerosa)
(Long-branched sage)
- **Sun or partial shade**
- **Any good fertile soil**
- **Early summer to late autumn flowering**

For many years this hardy herbaceous perennial was known

Above: *Salvia splendens 'Bonfire Scarlet' is frequently grown in summer-bedding displays, creating a dominant display.*

as *S. nemerosa*. Each erect 90cm (3ft) stem carries branching spikes of violet-purple flowers, with reddish-brown bracts (modified leaves). Today there are also dwarf varieties, such as 'Lubeca', with masses of spikes of violet-blue flowers, 75cm (30in) high; and 'East Friesland', violet-purple, and only 45cm (18in) tall. These salvias look well when planted on their own.

Salvias are both fully hardy and perennial, and will grow in any good fertile soil or on chalk, but

they dislike dry soils, and should not be allowed to dry out. Some form of support should be given, such as peasticks pushed in around the plants to allow them to grow through. Propagate salvias by division in spring or autumn.

Sambucus nigra 'Aurea'

(Golden elder, Golden European elder)
- **Full sun**
- **Any good garden soil**
- **Colourful foliage in summer**

Sambucus nigra 'Aurea' is a useful deciduous shrub that can light up a border. The foliage at first is greenish yellow, later changing to a golden-yellow which intensifies throughout the summer. It has large clusters of yellowish or dull white heavily fragrant flowers in summer followed by black berries. It reaches about 2m (6.5ft) high.

Even more striking is *S. racemosa* 'Plumosa Aurea', the golden cut-leaved elder. The species *S. racemosa* is the red-berried elder, but 'Plumosa Aurea' is grown for its deeply cut golden foliage. It has white flowers in spring, followed by red berries in autumn.

Both these elders can be pruned in spring, when they can be cut back to within a bud or two of the old wood. Propagate by taking hardwood cuttings in winter, inserted out of doors.

Salvia sclarea   Salvia splendens 'Flarepath'   Salvia x superba   Sambucus nigra 'Aurea'

Sanguinaria canadensis 'Flore Pleno'

(Bloodroot)

- Sun or semi-shade
- Leafy soil
- Herbaceous

Related to the poppy, this is a genus with a single species, from North America. The common name refers to the red liquid that oozes from the root when cut. In spring, this hardy herbaceous perennial develops heads of double white flowers about 10cm (4in) tall which poke through the soil, followed by the palmate greyish green leaves, which die down by the end of summer. The flowers of this double form last longer than the single flowers of the species.

Once planted, preferably in a leafy soil, they should not be disturbed. They enjoy either a sunny situation or some shade.

Propagation of the double form can only be by division in early spring, when great care should be taken.

Sanvitalia procumbens

(Creeping zinnia)

- Sow in spring
- Ordinary soil
- Sunny site

Very aptly named, the zinnia-like flowers of this hardy annual are

Above: Sanvitalia procumbens is a bright-faced hardy annual, forming a carpet of colour.

quite striking. Bright yellow single flowers have jet black cone centres. They are 2.5cm (1in) across, produced on semi-prostrate branching stems only 15cm (6in) high from early summer onwards. Leaves are ovate, pointed and a useful green.

For successful results, fork peat or other humus into the top layer of soil before sowing the seed. To have plants flowering through the summer months, sow seeds outdoors in spring or earlier under glass; the latter will produce stronger, earlier-flowering specimens. Take out shallow drills where the plants are to flower, and

lightly cover the seed with soil. Thin out the spring-sown seedlings as soon as they are large enough to handle. Those sown in heat should be hardened off for later planting. In either case, thin out to 7.5cm (3in) apart.

Saponaria ocymoides

(Soapwort)

- Open sunny situation
- Well-drained soil
- Evergreen

This is an invaluable, prostrate, hardy herbaceous perennial for rock gardens and natural stone walls, where it cascades over rocks. It is a plant of shingle banks in the Alps of south-western and

Above: Saponaria ocymoides is a prostrate rock garden plant that loves to cascade over rocks.

south-central Europe, which indicates its need for good drainage. The mats can be 30cm (12in) across and are covered with dozens of 1cm (0.4in) wide pink flowers that appear from midsummer to late summer.

There are two selected forms: 'Compacta', which is slower-growing and less vigorous; and 'Rubra Compacta', with rich carmine flowers.

Propagation is very easy by soft cuttings in summer, taken from non-flowering wood and placed in a sand frame. It is necessary to stop the young plants at least twice to get a tidy young plant.

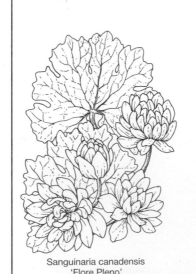

Sanguinaria canadensis 'Flore Pleno'

Sanvitalia procumbens

Saponaria ocymoides

Saponaria officinalis

Left: Saponaria officinalis is superb in herbaceous borders, creating a splash of colour during the summer.

Saponaria officinalis

(Bouncing bet, Soapwort)
- **Sunny location**
- **Well-drained soil**
- **Summer to early autumn flowering**

This hardy herbaceous perennial is called soapwort because a lather can be made from the foliage and used for cleaning old curtains. This wilding can be seen in hedgerows in summer and early autumn. It is a handsome perennial, but its roots can spread beneath the ground. It has panicles of large, fragrant, rose-pink flowers, 2.5-3cm (1-1.2in) across, carried on terminal loose heads on erect 60-90cm (2-3ft) stems. The three-veined leaves are 5-13cm (2-5in) long and 5cm (2in) wide. Double forms are 'Roseo Plena', which is pink, and the white 'Albo Plena'.

All do well in good well-drained soil, but lime or chalk soils should be avoided. Propagate by half-ripe cuttings in summer, or by division in spring.

Saxifraga cochlearis 'Minor'
- **Open position**
- **Well-drained limestone scree**
- **Evergreen**

The encrusted saxifrages form evergreen rosettes of grey-green leaves that are often attractively encrusted with spots of lime around the edges. *S. cochlearis* is found on limestone rocks in the Maritime Alps, which gives a lead to its requirements in cultivation: a well-drained situation, ideally on scree.

The form 'Minor' is ideal for planting in a trough, and forms an extremely neat hummock of grey-leaved rosettes, from which shoot sprays of 1.5cm (0.6in) wide milk-white flowers in early summer, no taller than 10cm (4in). This is a most attractive plant, for both its leaves and flowers.

Propagation is by detaching the side rosettes in August, preferably with some roots attached, and potting them on into a limy soil; or they can be planted out direct.

Saxifraga 'Southside Seedling'
- **Open situation**
- **Neutral soil**
- **Evergreen**

Another of the encrusted saxifrages but with larger leaves and evergreen rosettes, from the mountains of Europe from the Pyrenees through to Lapland and Iceland. It grows in the crevices of granite rocks, and so requires good drainage in cultivation, but not in the form of limestone chippings as for other saxifrages.

There are many geographical variants and garden hybrids, of which 'Southside Seedling' is one: it has strap-shaped leaves forming the rosettes, from which in summer are produced the arching sprays of white flowers, heavily spotted with red, on 30cm (12in) stems.

Propagate by dividing up the clump after flowering in late summer: plant the rosettes out direct or pot them up. Seed will not come true, but they can be tried.

Below: Saxifraga cochlearis 'Minor' enriches rock gardens with its grey-green leaves and milk-white early summer flowers.

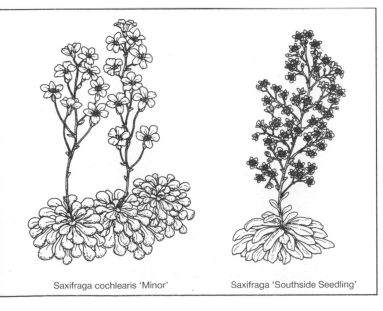

Saxifraga cochlearis 'Minor'   Saxifraga 'Southside Seedling'

Saxifraga umbrosa 'Elliott's Variety'

- **Shady situation**
- **Any soil**
- **Evergreen**

'Elliott's Variety' is a miniature rock garden plant which thrives in any shady corner, damp or dry. It does not enjoy full sun. It has neat foliage and deep rose flowers on 10-15cm (4-6in) stems in early summer.

This plant is not invasive, spreading not much beyond 20-30cm (8-12in). It is extremely useful for seemingly impossible corners in the rock garden.

Propagation is by division in early autumn, planting out direct or potting up individual rooted rosettes if you want quantity.

Schizanthus pinnatus 'Angel Wings'

(Butterfly flower, Poor man's orchid)
- **Sow in spring**
- **Ordinary well-drained soil**
- **Sunny position**

The very tall cultivars of this half-hardy annual are now being replaced by more manageable dwarfer forms for garden work. Use them as border plants or even in formal bedding. 'Angel Wings' is a cultivar well worth trying for all purposes. Only 30cm (12in) tall the plants are very free-flowering, compact and almost conical in shape, and will not require staking. Flowers are orchid-shaped and come in a wide variety of colours. The spotted petals and open throats of the blooms are most attractive. Stems and leaves are a light green, the latter being deeply cut and fern-like.

Sow seeds under glass in spring at a temperature of 16°C (60°F). Use a peat-based growing medium for sowing and for the subsequent pricking-off of seedlings. Harden off and plant out into flowering positions in early summer, 23cm (9in) apart. Avoid watering overhead in very hot weather.

Schizostylis coccinea

(Crimson flag)
- **Full sun**
- **Any moist fertile soil**
- **Early autumn flowering**

This rhizomatous perennial appears to grow and flower freely in most soils. In South Africa it grows near water, and it needs ample moisture to flower. It has long stems, 60-75cm (24-30in) or more. Pretty cup-shaped flowers open in a star-like fashion, not unlike small gladiolus flowers. *S. coccinea* has rich crimson blooms about 4cm (1.6in) across. The varieties 'Major' and 'Gigantea' are even brighter and larger; 'Mrs Hegarty' is pale pink, and 'Sunrise' has large pink flowers. The stems are excellent for cutting.

The rhizomatous roots need to be lifted, divided and replanted every few years to keep them thriving. A spring mulch of peat or well-rotted garden compost will help to retain moisture around the plants. Propagate by division in spring, always leaving four to six shoots on each portion.

Scilla peruviana

(Cuban lily, Hyacinth-of-Peru)
- **Warm sunny position**
- **Moist well-drained soil**
- **Plant 5cm (2in) deep**

This hardy bulbous plant has glossy strap-like leaves sometimes

Below: *Saxifraga umbrosa 'Elliott's Variety', with deep rose flowers in early summer, is ideal for small rock gardens.*

Above: *Schizostylis coccinea 'Major' bears large, cup and star-shaped, crimson flowers on long stems in early autumn.*

Saxifraga umbrosa
'Elliott's Variety'

Schizanthus pinnatus
'Angel Wings'

30cm (12in) tall. The flowers vary from white through blue to dark purple, in late spring. The flower heads have up to 100 star-shaped blooms, each about 2cm (0.8in) across.

The plants are easy to grow and need little after-care. They are recommended for rock and alpine gardens, growing in short grass. The bulbs should be planted 5cm (2in) deep in a moist but well-drained soil; add plenty of peat, leaf-mould or compost to improve the moisture-retention of the soil. The site should be warm and sunny. Put the bulbs out in late summer or early autumn, as soon as they become available. Scatter the bulbs over the area and plant them where they fall; this will give a casual and natural look. At this time offsets can be taken off mature plants and replanted.

Scilla sibirica 'Atrocoerulea'

(Siberian squill)
- **Sun or partial shade**
- **Moist well-drained soil**
- **Plant 5cm (2in) deep**

The leaves of this bulbous plant appear in early spring followed by the flower stems, of which there are three or four to each bulb. Each stem bears up to five brilliant deep blue bell-shaped flowers, almost 2.5cm (1in) long, in spring. Plant these separate from other blue flowers, as the vivid blue of

the scillas makes other blues look dull. The form 'Atrocoerulea' (also known as 'Spring Beauty') is a great improvement on the common form, with larger flowers and a more vigorous habit.

They will grow in any well-drained soil that holds moisture in drought periods. The bulbs should be planted in late summer or early

Left: Scilla sibirica 'Atrocoerulea' has deep blue bell-shaped spring flowers.

Below: Scilla tubergeniana brightens rock gardens with pale blue flowers in early spring.

autumn at a depth of 5cm (2in) in an area of sun or partial shade where they can be left undisturbed. Remove offsets from mature plants in autumn, and replant. Scatter the bulbs over the ground and plant where they fall to give a natural look.

Scilla tubergeniana
- **Sun or semi-shade**
- **Moist well-drained soil**
- **Plant 5cm (2in) deep**

This bulbous plant comes from the mountainous meadows and rocks of NW Iran and grows to a height of 10cm (4in), with a similar spread. The flowers are pale blue or white, and open as soon as they emerge from the soil.

The bulbs should be planted as soon as they are purchased, in late summer or early autumn, in a sunny or half-shaded area of the garden where the soil is moist but well-drained. Cover the bulbs with 5cm (2in) of soil. For a casual effect the bulbs can be cast gently over the area and planted where they fall. To increase the moisture-holding properties of the soil dig in a good supply of leaf-mould, peat or compost before planting. Once planted the bulbs can be left untouched, but, to increase stock, offsets can be taken from mature plants after the leaves have died down, and placed in a nursery bed to grow. Seed may take five years to reach flowering size.

Schizostylis coccinea

Scilla peruviana

Scilla sibirica 'Atrocoerulea'

Scilla tubergeniana

Sedum acre 'Aureum'
(Yellow biting stonecrop)
- **Sunny situation**
- **Any soil**
- **Evergreen**

This mat-forming evergreen is a rather invasive plant, best left to inhabit the crevices of old walls, where the yellow flowers make a bright splash of colour. The form 'Aureum' is still relatively active, but has the added attraction of golden yellow tips to its leafy shoots in spring.

This is an excellent subject for the alpine lawn and can be under-planted with bulbs. The flowers are yellow as in the species, but not of such importance in view of the useful foliage. It is not fussy about either soil or situation, though perhaps providing more foliage colour in a sunny spot.

Propagation is no problem. Almost any piece of the plant that is broken off will root, and division is possible at most times of year.

Sedum spathulifolium 'Cappa Blanca'
- **Sunny position**
- **Any soil**
- **Evergreen**

Sedum spathulifolium is a low, mat-forming evergreen species native to NW America, where it inhabits rocky ledges in the drier foothills from British Columbia

down to California. It makes dense mats of grey-green leaves in fleshy rosettes and is a good carpeting plant, spreading to 30cm (12in) or more and producing flat yellow flower heads, 5-8cm (2-3.2in) across in midsummer on 10cm (4in) stems.

The form 'Cappa Blanca' is from Cape Blanco in southern Oregon and has silvery grey foliage that is slightly smaller than the species. It behaves exactly like the species, and is a most attractive plant. Two

other forms – 'Purpureum', with larger purple leaves, and 'Aureum', with leaves tinted yellow, but less vigorous – are in circulation.

Propagation, as with most sedums, is easy: by division at any time or, if quantity is required, by detaching single rosettes and potting them up.

Below: Sedum acre 'Aureum' is a mat-forming rock garden evergreen with yellow flowers. It has bright yellow shoot tips.

Sedum spectabile 'Autumn Joy'
(Ice plant)
- **Full sun**
- **Well-drained soil**
- **Late summer/autumn flowering**

The name ice plant probably originated because this perennial species has glaucous glistening foliage. The leaves are opposite or in threes, and clasp stout erect

Above: Sedum spectabile 'Autumn Joy' is colourful in autumn, with large and nearly flat salmon-pink flower heads. It attracts bees.

Sedum acre 'Aureum'

Sedum spathulifolium 'Cappa Blanca'

Sedum spectabile 'Autumn Joy'

Senecio 'Sunshine'

stems 30-60cm (12-24in) high. Above these stems are borne flat plate-like unbranched flowers. *S. spectabile* has pale pink blooms. The varieties 'Carmen' and 'Meteor' are a deeper pink, and 'Brilliant' is a deep rose pink. 'Autumn Joy' is at first pale rose, gradually changing to a beautiful salmon pink.

These sedums can be grown with the minimum of attention. Propagate them by taking stem cuttings in midsummer, and rooting in sandy soil in a cold frame, or by division in late summer or autumn. Give these sedums room – about five plants to a square metre (square yard).

Above: Senecio 'Sunshine' displays bright yellow, daisy-like flowers in summer.

Senecio 'Sunshine'

(Senecio greyi, Senecio laxifolius)
- **Full sun**
- **Any soil**
- **Summer flowering**

This evergreen hardy flowering shrub is normally grown for its foliage rather than its flower. For many years it was known as *S. laxifolius* or *S. greyi*. It usually grows to 1-1.2m (3.3-4ft). It has leathery leaves up to 7cm (2.75in)

long and 3cm (1.2in) wide. The young foliage has at first a cobweb-like grey covering above (later becoming smooth), with white felt beneath. In summer upright panicles of golden-yellow daisy-like flowers are produced.

This bushy shrub does well in coastal areas. If damaged by frost, bushes can be cut hard back in spring; carry out such pruning at least every four or five years. Heavy snow may weigh branches down; prune in spring to regain its normal shape.

Propagate by half-ripe cuttings in late summer or early autumn.

Sidalcea malvaeflora

(Checkerbloom, Greek mallow)
- **Full sun**
- **Good ordinary soil**
- **Summer flowering**

These mallow-flowered beauties are most graceful hardy herbaceous perennials. The funnel-shaped flowers in varying shades of pink are carried in terminal branching spikes on stout stems 1.2-1.3m (4-4.5ft) high. The leaves are divided like a hand. Varieties to choose from include: 'Croftway Red', a deep rich red, 90cm (3ft) tall; 'Rose Queen', deep rosy pink, 1.2m (4ft); 'William Smith', salmon-pink, 1.05m (42in); and 'Sussex Beauty', a clear satiny rose-pink, 90cm (3ft).

They may be attacked by hollyhock rust, but there is no need

to worry. Spray the plants with zineb. Propagate them by division, in autumn or spring. Support the taller varieties with canes and cut down plants after flowering to encourage the development of lateral shoots.

Silene schafta

(Campion)
- **Any sunny position**
- **Any soil**
- **Evergreen**

This most accommodating hardy perennial is suitable for the rock garden, has few dislikes, and will give of its best in most situations. Mid-green lanceolate leaves form a tuft that spreads up to 30cm (12in) and produces sprays of rose-magenta flowers on 10-15cm (4-6in) stems over a very long period from midsummer to early autumn. Although it is easily grown, there is a slight coarseness about the plant that does not rank it among the aristocrats of the rock garden.

Propagation is fairly quick by seed sown in late winter; pot the seedlings up in early spring ready for planting out in early summer. Alternatively, cuttings taken in midsummer and placed in a sand frame make specimens ready for planting in autumn.

Below: Silene schafta brightens rock gardens from midsummer to autumn with rose-purple flowers.

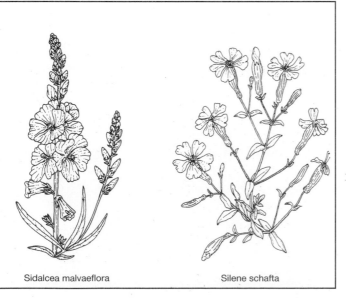

Sidalcea malvaeflora

Silene schafta

Skimmia japonica
- **Sun or partial shade**
- **Fertile moist soil; not chalk soils**
- **Spring flowers; autumn and winter berries**

This hardy, evergreen shrub has several cultivars. Male and female flowers are on separate plants, and both sexes must be grown if berries are to be produced. *S.j.* 'Foremanii' is a female form and bears a profusion of bright scarlet berries. The yellowish green foliage has lance-like leaves 8cm (3.2in) long and 2cm (0.8in) wide and tapered at each end, with reddish stalks. This bushy spreading shrub does best in shade. It will reach 1-1.5m (3.3-5ft) tall and 1.5m (5ft) or more wide.

'Rubella' is a compact male clone with deep green foliage. It bears large conical flower heads in spring and the panicles of ruby-red buds with their dark flower stalks are especially beautiful in winter. It reaches 1-1.2m (3.3-4ft) tall and equally wide. Propagate by seed sown in late winter, by half-ripe cuttings in summer, or by hardwood cuttings in autumn.

Below: Skimmia japonica forms a dome-shaped, evergreen shrub covered with fragrant flowers.

Sisyrinchium bermudianum
(Blue-eye grass)
- **Full sun**
- **Any good garden soil**
- **Evergreen**

Plants that seed themselves freely can sometimes be unpopular. Although the herbaceous perennial *S. bermudianum* is guilty of this habit, it is one that can be tolerated. The 15cm (6in) upright flat iris-like foliage is useful for giving some height to a flat area on the rock garden. Some of the leaves are in fact disguised flower stalks and small satiny blue flowers appear at the leaf tips from early summer.

This species is very easy to cultivate, growing even in shaded situations on the peat bed if you do not watch it. It is also very useful in a paved area where it can seed in the cracks.

Its habit of seeding about makes propagation easy: just gather up the seedlings and pot them on. Alternatively, you can sow seed in midwinter, or divide in early spring or early autumn.

Above: Sisyrinchium striatum is superb in midsummer with its pale flowers that cling to upright stems.

Sisyrinchium striatum
- **Sunny location**
- **Well-drained soil**
- **Summer flowering**

This Chilean perennial is evergreen, and it gives grey-green sword-like foliage throughout the year. In winter its 45-60cm (18-24in) iris-like foliage makes a handsome fan in the borders, and in summer the 75-90cm (30-36in) rigid slender stems are closely packed with many pale yellowish-white flowers; the reverse of the petals is striped with purple. The flowers are carried on about half the total length of the stems. Grow it in a sunny place in well-drained soil with added leaf-mould or peat.

After a year or so plants suddenly die, but they seed themselves freely. Transplant self-sown seedlings to form a tidy clump. Cut down the faded flower stems and any dead leaves during the autumn. Propagate by division in autumn.

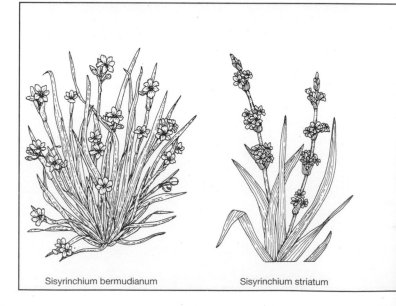

Sisyrinchium bermudianum

Sisyrinchium striatum

Smilacina racemosa

(False Solomon's seal, False spikenard, Treacleberry)

- **Shade**
- **Moist rich soil**
- **Spring flowering**

This hardy herbaceous perennial enjoys similar conditions to the well-known lily of the valley. Its slender, pointed, fresh green, spear-like leaves are downy beneath, and stick out right and left alternately from the stem. The little trusses of creamy-white scented frothy flowers are also arranged alternately, and are distributed on the underside of the arching 75cm (30in) stems. In autumn the flowers are followed by red berries.

Provided it is given shade and moisture, and no lime, this species will not be any bother. It must not be allowed to dry out during summer. Propagate by division of the rhizomatous roots in autumn. Do not divide in the first year after planting; the roots spread slowly underground and should not be disturbed until the plant is fully established.

Above: Solidago brachystachys, with tiny golden-yellow flowers, grows well on rock gardens.

Solidago brachystachys

- **Sunny situation**
- **Any well-drained soil**
- **Herbaceous**

This hardy herbaceous perennial is thought to be a variety of *S. cutleri*. It has a dwarf habit and is suitable for the rock garden. It is a dependable plant for flowering in early autumn. It makes a small clump, which when in flower is 15-20cm (6-8in) tall. The flowers are a miniature golden-yellow version of the larger golden rod. It does well in any soil, provided it has some good drainage and is in full sun. This plant is not invasive but do not plant it too close to other spreading plants.

Propagation is best by division in spring, planting direct or potting up. Seed sown in midwinter tends to be unreliable. Self-sown seedlings do not come true.

Above: Solidago 'Goldenmosa' is dominant in an herbaceous border, displaying frothy, yellow flowers on tall stems in late summer.

Solidago 'Goldenmosa'

(Aaron's rod, Golden rod)

- **Sun or partial shade**
- **Good ordinary soil**
- **Late summer flowering**

It is the garden hybrids of this well-known hardy herbaceous perennial that are grown. This includes 'Goldenmosa' with pretty frothy flowers, miniature heads of the original golden rod, and similar to mimosa. The rough hairy flower spikes are 75cm (30in) tall. Two smaller varieties are the 45cm (18in) 'Cloth of Gold', with deep yellow flowers, and 'Golden Thumb', with clear yellow flowers on 30cm (12in) stems, which produces neat little bushes ideal for the front of the border.

These vigorous plants will thrive in any good soil well supplied with nutrients. A sunny location or one in partial shade will suit them equally well. Propagate them all by division in spring.

Skimmia japonica

Smilacina racemosa

Solidago brachystachys

Solidago 'Goldenmosa'

Spiraea × arguta
(Bridal wreath, Foam of May)
- **Sunny position**
- **Any good garden soil**
- **Spring flowering**

This hardy, graceful, deciduous shrub is spring-flowering. It grows to about 1.5-2m (5-6.5ft) high, with slender twiggy growth, and dainty pure white flowers produced in clusters on arching sprays.

S. media is an erect shrub up to 1.2-2m (4-6.5ft) tall that bears long-stalked racemes of white flowers. S. prunifolia is the same height as S. media; the double white flowers in rosette-like clusters are borne along arching stems. Lastly, the pale green S. thunbergii has pure white flowers produced on wiry leafless stems in clusters of two to five; the shrub is about 90cm-1.5m (3-5ft) tall.

Once flowering has finished, remove old flowering shoots and shorten any long shoots. Propagate by half-ripe cuttings in summer.

Spiraea × bumalda
- **Sunny position**
- **Any good garden soil**
- **Summer flowering**

This hardy deciduous summer-flowering shrub is very popular, and best known is the variety 'Anthony Waterer'. It is 1.2-1.5m (4-5ft) high. Above the dark green

toothed leaves are flat branching clusters of carmine flowers 8cm (3.2in) wide, borne on the current season's growth from summer to autumn. In spring the cultivar 'Gold Flame' has unfolding leaves of rich bronze-red, later a light russet-orange, and crimson flowers in late summer. S. nipponica 'Snowmound' has small clusters of white flowers with green centres, each cluster borne at the end of a leafy twig on the previous year's growth; this shrub will reach a height of 1.2-1.5m (4-5ft). S. ×

vanhouttei is a 2m (6.5ft) vigorous shrub that is covered with umbels of pure white flower heads in early summer.

Prune all these spiraeas fairly hard each year in late winter, reducing the previous year's growth to several eyes of the old wood. Propagate by half-ripe cuttings in summer.

Below: Spiraea thunbergii is a graceful deciduous shrub with pure white flowers borne on leafless stems in spring.

Above: Spiraea × bumalda has a deciduous nature, with dominantly coloured flowers.

Stachys olympica 'Silver Carpet'
(Stachys lanata)
(Lamb's ear, Lamb's tongue)
- **Full sun**
- **Well-drained soil**
- **Non-flowering**

Stachys olympica (once S. lanata) flowers very freely, but 'Silver Carpet' is a non-flowering variety. It makes excellent ground cover and does not have the

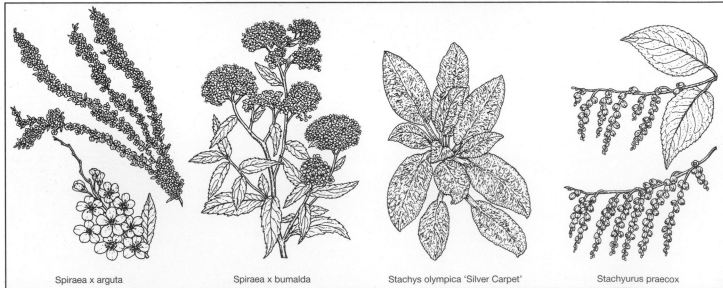

| Spiraea x arguta | Spiraea x bumalda | Stachys olympica 'Silver Carpet' | Stachyurus praecox |

Stachyurus praecox
- Sun or semi-shade
- An acid humus fertile soil
- Late winter flowering

A hardy deciduous flowering shrub that brightens gardens in late winter. The flowers are formed in autumn and open in late winter or very early spring. The oval lance-shaped leaves are 8-15cm (3.2-6in) long. The stiff drooping racemes are composed of 12 to 20 cup-shaped greenish-yellow flowers, borne on the reddish-brown naked branchlets.

As frost can damage the flowers, choose a sheltered spot, in well-drained soil with plenty of humus. A sunny or semi-shaded position is best. No regular pruning is needed. Propagate, by layering or by half-ripe cuttings, in summer.

disadvantage of producing flower stems, which look untidy once the plant has finished flowering. If you have *S. olympica*, cut off the flowers heads as soon as they are over. Both *S. olympica* and 'Silver Carpet' are evergreen.

A quite different stachys is *S. macrantha* (syn. *S. grandiflora*), or big betony. This has heart-shaped hairy white foliage which is a soft green and very wrinkled. The rosy-violet flowers are held on erect stems 30cm (12in) high. They flower during summer.

Propagate stachys by division, in spring or autumn. Do not let them encroach on other perennials.

Above: Stachys olympica 'Silver Carpet' has an attractive woolly and silvery appearance.

Sternbergia lutea
(Lily of the field, Winter daffodil, Yellow star flower)
- Full sun
- Well-drained soil
- Plant 10-15cm (4-6in) deep

This hardy bulbous plant from the eastern Mediterranean and Iran looks like a crocus but flowers in autumn, with bright blooms up to 5cm (2in) long on a true stem. The strap-like leaves appear with the flower but remain small and immature until the following spring. The plant will reach a height of 15cm (6in), with a similar spread.

Plant the bulbs in late summer, 10-15cm (4-6in) deep in a well-drained soil, in a sunny part of the garden. Leave undisturbed until they become overcrowded, when they can be lifted in late summer, divided, and replanted immediately to prevent drying out. The offsets can be removed and grown separately, and will mature and come into flower in one year. This plant can be grown with, or as an alternative to, autumn-flowering crocuses and will provide a show of brilliant yellow. If slugs attack young growth, use a slug bait.

Above: Sternbergia lutea is a brightly coloured bulbous plant with yellow flowers in late summer and autumn.

Styrax japonica
(Japanese snowbell)
- Sun or semi-shade
- Moist fertile lime-free soil
- Early summer flowering

This handsome deciduous shrub or small tree, seldom taller than 5.5m (18ft), has oval leaves of a dark glossy green, and creamy white fuchsia-like flowers borne on short lateral shoots. Shade it from early morning sun, as the young shoots and flower buds can be injured by frost.

This species needs moist loamy soil to which leaf-mould or moistened peat has been added. It is quite hardy except in frost-prone gardens. No regular pruning is necessary. Although an occasional thinning of overcrowded growth may be given, the natural beauty will be lost if it is pruned heavily.

Propagate by seeds sown out of doors as soon as ripe, by half-ripe cuttings in summer, or by layering in autumn.

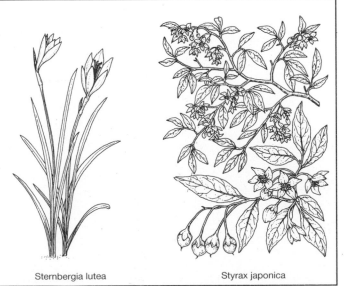

Sternbergia lutea   Styrax japonica

Above: Syringa meyeri 'Palibin' is a lilac for small gardens, creating a wealth of small, highly fragrant, lavender-purple flowers in early summer.

Syringa meyeri 'Palibin'

- **Open situation**
- **Any soil**
- **Deciduous shrub**

This deciduous shrub usually grows no more than 1.2m (4ft) high by 1m (3.3ft) across. It makes a twiggy bush, which blooms freely at the usual time for lilacs, in early summer, producing slightly scented lavender-purple flower panicles.

It is not fussy about soil, though it prefers not to grow in wet boggy conditions. It requires no pruning.

Propagation is by heel cuttings, 7-10cm (2.75-4in) long, taken from non-flowering shoots in midsummer. Insert these in a peat and sand frame. If mist propagation is available, this is a help. Pot the rooted cuttings into a loam-based compost. Although it takes some time to reach its ultimate height, allow space when planting.

Syringa vulgaris

(Common lilac)
- **Full sun**
- **Good fertile soil, including chalk soils**
- **Late spring to early summer flowering**

These hardy deciduous shrubs and small trees are renowned for their flowers and fragrance. Single varieties include 'Souvenir de Louis Spaeth', a deep wine red, flowering in mid-season; 'Maud Notcutt', with large pure white flowers; 'Vestale', white, with light-green foliage; and 'Congo', lilac-red, free-flowering, and compact. Double varieties include 'Katherine Havemeyer', deep purple, large and strongly scented; 'Michael Buchner', lilac, with a lovely scent; 'Madame Lemoine', heavy white panicles; and 'Charles Joly', dark purplish red.

Lilacs thrive on well-drained loamy soil or chalk. Bushes can be as high as 5.5m (18ft). Plant them 3-4.5m (10-15ft) apart. Remove old flower trusses as soon as they are over. No regular pruning is needed. Propagate by layering in spring and remove suckers from grafted plants.

Tagetes erecta 'Orange Jubilee' F1

(African marigold, Aztec marigold)
- **Sow in spring**
- **Any soil**
- **Open and sunny site**

These half-hardy annuals are very reliable, and the cultivar 'Orange Jubilee' is no exception. One of a strain of Jubilee types growing to 60cm (24in) tall, they are often referred to as 'hedge forms' because of the dense foliage. 'Orange Jubilee' is an F1 Hybrid and although seeds are relatively expensive they are worth the extra cost because of the reliable uniformity of flower. Carnation-shaped double blooms are produced on the almost erect stems of very sturdy plants. Light orange in colour, individual flowers can be 10cm (4in) in diameter. Dead-head to prolong flowering. Foliage, kept below the flowers, is light green and deeply cut. All parts of the plant are very pungent.

Sow seeds in warmth in late winter. Prick out the seedlings into seed boxes and later harden off before planting out as soon as all risk of frost has passed.

Below: Tagetes erecta 'Orange Jubilee' is majestic, displaying large, orange flowers.

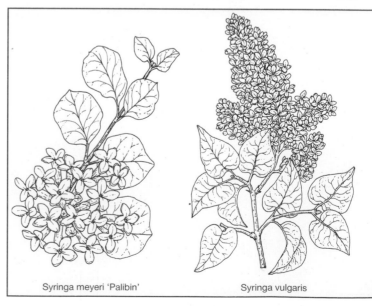

Syringa meyeri 'Palibin'   Syringa vulgaris

Tagetes patula 'Yellow Jacket'

(French marigold)
- **Sow in spring**
- **Ordinary, even poor soil**
- **Open and sunny site**

Few half-hardy annuals provide such good value as the marigolds. They tolerate most conditions except shade, and even on poor soils they do remarkably well. Continual dead-heading of plants will give a longer flowering season. Recent introductions - and there have been many – can make it difficult to choose, but 'Yellow Jacket' is strongly recommended for its dwarfness. Only 15cm (6in) in height, it has large, double, carnation-like flowers of bright yellow, which shine.

Sow under glass in spring. Use any good growing medium to raise the seed. Keep in a temperature of 18°C (65°F). Prick off the young seedlings in the usual way. Harden off and plant out in early summer, 15cm (6in) apart, after the risk of frost. Spray against aphid attacks.

Tagetes signata pumila

(Tagetes tenuifolia)
- **Sow in spring**
- **Ordinary well-cultivated soil**
- **Open sunny location**

Also known as *T. tenuifolia*, this half-hardy annual creates a wealth of colour during midsummer and late summer. There are many varieties to choose from. Colours range from lemon to yellow, orange-brown and mahogany, with many different markings. The finely divided light green leaves are pleasantly scented.

Seeds may be sown in seed mixture under glass from early spring in a temperature of 16-18°C (60-65°F) and lightly covered until germination, which should take about one week. Prick off into trays and grow on in a lower temperature until ready for hardening off; plant out in early summer after frost. Space plants about 20cm (8in) apart.

Above: *Tagetes patula 'Glowing Ember'* has bright flowers, orange with crimson blotches.

Take care not to overwater or overfeed, which will result in too much foliage.

Taxus baccata 'Fastigiata Aurea'

(Golden Irish yew)
- **Open site**
- **Well-drained soil**
- **Slow-growing large shrub**

This evergreen conifer has a very neat upright form, and golden leaves. It forms a narrow bowl shape with very tight foliage, which gives it a solid look. A ten-year-old plant will reach 2m (6.5ft) tall with a

spread of 65cm (26in), and it will eventually reach 4.9m (16ft) high. The foliage is a glorious yellow-gold, holding its colour right through the winter.

Propagate by cuttings in autumn; set them in a half-and-half mixture of peat and sand, and in the following spring move the rooted cuttings to a nursery bed. Grow on for two years and then plant out into their final positions. Choose a soil that is well-drained, either acid or alkaline, and in full sun. If using them for a hedge, plant at least 35cm (14in) apart; a feed of a general fertilizer will give them a good start. Take care for this is a poisonous plant.

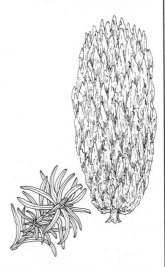

Right: *Taxus baccata 'Fastigiata Aurea'*, a slow-growing conifer, forms a golden column.

Tagetes erecta 'Orange Jubilee' F1

Tagetes patula 'Yellow Jacket'

Tagetes signata pumila

Taxus baccata 'Fastigiata Aurea'

Taxus baccata 'Repens Aurea'

- **Full sun**
- **Well-drained soil**
- **Slow-growing ground cover**

This evergreen conifer is similar in habit to *Taxus baccata* 'Repandens', but it also has variegated leaves. It grows slowly, to make a plant 35cm (14in) high with a width of 1m (3.3ft) in ten years; over the years it reaches about 3m (10ft) wide and 90cm (3ft) tall. The spreading branches can be trimmed back to a domed shape. The foliage is dense, and each leaf is green with a margin of gold – pale gold in spring but gradually becoming deeper. The branches spread, with drooping tips.

Grow from cuttings taken in autumn, struck in a half peat and half sand mixture and over-wintered in a cold frame. In spring set the rooted cuttings in a nursery bed for two years. The plants should be placed in well-drained soil in full sun; shade would make the plant lose its golden colour and revert to green. This plant is poisonous so only grow it in an area without children or animals.

Below: Taxus baccata 'Repens Aurea' is prostrate, with golden-yellow foliage. Plant in a dwarf conifer garden.

Tecophilaea cyanocrocus

(Chilean crocus)

- **Warm sunny place**
- **Rich sandy soil**
- **Plant 5cm (2in) deep**

This bulbous plant has a few slender twisted leaves growing to a height of 12.5cm (5in). Its deep blue to purple petals have white throats. In their natural habitat in Chile these plants grow on stony well-drained slopes.

Plant them out of doors in a rich sandy soil that drains well, in a sunny and warm position with some protection from hard frost. In wet areas cover with a cloche to keep the plant dry during the winter months; this will stop the growth of the leaves, which are susceptible to low temperatures, and the plant will pick up in the spring. Plant the corms 5cm (2in) deep in mid-autumn. They can also be grown as pot plants in a cool greenhouse: place six corms in a 15cm (6in) pot of moist potting mixture, leave without water until the leaves shoot, then water until the leaves die. Allow the plants to dry out in the greenhouse, remove any offsets and grow on.

Below: Tecophilaea cyanocrocus, with deep blue flowers and white throats, thrives in well-drained and sunny rock gardens.

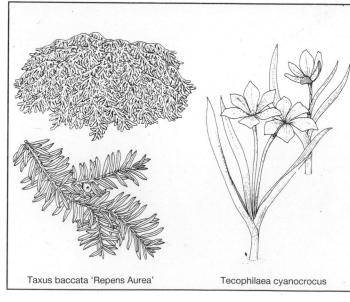

Taxus baccata 'Repens Aurea'　　Tecophilaea cyanocrocus　　Teucrium pyrenaicum　　Thalictrum speciosissimum

Teucrium pyrenaicum
- **Sunny exposure**
- **Light, well-drained soil**
- **Evergreen**

Some shrubby members of this genus have aromatic foliage, but not so *T. pyrenaicum*, which is a trailing plant with crinkly woolly leaves forming a neat mat about 30cm (12in) across. It is low-growing, and when in flower is only 5-8cm (2-3.2in) high. The flowers are curiously hooded, mauve and cream, in flat heads about 2.5cm (1in) across, and they appear from midsummer to late summer.

This hardy perennial, ideal for a rock garden, needs a well-drained soil, preferably on the light side, and a sunny situation. It is basically hardy, but may succumb to a particularly wet cold winter. A pane of glass over this plant in a wet winter may assist it.

Propagation is by division in spring; pot up rooted rosettes into loam-based compost and plant in six to eight weeks.

Thalictrum speciosissimum
(Thalictrum flavum glaucum)
(Meadow rue)
- **Sun or light shade**
- **Any good fertile soil**
- **Summer flowering**

This hardy herbaceous perennial is much sought after by flower arrangers for its foliage. Also known as *T. flavum glaucum*, it has lovely glaucous leaves pinnately cut and divided. The foliage lasts longer than the frothy pale yellow flowers carried on huge panicles at the top of stout 1.5m (5ft) stems. This is a back of the border perennial.

T. dipterocarpum is another lovely meadow rue, with branching panicles of rosy mauve flowers with bright yellow stamens. It needs rich well-cultivated soil, and staking if planted in a windy site. The form 'Hewitt's Double' has rich mauve flowers.

Propagate by division in spring, and 'Hewitt's Double' by offsets also in spring.

Above: Teucrium pyrenaicum creates mats of crinkly, woolly leaves. Mauve and cream flowers appear during the summer.

Above: Thuja occidentalis 'Danica' creates bright green, bun-shaped hillocks.

Thuja occidentalis 'Danica'
- **Full sun**
- **Deep moist soil**
- **Slow-growing dwarf bush**

This evergreen conifer forms a small slow-growing bun that looks fine on a rockery or among heathers. It will grow to 30cm (12in) tall with a spread of 45cm (18in) in ten years, and eventually reaches about 75cm (30in) high and 1.2m (4ft) wide. The scale-like foliage is carried on fans in vertical sprays. The bright green leaf colour turns bronze during the winter months, and if crushed the leaves give off an apple-like scent. Cones are yellow-green, ripening to brown.

To obtain plants with the characteristics of the parent, take cuttings in autumn, set in a mixture of half peat and half sand, and keep in a cold frame during the winter. Put rooted cuttings into pots of potting compost and plunge out of doors into a nursery bed for two years. Plant out in a sheltered position in full sun in a deep moist soil.

Thuja occidentalis 'Holmstrupii'
- **Full sun in sheltered position**
- **Deep moist soil**
- **Slow-growing medium bush**

This evergreen conifer forms a pyramidal bush that grows well in a border or rockery. At ten years old the plant will be about 1.5m (5ft) tall with a width of 60cm (24in) across the base, and its ultimate height is around 3m (10ft). This slow-growing shrub has bright yellow-green foliage in closely packed fans of scale-like leaves. The leaves bronze slightly during the winter in cold areas, but this cultivar is one of the best to keep a good green colour. The cones are green, ripening to brown, and about 2.5cm (1in) across.

The plants can be grown from cuttings taken in autumn, set into a half peat and half sand mixture, and kept in a cold frame over winter. Then put the rooted cuttings into pots and plunge these into a nursery bed for two years. After this period transplant them into deep moist soil in a sheltered position in full sun. A spring feed of a general fertilizer and a mulch of peat and compost will keep the plants growing well.

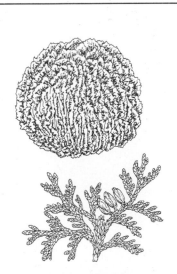

Thuja occidentalis 'Danica'

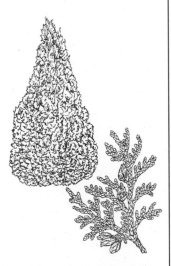

Thuja occidentalis 'Holmstrupii'

Thuja orientalis 'Aurea Nana'
- **Full sun**
- **Deep moist soil**
- **Slow-growing small shrub**

This evergreen conifer makes a rounded cone shape of yellow-green foliage that fits in with rockeries, borders, scree or heather gardens. It is a dwarf conifer growing to 60cm (24in) tall with a spread of 50cm (20in) in ten years, and it rarely reaches higher than 1m (3.3ft). The foliage is in vertical fans of densely packed scale-like leaves of yellow-green, which turn gold in winter. It hardly ever needs trimming. The small cones are about 1.8cm (0.7in) wide, ripening from green to brown in autumn, and have six hooked scales.

This plant is increased by cuttings. Take these in autumn, set into a half-and-half mixture of peat and sand, and over-winter in a cold frame. The rooted seedlings should be potted and sunk into a nursery bed for two years. Put out the plants into their final positions, choosing a deep moist soil in full sun. Generally this shrub is trouble-free.

Thuja plicata 'Rogersii'
- **Sunny position**
- **Deep moist soil**
- **Slow-growing dwarf shrub**

This dwarf evergreen conifer has a fine conical shape and golden foliage, and is ideal for rockeries, scree or heather gardens, or containers. In ten years this slow-growing plant will reach 70cm (28in) high with a spread of 40cm (16in), and in 30 years it can grow over 1m (3.3ft) tall and almost as wide, but careful pruning will make a columnar form or wide-spreading bun shape. The fine foliage is densely packed in tight clusters, green in colour, with the edges of the scale-like leaf fans gold, and in winter this turns to bronze. Keep it in full sunlight to retain the gold.

Propagation is by cuttings, taken in autumn. Set in a half-and-half mixture of peat and sand, and over-winter in a cold frame. In spring pot the rooted cuttings and plunge them into a nursery bed for two years. They can then be planted out into permanent positions in full sun and a deep moist soil. These plants are trouble-free.

Thuja plicata 'Stoneham Gold'
- **Full sunlight**
- **Deep moist soil**
- **Slow-growing small shrub**

This slow-growing evergreen conifer's rich golden-yellow foliage is as bright in winter as in summer. In ten years this compact plant will have reached just over 70cm (28in) tall and 35cm (14in) wide; its ultimate size is estimated at just over 2m (6.5ft). The foliage is dark green in the depths of the closely packed scale-like leaf sprays, but on the outer edges the colour pales to a bright orange-yellow. It can be trained to form a definite cone or ball shape.

The plant is grown from cuttings taken in autumn and set in a mixture of peat and sand. Keep these in a cold frame during the winter and pot up the rooted cuttings in spring. Place in a nursery bed for two years and then plant out in full sun in a deep moist soil. In dry weather, keep young plants watered until established. These plants are usually free from pest and disease attack.

Thunbergia alata
(Black-eyed Susan, Clock vine)
- **Sow in spring**
- **Ordinary, well-drained soil**
- **Sunny and sheltered position**

Surely one of the finest annual climbers, this half-hardy annual comes from South Africa. It freely produces 5cm (2in) wide tubular flowers of orange-yellow, the centre of the tube being dark purple-brown. Blooms are formed from the axils of the ovate light green leaves, which are carried on twining stems up to 3m (10ft) long. This is an ideal climbing plant for the cool greenhouse. If given a sheltered sunny site it will do equally well in the garden: grow it against a south-facing wall, or on tall peasticks in an annual or mixed border.

If space and position allow, let this species twine amongst a blue clematis – it creates a lovely combination of colour.

Sow seeds in spring under glass in a temperature of 16-18°C (60-65°F). Use any good growing medium. Keep young plants well spaced under glass to prevent

Above: *Thuja orientalis 'Aurea Nana' is cone-shaped, with* yellowish-green foliage held in upright sprays.

Thuja orientalis 'Aurea Nana'

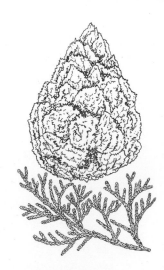

Thuja plicata 'Rogersii'

Above: Thymus 'Doone Valley' is low and spreading, with small, lavender flowers in summer borne above olive-green leaves.

tangling. Prick off the seedlings singly into individual small pots and place a split cane in each to give support. Plant out after hardening off in summer.

Thymus 'Doone Valley'

(Thyme)
● **Open, sunny situation**
● **Any soil**
● **Evergreen**

This small, aromatic, evergreen plant loves the sun in an open

Above: Thymus serpyllum, an aromatic and compact low-growing shrub, has small, pink-violet flowers.

position and is not fussy over soil, although obviously it would not be happy in waterlogged conditions. It forms flat mats, ideal for the alpine house and can be under-planted with bulbs. The foliage is aromatic and does well where it can be stepped on to draw out its fragrance.

'Doone Valley' is of doubtful

parentage but of undoubted worth, with its olive-green leaves flecked with golden spots. Rounded heads of lavender flowers are borne on 10cm (4in) stems in summer.

Propagation is by division in late summer; pot up the small pieces or plant them out direct. Do not plant 'Doone Valley' in shade, or it will lose its variegation.

Thymus serpyllum

(Wild thyme)
● **Open sunny situation**
● **Any soil**
● **Evergreen**

This aromatic evergreen shrub forms a prostrate mat, perfect for the alpine lawn and for under-planting with bulbs. It is a very variable plant, both in its native habitats throughout Europe and in cultivation, where there are several named forms. The mats can spread to 60cm (24in) or more, but are beautiful when smothered with the 1cm (0.4in) heads of flowers that range from pink to rich rose.

Of the named forms 'Coccineum', with deep red flowers, is outstanding; 'Minus' is useful for sinks and troughs because of its compact habit; and 'Silver Queen' has silver and green variegated foliage.

Propagation is by division in spring or autumn, potting up the divisions or planting direct. Remember its spreading habit and allow plenty of room.

Thuja plicata 'Stoneham Gold'

Thunbergia alata

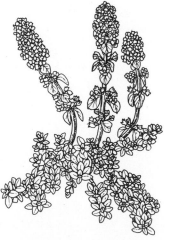

Thymus 'Doone Valley'

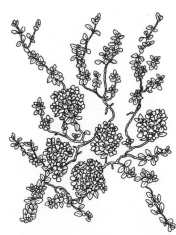

Thymus serpyllum

Tigridia pavonia

(Peacock tiger flower, Tiger flower)
- **Sunny location**
- **Rich well-drained soil**
- **Plant 7.5-10cm (3-4in) deep**

These spectacular half-hardy cormous plants from Mexico and Peru can reach 60cm (24in) tall, with long sword-shaped pleated leaves of mid-green. The flowers last only a day, but each stem produces a succession of up to eight blooms in summer. These are up to 10cm (4in) wide, and have three large petals with three small petals in between, surrounding a cup-shaped base. The larger petals are plain but the smaller ones are spotted in white, yellow or red, which gives them the common name of peacock tiger.

Plant the corms in spring, 7.5-10cm (3-4in) deep in a rich well-drained soil, in a position where there is plenty of sun. Lift them in autumn and keep dry and frost-free until replanting time next spring. At this time cormlets can be removed and grown separately, to reach flowering size in a couple of years. During winter guard against mice eating the stored corms. Keep plants moist in dry weather.

Above: Tigridia pavonia 'Rubra' is eye-catching, with large, orange-salmon petals and purple throats spotted with white.

Tradescantia virginiana 'Isis'

(Spiderwort, Trinity, Widow's-tears)
- **Sun or partial shade**
- **Any good fertile soil**
- **Summer and autumn flowering**

The spiderworts are probably better known as house plants, but the hardy herbaceous perennials are much larger. *T. virginiana* has a number of varieties from which to choose. These perennials have smooth almost glossy curving strap-shaped leaves, ending in a cradle-like effect, where a continuous display of three-petalled flowers emerges throughout summer and autumn.

The variety 'Isis' has deep blue flowers and is 45cm (18in) high. The pure white 'Osprey', has three-petalled crested flowers, and another pure white of similar height is 'Innocence'. Two 50cm (20in) varieties are the carmine-purple 'Purewell Giant' and the rich velvety 'Purple Dome'.

Plant them in clumps, not singly; on their own they are not effective, but clumps make a splash of colour. Plant near the front of a border. Propagate them by division in spring or autumn.

Above: Tradescantia virginiana 'Isis' displays deep-blue flowers amid sword-shaped, glossy leaves.

Trillium grandiflorum

(Wake robin, White wake robin)
- **Shady situation**
- **Moist well-drained soil**
- **Plant 10cm (4in) deep**

This trillium can grow to a height of 45cm (18in). It has pale to mid-green leaves, and large flowers

Tigridia pavonia

Tradescantia virginiana 'Isis'

Trillium grandiflorum

Trillium sessile

7.5cm (3in) across with the petals slightly turned back, blooming from mid-spring. The blooms are white on opening, gradually changing to pink; double varieties are available in white and pink.

Trilliums are hardy, rhizomatous, herbaceous perennials that need a moist well-drained soil in a shady situation; added peat, leaf-mould or compost is beneficial. Rhizomes should be planted in late summer, as soon as they become available, at a depth of 10cm (4in). Planting in groups, with the bulbs 15cm (6in) apart, gives a massed effect. When leaves die down in late summer the plant can be lifted, and the rhizomes divided and replanted. Seeds can take up to six years to reach flowering size, so it is better to grow from rhizome sections, but make sure that each piece has a growing shoot on it.

Trillium sessile
(Toad lily, Toadshade, Wake robin)
- **Cool position**
- **Moisture-holding soil**
- **Herbaceous**

It is hard to believe that trilliums belong to the lily family, because they are so different in looks. Strong stems emerge, 15-30cm (6-12in) tall, on top of which are three dark green oval leaves, marbled grey. Where these three leaves meet, the stemless purple-pointed flowers appear in spring.

They are hardy, rhizomatous, herbaceous perennials that will be long-lived if given the right conditions: a cool, shady position that never dries out, with a leafy, peaty soil, although they will accept a heavier soil with equanimity.

Propagation is by division in late summer; make certain that the roots do not dry out when they are dug up. Plant out directly, or pot up in a leafy soil. Seed can be sown in spring in a fine leafy compost.

Tritonia crocata
- **Full light**
- **Good potting mixture**
- **Plant 5cm (2in) deep**

This cormous plant has fans of slender, sword-shaped mid-green leaves, and will grow to a height of 45cm (18in). In late spring it will produce a number of cup-shaped flowers up to 5cm (2in) wide, in white, yellow, pink, orange or copper.

Most of this group of plants are best grown as pot plants, although they can be used in late spring as container plants in the garden. Corms should be planted in moist potting mixture, five to a 15cm (6in) pot. After planting in early autumn, the pot should not be watered until the leaves start to shoot, unless the mixture dries right out. Keep a temperature of over 7°C (45°F) and put the plant in full light.

After flowering keep well watered until the leaves die back, then let the soil dry out in greenhouse heat until early autumn, when it should be repotted. At this time offsets can be removed from the larger corms and grown on. Support leggy plants with canes.

Trollius × hybridus
(Globe flower)
- **Sun or dappled shade**
- **Moist soil**
- **Spring flowering**

These hardy herbaceous flowers thrive best in moist soil, and they need plenty of humus such as leaf-mould, well-rotted farmyard manure or good garden compost, especially in drier ground.

The following varieties are worth considering: 'Fire Globe' is 75cm (30in) tall, with deeply cut large dark green foliage and rich orange-yellow globular flowers; of similar height, 'Goldquelle' is a vigorous plant with pale buttercup-yellow globular flowers; 'Canary Bird' is not quite 60cm (24in) high, with coarsely divided dark green foliage and large cup-shaped bright golden-yellow flowers. If your soil does not dry out, plant 45cm (18in) 'Earliest of All', with medium-size foliage, and bright golden-yellow, cup-shaped flowers in early spring.

Propagate all varieties by division in spring.

Below: Trillium grandiflorum has large flowers with slightly recurving white petals.

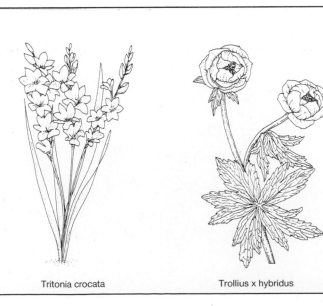

Tritonia crocata

Trollius x hybridus

Tropaeolum peregrinum

(Tropaeolum canariense)
(Canary creeper)
● Sow in spring
● Average soil
● Sun or partial shade

Also known as *T. canariense*, this choice climber, related to the nasturtium, is well worth a place in the garden if you have a suitable site. Strictly short-lived perennials they are treated as annuals for cultivation purposes. The elegantly fringed yellow flowers, 2.5cm (1in) across, have graceful green spurs, and are produced freely from thin twining stems that can reach a height of 4m (13ft) in a single season. Peltate leaves of five lobes, and green-blue in colour, are carried on the full length of the stems. This species is useful and looks attractive over trellis work or on wires.

Sow seeds in early spring to produce flowering plants in the summer. Use any good growing medium, plant two seeds per pot, and keep in a temperature of 13°C (55°F). Place a split cane in each pot to provide support; plant out in early summer, after hardening off. Avoid overwatering and do not feed: otherwise plants will make leaves but very few flowers.

Below: Tropaeolum peregrinum, a scrambling, twining climber, has greenish-blue leaves and elegantly fringed yellow flowers.

Tropaeolum polyphyllum

● Sunny situation
● Deep, well-drained soil
● Herbaceous

This is a spectacular herbaceous perennial that seems difficult to establish, but it is worth the effort, as it is so distinctive and showy. It is a tuberous-rooted perennial, which sends up long trailing or arching stems of grey leaves, in the axils of which are produced large rich yellow nasturtium-like flowers in early and midsummer. It dies away after flowering and is likely to come up in a completely different spot the following year.

The secret of success is to plant the tuber at least 30cm (12in) deep, in a position where its trailing stems can hang down over a rock or wall. Its hardiness has long been proven.

Once the plant is established, propagation is simple, by digging up the tubers as required.

Tropaeolum speciosum

(Flame creeper, Scotch flame flower)
● Shade and sun
● Retentive moist soil
● Summer and autumn flowering

This beautiful deciduous perennial can be bitterly disappointing, because its fleshy roots are difficult to establish. Once settled it is a joy. Pretty six-lobed leaves are carried on twining stems that are best seen rambling over evergreen shrubs or hedges. From midsummer through to the autumn the plant is covered with superb scarlet flowers about 4cm (1.6in) across and with attractive spurs. The plant is best suited to cool moist country gardens; it is not ideal for towns and cities.

Propagate by seed sown in spring in a cold frame, or by division in spring.

Below: Tropaeolum polyphyllum covers large rocks or dry stone walls with rich yellow flowers and arching grey leaves.

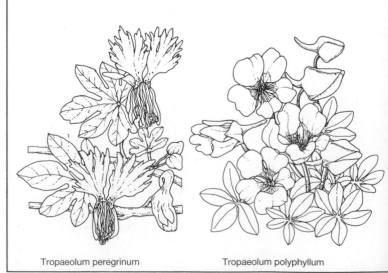

Tropaeolum peregrinum

Tropaeolum polyphyllum

Tsuga canadensis 'Bennett'

- Partial shade
- Moist well-drained soil
- Slow-growing dwarf shrub

This evergreen conifer is dwarf in character, making a low spreading plant with small yew-like leaves. It will grow slowly to just over 30cm (12in) tall with a spread of 60cm (24in) in ten years, and eventually makes a shrub about 1.2m (4ft) high and 2.4m (8ft) wide. The foliage is a fresh mid-green. The flat leaves are 1.25cm (0.5in) long.

The plant is propagated by cuttings in autumn. Set them in a half-and-half mixture of peat and sand and over-winter in a cold frame. In spring put the rooted cuttings into pots and plunge them into a nursery bed for three years. Keep the bed clear of weeds, and water the young plants in dry weather. Plant out into a moist well-drained soil in partial shade, sheltered from dry winds.

Tsuga canadensis 'Pendula'

- Sunshine or partial shade
- Moist well-drained soil
- Slow-growing medium shrub

This evergreen conifer has a distinctive habit of growth, forming a mound of overlapping weeping branches, and it makes a fine specimen plant for the lawn, or set high on a rockery. It forms a shrub 1.5m (5ft) across in ten years. A good plant should grow to 3m (10ft) tall and 9m (29.5ft) across. The foliage is mid-green and looks magnificent with the spring growth of pale lime-green tips.

It is propagated by cuttings taken in autumn, set in an equal mix of peat and sand, and put into a cold frame until spring. The rooted cuttings are put into pots and sunk into a nursery bed for three years. Plant out into the open or in partial shade in moist well-drained soil. Protect from drying winds.

Left: Tsuga canadensis 'Bennett' has fresh, yew-like foliage.

Tulipa – Double Early

(Tulip)
- Full sun
- Alkaline soil
- Plant 15cm (6in) deep at most

This group of tulips has early-blooming flowers in spring, and if forced under glass can be in flower in late winter. The form is double, with blooms often reaching 10cm (4in) across. The plants grow to 30-38cm (12-15in), and leaves are often grey-green. The colours available are white, yellow, pink, orange, red, violet and purple, with many multicolours.

Plant out bulbs in late autumn in a slightly alkaline soil, 15cm (6in) deep. Tulips thrive in direct sunlight but keep bulbs moist

Above: This is a beautiful pink-coloured Double Early tulip called 'Peach Blossom'.

while growing. When the petals fall, dead-head the plant but leave the stem and leaves to feed the bulb for the coming season. When the leaves turn yellow the plant can be lifted and stored for replanting in late autumn. Offsets can be taken at lifting time and grown on.

Tropaeolum speciosum

Tsuga canadensis 'Bennett'

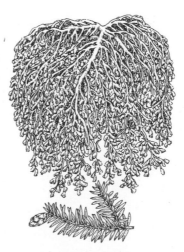
Tsuga canadensis 'Pendula'

Tulipa – double early

Tulipa – Greigii Varieties
(Tulip)
- **Sunny site**
- **Add lime if soil is acid**
- **Plant 15cm (6in) deep at most**

These hybrids are becoming popular for their decorative leaves and brilliant long-lasting flowers of red, yellow and near-white. The leaves are beautifully marked with stripes and mottles in browny purple, and the short sturdy growth helps plants to stand up to high winds, which makes them ideal for exposed sites. Generally growing to 25cm (10in), they flower in mid-spring. The petals reach 7.5cm (3in) long when the bloom opens fully in direct sunshine.

Where soil is acid, add some lime; where there is heavy clay, add plenty of sharp sand and fibrous material to help drainage. The bulbs should be planted in groups of up to a dozen to give a good display. Pick off the dead heads to build up the bulb for the next year. Keep the area around the bulbs weed-free.

Dust soil with an insecticide to deter pests. Most diseases are due to excessive moisture. If disease appears other than rot, destroy bulb.

Below: Tulipa greigii 'Red Riding Hood' creates a sea of brilliant red flowers and variegated leaves during the spring.

Tulipa – Kaufmanniana Varieties
(Tulip)
- **Sunny sheltered site**
- **Well-drained soil**
- **Plant 15cm (6in) deep at most**

These small tulips have been developed from the parent plant *T. kaufmanniana*, which comes from Turkestan. They have fine pointed flowers that open out almost flat, which gives them the appearance

Above: Tulipa kaufmanniana develops long, elegant flowers

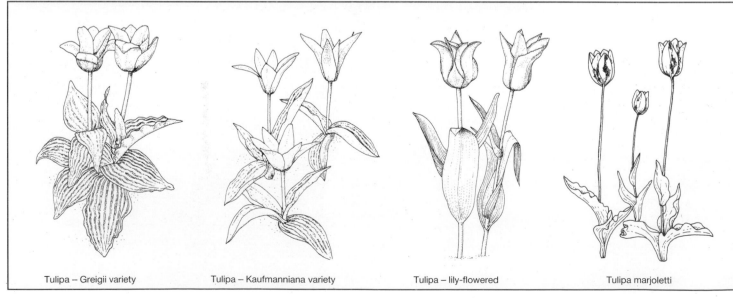

Tulipa – Greigii variety   Tulipa – Kaufmanniana variety   Tulipa – lily-flowered   Tulipa marjoletti

of a water-lily. Some open early in spring and they grow to only 10-25cm (4-10in). They are sturdy, and some have attractively striped and mottled leaves. Most have two-coloured flowers almost 10cm (4in) long. These tulips are suitable for rock gardens, the front of borders or containers where they can be left undisturbed.

Plant in well-drained soil in sunshine, at a depth of 15cm (6in). Keep them moist during spring, and dead-head after flowering.

flushed red and yellow on the outside in spring.

Tulipa — Lily-flowered
(Tulip)
- **Full sun**
- **Slightly alkaline soil**
- **Plant 15cm (6in) deep at most**

These tulips are noted for their flower shape, being slightly waisted with pointed petals that curl outwards. Blooms open in mid-spring and often reach 20cm (8in) wide. The leaves are green, some with a grey cast; the plants reach 60cm (24in) tall, and look very effective when massed. Colours include white, yellow, orange, red and multicoloured.

These tulips enjoy full sun and a slightly alkaline soil. Add lime to an acid soil. Plant 15cm (6in) deep in a sunny place in late autumn, and keep it moist while growing. Once the flower petals fall, cut off the heads. When leaves turn yellow, lift the plant, remove the offsets and grow them separately until mature.

Tulipa marjolettii
(Tulip)
- **Sunny situation**
- **Well-drained soil**
- **Bulbous**

Although rather tall — at 35-45cm (14-18in) — for the smaller rock garden, this tulip has much grace. It is reputed not to be a true species, but a garden hybrid from southern France. It has grey leaves and soft primrose-yellow flowers

slightly stained red on the exterior of the petals.

The bulb frame is an excellent place for tulips. This structure, usually raised up off the ground, is covered by tall frame lights to allow for growth. The lights are removed during the growing period in spring, and replaced when the foliage has died down, to simulate the summer baking the bulbs would receive in the wild. The frames are removed in early autumn for some moisture, and then replaced for the winter; open them on fine frost-free days. An annual feeding of bonemeal in autumn before watering is a help.

Tulipa — Parrot
(Parrot tulip, Tulip)
- **Full sun**
- **Good limy garden soil**
- **Plant 15cm (6in) deep at most**

These tulips are easily recognized by their heavily fringed and feather-like petals. The blooms are large, reaching 20cm (8in) across, and appear in a range of brilliant white, yellow, pink, orange, red and purple in mid-spring. Plants grow to 60cm (24in) tall.

Place bulbs in a sunny position, 15cm (6in) deep in an ordinary limy soil. Keep moist during the growing period, and when the petals fall off, dead-head the plants. When the leaves turn yellow, plants can be lifted and stored in a dry place until late

autumn. Offsets can be removed and replanted in nursery beds to mature. Keep tulips free from attack with a pesticide and fungicide.

Tulipa — Rembrandt
(Tulip)
- **Full sun**
- **Soil that is slightly alkaline**
- **Plant 15cm (6in) deep at most**

These are tulips with 'broken colours', usually Darwin types, which can be seen in old Dutch paintings. The rounded flowers open in mid-spring and are often 12.5cm (5in) wide. The plants stand 75cm (30in) tall, with leaves sometimes having a blue-green cast. The vividly coloured blooms can be white, yellow, orange, red, pink, violet or brown.

Plant bulbs in late autumn, 15cm (6in) deep, in a good garden soil that is slightly alkaline, and in full sun. If the soil is dry at the time of planting, water it well, and leave until the plant starts growing; then keep moist until the leaves turn yellow. Once the flowers have finished, cut off the heads to allow the bulbs to take up food. When the leaves turn yellow, lift the plants, remove and replant the offsets, and store the parent bulbs for replanting in late autumn.

Below: Tulipa 'Flaming Parrot' is spectacular, with heavily fringed petals, yellow with red stripes.

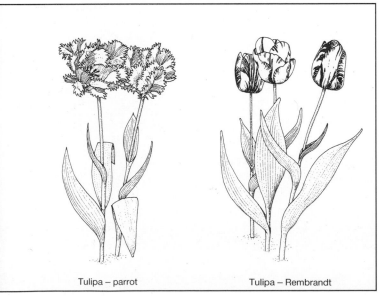

Tulipa — parrot   Tulipa — Rembrandt

Tulipa – Single Early
(Tulip)
- **Full sun**
- **Slightly alkaline soil**
- **Plant 15cm (6in) deep at most**

Tulips were introduced into Europe from Turkey over 300 years ago and an industry for developing bulbs and hybrids has centred in Holland.

Single Early types have single blooms in spring when grown out of doors, or in winter if forced under glass. The flowers grow to 12.5cm (5in) wide, and sometimes open flat in direct sunshine. A wide range of colours is available, in white, yellow, pink, red, orange, purple and mixtures. The plants, 15-38cm (6-15in) tall, are ideal for bedding or border planting.

Plant in late autumn in a slightly alkaline soil, in full sunlight, 15cm (6in) deep. When the petals fall, cut off the head to allow leaves and stem to feed the bulb for the following season. Offsets can be removed in late autumn.

Tulipa sylvestris
(Tulip)
- **Open situation**
- **Any soil**
- **Bulbous**

This is not quite such a free-flowering species, but is suitable for both the rock garden and borders, and will naturalize in woodland conditions or grass. It has narrow grey-green leaves and scented yellow flowers on 30cm (12in) stems. When fully open the flowers are 6-8cm (2.4-3.2in) across. There is a form from northern Iran that flowers more freely, offered as *Tulipa sylvestris* var. *tabriz*.

Propagation is by increased bulbs or by seed sown in late winter. If germination does not take place the first year, then the seed pots should be left outside another winter for a frosting.

Below: *Tulipa 'Hadley' is a Single Early tulip, rose-pink with an orange tinge.*

Tulipa tarda
(Tulip)
- **Sheltered and sunny position**
- **Well-drained soil with some lime**
- **Plant 15cm (6in) deep at most**

This small plant from central Asia is only 10cm (4in) tall and has up to six blooms on each stem. These are star-shaped, and the yellow petals, 5cm (2in) long, have prominent white tips and a green flush on the outside. When planted 7.5cm (3in) apart, these tulips form a carpet of blooms in spring. The narrow leaves are mid-green in colour.

Plant the bulbs in late autumn, in a sunny sheltered position, 15cm (6in) deep in a good well-drained soil that has some lime in it. Plant them in groups of up to a dozen for good effect. During the growing season make sure that the soil does not dry out. Cut off dead heads to make the plant's strength go into the bulbs. The plants can be left in the soil, but when they become crowded, lift and divide.

Below: *Tulipa tarda is an easily grown dwarf tulip, with star-shaped yellow flowers.*

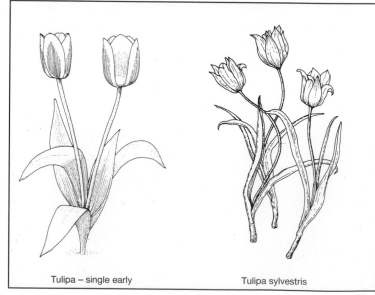

Tulipa – single early

Tulipa sylvestris

Above: Ursinia anethoides 'Sunshine Mixed' has yellow flowers with maroon centres.

Ulex europaeus
(Common gorse, Furze, Gorse, Whin)
- **Full sun**
- **Ordinary, poor dry or limy soil**
- **Flowers in spring**

The spine-tipped shoots and dark green foliage of this shrub are almost evergreen. Although gorse is at its best in spring, the golden-yellow fragrant flowers can be seen on bushes almost throughout the year. The cultivar 'Plenus', the double-flowered gorse, is slower growing than the common gorse, and more compact.

This hardy shrub grows happily in the bleakest of localities, and makes an excellent windbreak. Bushes can be badly frosted, but if they are cut back in spring, they will soon regenerate. Keep bushes under control. Common gorse can grow up to 1.5m (5ft) tall; double gorse will reach a height of only 1.2m (4ft). As this genus transplants badly, it is best to put out pot-grown plants.

Propagate the common gorse by seed sown out of doors in spring. The double cultivar does not produce seed; cuttings must be taken from the current year's growth during the summer months.

Ursinia anethoides
- **Sow in spring**
- **Ordinary or dry soil**
- **Sunny location**

Blooms of this half-hardy perennial, usually grown as a half-hardy annual, are daisy-like and come in shades of golden-yellow or orange. Often they are banded towards the base of each flower in black or maroon. Blooms will be up to 5cm (2in) across. Stems are 30cm (12in) in height.   It is very important to grow ursinias in full sunshine, because they tend to close their flowers in dull weather and at night.

Sow seeds under glass in spring, and keep a constant temperature of 16°C (60°F). Use any good growing medium that is free-draining. Add sand to heavy soils. Prick off the seedlings into boxes. Harden off in late spring and plant out into flowering positions in early summer, 23cm (9in) apart.

Above: Uvularia perfoliata has delicate, pendent, pale yellow flowers and heart-shaped leaves.

Uvularia perfoliata
(Strawbell, Throatwort)
- **Light shade**
- **Leafy soil**
- **Herbaceous**

This small genus of hardy plants, from the woods of North America, is related to the lily, and has a rhizomatous root system. They are ideal for a shady part of the rock or peat garden. A single upright stem, about 20-25cm (8-10in) tall, appears in late spring, with sessile pointed heart-shaped leaves on the upper part. Numerous pendent pale yellow narrow bell-shaped flowers are found, singly or in pairs, at the tips of branchlets. The leaves are perfoliate; that is, the main stem appears to pass through them.

The best time for propagation is in summer when the plants can be divided and potted up in leafy soil and kept moist and shaded. Division in mid-autumn is possible but brings the possibility of greater loss in winter.

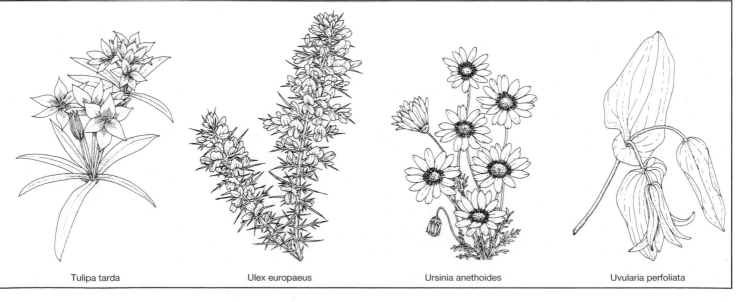

Tulipa tarda   Ulex europaeus   Ursinia anethoides   Uvularia perfoliata

Veronica teucrium 'Trehane'

- Open situation
- Well-drained soil
- Herbaceous

This is a very attractive hardy herbaceous perennial. In the form 'Trehane' the foliage is golden-yellow and this contrasts pleasantly with the blue flowers. It is not as vigorous as the species and so does not spread to much more than 20-25cm (8-10in). If this plant is put in a shady place, it will rapidly lose the yellow colouring of its leaves.

Other good varieties include: 'Crater Lake Blue' with deep blue flowers; 'Kapitan' with bright blue flowers on short spikes; and 'Shirley Blue' with blue flowers.

Propagation is by any type of cutting from midsummer to late summer. Pot up when rooted, to over-winter in a cold frame.

Viburnum × bodnantense

- Sunny position
- Any good fertile soil
- Flowers in autumn and winter

This vigorous deciduous flowering shrub is a hybrid between *V. farreri (V. fragrans)* and *V. grandiflorum*. It appears to sulk for a few years at first, but once established there is no holding it. The frost-resistant hybrid named 'Dawn' has buds that are at first rose-red, and then open into clusters of sweetly fragrant rose-tinted white flowers on the naked branches, followed by deep green foliage with red stalks. The height of this hybrid is around 2.5-3m (8-10ft), sometimes more.

When pruning is needed, remove complete old or weak branches at ground level; this will encourage new growth from the base.

Propagate by layering; rooted branches often layer naturally, otherwise layers can be put down during early summer. Give this viburnum ample space to spread itself.

Viburnum plicatum 'Mariesii'

- Prefers partial shade
- Any moist fertile soil
- Flowers in late spring and early summer

This deciduous horizontal-branched flowering shrub seems happier with some shade, rather than in full sun. The oval pointed leaves are toothed except at the base, 5-10cm (2-4in) long, up to

Above: *Viburnum tinus is an evergreen winter-flowering shrub. Plant in light shade or full sun.*

Left: *Viburnum × bodnantense is famed for its fragrant winter flowers, borne on naked stems.*

6.5 (2.5in) wide, dull dark green above, pale greyish beneath, and slightly downy. Bushes can be 1.5-3m (5-10ft) high, and wider. The large inflorescences have ray flowers about 4.5cm (1.8in) wide with the pinhead fertile flowers in

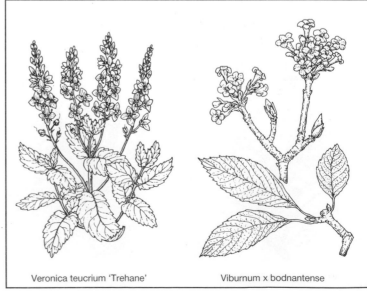

Veronica teucrium 'Trehane'   Viburnum x bodnantense

the centre. The foliage in autumn turns to dull crimson.

No regular pruning is needed. Propagate by summer layering, or by half-ripe cuttings of the current year's growth taken in summer.

Viburnum tinus
(Laurustinus)
- **Full sun or partial shade**
- **Any good garden soil, including chalk**
- **Winter and spring flowers**

Viburnum tinus is an evergreen flowering shrub that makes a dense rounded bush. The opposite leaves, dark glossy green above and paler beneath, are borne on red stalks. The main shoots are red above, green beneath and warted. At the ends of the leafy shoots are terminal flower clusters 5-10cm (2-4in) across. The greeny buds are tinged with mauvy pink before opening white in winter and spring, followed by deep blue fruits that become black. Bushes will reach a height of 2-3.6m (6.5-12ft). The cultivar 'Eve Price' is of more compact habit, with smaller leaves.

Laurustinus does well on chalk or non-chalk soils and is excellent in coastal areas. Prune bushes that have grown out of hand or are frost damaged by cutting them hard back to the oldest wood near ground level in late spring.

Propagate by seed sown in late winter, or by half-ripe heel cuttings taken in early to late summer.

Above: Viola cornuta brings a lovely lavender colour to rock gardens in summer.

Viola cornuta
(Horned viola)
- **Sow in early spring**
- **Fertile and moist but well-drained soil**
- **Sun or partial shade**

This herbaceous perennial viola comes from the Pyrenees and is therefore quite hardy for most garden purposes. The species is usually represented by the lovely lavender- or violet-coloured flowers, although there is the white form 'Alba'. Blooms are angular, and about 2.5cm (1in) across, carried on semi-prostrate soft stems not much longer than 30cm (12in). Leaves are oval to ovate, and green. Use them as an early or midsummer annual for the edge of a border or bed and for the odd pocket in the rock garden. They will tolerate dappled shade as long as the soil is moist.

Sow seeds during early spring under glass, in a temperature of 16°C (60°F). Use a soil-based growing medium. Prick off

seedlings into boxes or trays, harden off in the usual way and plant out in late spring, 23cm (9in) apart. Alternatively, broadcast the seeds where they are to flower and thin out later.

Viola wittrockiana
(Pansy)
- **Sow in early spring and summer**
- **Well-cultivated soil**
- **Sun or partial shade**

This viola is grown as a hardy biennial, and will flower in sun or partial shade. Many large-flowered F1 and F2 hybrids have recently been introduced. There are several strains able to flower during winter and early spring.

For summer and autumn flowering, seed may be sown in gentle heat under glass in late winter or early spring, or under cold glass in spring. The seedlings should be pricked out and grown cool ready for planting out when large enough. Summer and autumn sowings can be made in a sheltered position in the open or in cold frames for the following year. Pansies appreciate good fertilized soils enriched with well-rotted compost or manure. Prompt removal of dead flowers will promote continual flowering. Keep watered in dry weather and watch for aphids, which check growth. Plant on a fresh site each year to avoid soil diseases.

Viburnum plicatum 'Mariesii' Viburnum tinus Viola cornuta Viola wittrockiana

Viscaria elegans

(Lychnis coeli-rosa, Silene coeli-rosa)

(Rose of heaven, Viscaria)

- **Sow in autumn or spring**
- **Ordinary soil**
- **Sun or partial shade**

Also known as *Silene coeli-rosa* and *Lychnis coeli-rosa*, this hardy annual is represented in gardens by several varieties. Salver-shaped and 2.5cm (1in) across flowers in a wide colour range are carried on slender stems 25cm (10in) high during summer. Leaves are grey-green and tend to be oblong in shape.

These plants are easily raised from seed. Sow them where they are to flower. Take out shallow drills during autumn or spring, and lightly cover the seed. Thin out seedlings to 15cm (6in) apart when they are large enough to handle. Autumn-sown plants will be stronger and flower slightly earlier. Avoid watering overhead in hot sunny weather.

Below: Viscaria elegans is a hardy annual that creates a feast of rich colour during summer.

Waldsteinia fragarioides

(Barren strawberry)

- **Sun or light shade**
- **Any soil**
- **Evergreen**

This hardy evergreen perennial from the eastern United States has a long flowering period in the summer. It is a mildly spreading plant that is at home in any soil. It is similar to a strawberry in looks and behaviour, hence its common name. The creeping stems produce dark green, three-lobed, toothed leaves, and 1cm (0.4in) wide golden-yellow flowers in early summer. It mingles quite unobtrusively with other plants, causing them no harm. If it becomes too invasive it can be controlled quite easily.

This species can be divided in late summer, by taking rooted stems at the edge of the mat and potting them in normal soil. Seed can be sown in spring. Young plants should be shaded.

Weigela Hybrids

- **Full sun**
- **Rich fertile soil, including chalk**
- **Summer flowering**

These are trouble-free deciduous flowering shrubs of which there are a number of attractive hybrids. The flowers are similar to those of honeysuckle except that all are scentless. Hybrids that are usually available include: 'Abel Carriere', a deep rosy carmine with a yellow throat, and a strong grower that can be 2m by 2m (6.5ft by 6.5ft); 'Bristol Ruby', a bright ruby red with almost black buds, fairly upright in habit, 2m by 1.5m (6.5ft by 5ft); 'Candida', pure white with bright green foliage, 2m by 2m (6.5ft by 6.5ft) or even wider; and 'Newport Red', bright red.

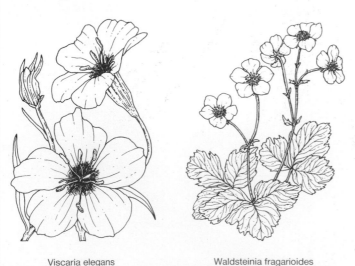

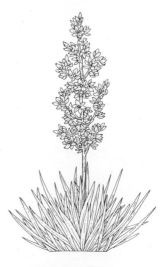

| Viscaria elegans | Waldsteinia fragarioides | Weigela hybrid | Yucca flaccida 'Ivory' |

They are all easily grown, provided they have rich soil with ample moisture at their roots. Prune regularly as soon as they have finished flowering, and then remove old flowering side branches.

Propagate by hardwood cuttings in autumn, inserted out of doors.

Below: Waldsteinia fragarioides has a strawberry-like appearance, with bright yellow flowers.

Yucca flaccida 'Ivory'
- **Full sun**
- **Any soil, especially sandy loam**
- **Summer flowering**

This low-growing evergreen hardy flowering shrub with its architectural foliage helps to create a subtropical atmosphere in the garden. The bluish green leaves are 3-4.5cm (1.2-1.8in) wide. The long spikes of creamy white bells are poised horizontally – unlike most yuccas, whose flowers hang down. The bells are borne at right angles on 1.2m (4ft) long stems, and they have well-formed pointed petals. This is an ideal plant for the gardener who has limited space.

Propagate by division. Or the tops can be induced to root by trimming off half the leaves and inserting the stems in earthenware pots filled with a sandy compost; place them in a greenhouse. Yuccas do need a sunny aspect.

Zantedeschla aethiopica 'Crowborough'
(Arum lily)
- **Sunny location**
- **Dry or wet soil**
- **Summer flowering**

This is a hardy arum lily, but during its first few years after planting some form of protection should be given. This hardy variety is about 90cm (3ft) high and has white fleshy spathes with spear-shaped foliage. The bright yellow 'true' flowers are borne on a fleshy spadix enclosed by the large white spathe, which is a modified bract.

In future years, once the plants are established, give a good thick mulch of leaf-mould or bracken. When planting, place the roots about 10cm (4in) below soil level. As plants mature it will be found that the roots will penetrate more deeply. 'Crowborough' will put up with dry as well as moist conditions, and will flourish in heavy soil.

Propagate in late spring, by removing young offsets at the base of the plants.

Below: Zantedeschia aethiopica 'Crowborough' has large, white, arum-like flowers borne above rich green leaves.

Zantedeschia aethiopica 'Crowborough'

Zinnia elegans

Zinnia elegans
- **Sow in spring**
- **Ordinary well-drained soil**
- **Sunny location**

This well-known half-hardy annual is one of the brightest plants for borders during summer. The range of varieties is wide, with large daisy-like flowers in many colours – white, purple, orange, yellow, red and pink.

Sow under glass in spring at a temperature of 16°C (60°F). Use any good growing medium. When pricking off, use individual peat pots for each single seedling; this will avoid any major disturbance of the roots or stems at planting-out time. Harden off carefully in the usual way at the end of spring and plant out in early summer, 30cm (12in) apart.

INDEX OF COMMON NAMES

INDEX OF LATIN NAMES

The plant names in **bold** in the following listing indicate alternative Latin names for the main plants featured alphabetically in the book. In addition, there are other plants listed here which are mentioned in the book but not given full description.

PICTURE CREDITS

The majority of the photos in this book are the copyright of Salamander Books Ltd. Other photographs are credited as follows on the page: (T) Top; (B) Bottom; (R) Right; (L) Left.

David Squire: 3, 5, 7B, 8, 15, 21L, 28R, 30, 32R, 36, 38B, 42B, 45L, 46R, 48R, 55R, 61L, 69R, 70-71, 73, 78R, 83, 90R, 93T, 96L, 97, 98R, 100, 103R, 112, 115, 119, 120-121, 122L, 123, 130L, 132L, 136R, 146L, 148, 150R, 151, 153, 154L, 157T, 165L, 166, 168-169, 177, 182R, 188-189, 189R

Eric Crichton: 1, 38T, 59R, 92R, 108L, 114, 127, 173R, 179R, 180L